WITHDRAWN
UTSA Libraries

GOVERNMENT IN BUSINESS

GOVERNMENT IN BUSINESS

BY

STUART CHASE

GREENWOOD PRESS, PUBLISHERS
WESTPORT, CONNECTICUT

Library of Congress Cataloging in Publication Data

Chase, Stuart, 1888–
   Government in business.

   Reprint of the 1935 ed. published by Macmillan, New York.
   1. Industry and state--United States. 2. Collectivism. I. Title.
   HD3616.U47C45 1973   338.973   71-136849
   ISBN 0-8371-5283-6

Copyright, 1935, by
STUART CHASE

All rights reserved—no part of this book may be reproduced in any form without permission in writing from the publisher, except by a reviewer who wishes to quote brief passages in connection with a review written for inclusion in magazine or newspaper.

Originally published in 1935
by The Macmillan Company, New York

Reprinted in 1973 by Greenwood Press,
a division of Williamhoue-Regency Inc.

Library of Congress Catalogue Card Number 71-136849

ISBN 0-8371-5283-6

Printed in the United States of America

Acknowledgments

THANKS are due to *Current History, Harper's Magazine,* and the *New Republic,* for their courtesy in allowing me to reprint certain material first published in these magazines; and to my wife, Marian Tyler, who wrote the first draft for Chapter XVI, On Changing Human Nature, and rendered invaluable assistance in editing the whole manuscript. No formal bibliography has been prepared because there are no books devoted primarily to this field, or none that I could find. Useful references on various phases of the problem will be found scattered through the footnotes, and I am deeply indebted to the authorities cited.

STUART CHASE

Redding, Connecticut
June, 1935

Contents

CHAPTER		PAGE
I	WHAT IS PUBLIC BUSINESS?	1
II	THE TREND TOWARDS COLLECTIVISM	17
III	NEW DEAL COLLECTIVISM	33
IV	MORE NEW DEAL COLLECTIVISM	51
V	PUBLIC BUSINESS ABROAD	70
VI	SIX STUDIES OF CAPITALIST DECAY	93
VII	AGENDA OF THE STATE	118
VIII	A BUDGET	131
IX	THE FIELD FOR INDIVIDUAL INITIATIVE	154
X	NOBODY'S BUSINESS	171
XI	OLD MAN RIVER: PUBLIC BUSINESS AND NATURAL RESOURCES	182
XII	BIG BUSINESS	198
XIII	MODELS FOR REGULATION AND CONTROL	216
XIV	MODELS FOR PUBLIC OWNERSHIP	233
XV	THE ADMINISTRATION OF PUBLIC BUSINESS	244
XVI	ON CHANGING HUMAN NATURE	258
XVII	AN ORDER OF BUSINESS	275
	INDEX	291

GOVERNMENT IN BUSINESS

CHAPTER ONE

What Is *Public Business?*

EARLY in 1935, the Supreme Court handed down its decision on "hot oil." The Secretary of the Interior, it was declared, did not have legal authority to regulate the flow of petroleum from American wells. Were the big oil men delighted? They were not. They waste no love on Mr. Ickes, but the alternatives disturbed them deeply. They were faced either with more specific and probably more drastic government control, or with a bitter and demoralizing price war. It was even suggested that oil be declared a public utility in order to legalize the necessary regulation. A retreat to individualism appeared as alarming as an advance to collectivism. Thus the oil industry stands —or shudders—between the devil and the deep sea. This same shudder is traversing the whole economic system, both here and abroad.

The coal industry, following the voiding of its code by the NRA decision, promptly demanded special legislation to take its place, and President Roosevelt put the Guffey coal bill on his "must" list. Apparently both miners and operators are more afraid of free competition than of federal control.

Consider again the unhappy position of the Supreme Court in the famous gold clause case. Decided one way, the central pillar of the edifice of private property is wrenched loose. If the flat promise to pay in gold is held invalid, a contract is not a contract; twenty-five stipulated grains of gold turn out to be only fifteen grains of gold. Decided the other way, the domestic debt burden marches up a cool 70 billions, spreading bankruptcy and financial ruin, if the Attorney General is to be believed. The recovery gained over twenty painful months would be wiped out over night. The Court decided against the sacredness of contracts, thus saving a devastating deflation, at the price of portentous inroads upon property relationships in the future. "The Constitution is gone, and I am filled with shame and humiliation," cried Mr. Justice McReynolds, in delivering the minority opinion.

These are harrowing, critical decisions. There will be more of them. The public interest and traditional rights of private property are locked in gigantic combat of which no man can clearly see the end. "All modern progressive and revolutionary movements," says George Bernard Shaw, "are at bottom attacks on private property. A Chancellor of the Exchequer apologizing for an increase in the surtax, a Fascist dictator organizing a Corporative State, a Soviet commissar ejecting a kulak, are all running the same race, though all except the commissar may be extremely reluctant to admit it." The New Deal is but a single engagement on a world-wide battle front. In Russia the forces of private income producing property are in disorderly retreat, but in all other industrial nations the struggle is grim and unremitting. Fascism in Italy and Germany is an unstable compromise between state control and private enterprise. In Sweden, England, Poland, Canada, Japan, Australia, Mexico, Argentina—

WHAT IS PUBLIC BUSINESS? 3

wherever you choose to look—collectivism, with its centralized credit policies, agricultural subsidies, arbitrary control of exports and imports, public works, relief programs, surtaxes, social insurance, is cutting deeply into the cherished freedom of private business.

Up to the War, particularly in the United States, there were few harrowing decisions to make between public interest and private. (Lincoln, of course, had a major decision in 1861.) Private enterprise could look over its great realm without a qualm. In spite of bitter criticisms by socialists and humanitarians, the system met the pragmatic test. It was above the line of social toleration. Lecture hall debates as to the virtues of government ownership against private ownership were exercises in dialectics, irrelevant to economic realities. The defenders of private enterprise, impregnable though their position was at the time, looked anxiously for thin entering wedges and for camels' noses under the tent. There were few to find—a municipal water works and a sewage system here and there. The Post Office Department was periodically withered by rhetorical scorn, but mail deliveries were not affected.

Then came the War. It was found, to the astonishment of the several general staffs, that war in the machine age meant the husbanding and control of nearly every variety of raw material; the planned direction of the bulk of agriculture, industry and transport. Private business, congenitally intolerant of planned direction, could not meet the military test. The State took over the economic complex. Now the parlor debates began to have tangible meaning. If collective effort was an effective way to wage wars, why not to abolish poverty? In Europe the lesson was driven home to a degree; the State, as we shall see, never went back to the status quo ante. In America, President Harding made a valiant effort to return, but government budgets did not shrink to the placid proportions of 1912, and a number of new public services remained. Private business, however, resumed its economic supremacy, and from 1920 to 1929 touched heights both temporal and spiritual hitherto undreamed of.

But the uprush was too dizzy; the latter days of the New Era and its fantastic stock market were like the world of a fever patient. Suddenly the end came. Revivals have been announced for six long years, one after another, but none has come as I write. Little consumer goods boomlets, then little cascades. Some 22 million Americans are still on public relief.* Relief and other interference are heralded as rampant paternalism. While the form of this collective activity is neither so complete nor so dramatic as in 1918, it is historically more significant. How long is it to last? Will private business come back, if and when the depression ends, as it did when the War ended? Is the State in for good and all? What is the function of the State, of collectivism generally, in respect to economic activity in the power age?

Agenda of the State

As long ago as 1926, John Maynard Keynes announced the end of laissez-faire, and quoted Bentham's distinction between *Agenda* and *Non-Agenda*. The former was the field for collective enterprise, the latter for private. Where should the line run? "Perhaps the chief task of economists at this hour is to dis-

* June, 1935.

WHAT IS PUBLIC BUSINESS? 5

tinguish afresh the *Agenda* of government from the *Non-Agenda.*" If this was a major task in 1926, with post-war prosperity in flood, how much more so is it in 1935, with six years of depression forcing the issue? What are the *Agenda* today?

Probably all Europeans and most Americans are now prepared to admit that the line that ran in 1912 has gone forever. The growth of the motor car alone has forced governments into extensive new functions of highway building and traffic control, and so driven the line to the left—if you please to call government activity leftward. This is no parlor debate. Collectivism is upon us, horse, foot and guns. Today we have no time to waste on academic arguments as to whether municipal power plants lose more money than private plants, or whether the Post Office surplus is really a deficit, or whether the government-owned Inland Waterways Corporation should be abandoned because of the "hidden costs" of clearing the channel of the Mississippi. There is no important economic activity in America which the New Deal does not touch. Upwards of 70 percent of all Europeans are now living in the shadow of state controlled enterprise.

"Towering above all problems," says Charles E. Merriam, "is the larger question of how the division of power and responsibility under our complicated economic and political order shall be brought about. Of particular importance will be the type of rapprochement and rapport on the border line between industry and government. Shall business men become rulers, or rulers business men, or shall labor or science rule the older rulers? . . . What forms of government-owned corporations may emerge between the lines of the purely political and the purely economic? How shall business bureaucracy be held to greater public responsibility? ... The whole delicate structure of modern industry is increasingly intertwined with governmental functions, and will continue to be so in the future, not as a result of any theory whatever, but as the inevitable consequence of the closer integration of social and political life." *

Advocates of private business are apparently convinced that the wholesale slide towards collectivism is the work of "agitators," of reds, of borers from within. A safe and sane intellectual like Rexford Tugwell is made a symbol for socialistic penetration. The business camp thus mistakes the word for the thing, a dangerous error. If private business really desires to retain power in the future, its advocates had best forget about Tugwell and the reds, and concentrate on the march of tangible events. It is not with a few personalities that they must come to terms, but with a maelstrom of impersonal, historical forces.

Definitions

What do we mean by "business," and how does public business differ from private? Thorstein Veblen was in the habit of using the word "business" somewhat rigorously as the buying and selling of commodities with a view to personal pecuniary profit. Over against it, he put the word "industry," as the tangible workmanship involved in producing goods. His distinction was one of purpose—vendibility opposed to serviceability. I shall use a wider and more common definition. Business is here considered to be any form of keeping busy on the economic front, whether the

* Charles E. Merriam: *Political Power*. McGraw-Hill, 1934.

WHAT IS PUBLIC BUSINESS? 7

aim of that activity is to make money or to render service. When my mother urged me as a youth to become a good business man, she was not thinking in terms of Veblen, where "the highest achievement in business is the nearest approach to something for nothing"; she was hoping that I might become accurate, punctual, and efficient. Broadly speaking, business means getting things done, specifically getting economic goods produced. One may speak of a business-like housewife, or club, or Russian oil trust, or cooperative association.

What is the State? Merriam describes it as a group which is permitted a wider latitude in the direction of pains and penalties than any other in the social organization.* These sanctions may be juristically without limit, but if the State overworks them, revolution results. They include control over persons and property, restraint, immobilization—normally in jail; limitation of status, deportation, and even the taking of life itself in war or as a penalty for certain crimes. "This blanket power is recognized in the political relationship alone, although its forms may be employed by other groups as well, under certain conditions, as in secret societies." The Church has weapons to punish both here and hereafter. Fraternal organizations can make life very uncomfortable for the wayward. Gangsters who violate their code may be "taken for a ride."

Fortunately in this country the State coincides roughly with a self-sustaining economic community. This makes more sense than does such a region as Europe, where one economic community is split among a score of sovereign States.

From the larger point of view, that of an interplane-

* Charles E. Merriam: *Political Power*. McGraw-Hill, 1934.

tary traveler, for instance, there is no *physical* difference between public business and private. The State, the cooperative association, or any other collective organization, employs labor, raw materials and technical skill to produce goods and services, which output is distributed to the community, even as the output of private business, also produced by labor, raw materials and technical skill, is distributed to the community. Modern specialization of labor applies in both cases. Certain workers feed, clothe or shelter other workers in exchange for motor cars, highroads, permanent waves, fire protection, newspapers, water supply, phonographs, public school education, golf balls, public health service, and so on. In the United States today the private area is larger than the public both in manpower and in investment, but the output is intrinsically no more important and no less. We must have the farmer's food, the garment maker's overcoat, the municipality's water and the Treasury's certification of ten dollar bills. The public sector runs more to services than to goods, but services are almost as essential as goods under power age conditions. Deprived of its fire department for only a few hours, any large modern city might find its goods reduced to ashes. There is a persistent notion that private business is "productive," and government business parasitic—a kind of old man of the sea. This is nonsense, as a moment's calm reflection will show. The carriage of mails is no more parasitic than the dispatching of telegrams, while as between Boulder Dam and the upper reaches of the cosmetic trade, I will let the reader choose his parasites. Both divisions have productive functions of the first importance, and both, alas, carry their due complement of fungoid growths.

WHAT IS PUBLIC BUSINESS? 9

Public business in Yucatan

It is helpful in this connection to look at a primitive community. Here is the village of Chan Kom, in eastern Yucatan, a community of 200 people.* Its economy is essentially one of barter and it is largely self-sufficient, with maize as its main food supply. In the spring the air is pungent with burning jungle in preparation for planting the *milpas*. There is almost no private business in Chan Kom, in the sense of producing for profit. One or two citizens try to raise cattle for an outside market. Private business here becomes the work of each family on its own fields and in its own house. Public business falls into two classes: the communal labor required of every citizen as a matter of ancient right and duty; voluntary labor devoted to helping friends and relatives at harvest time or when a house is built. The former is the equivalent of our government service, the latter of our clubs, associations, cooperative societies and the like. North of the Rio Grande, the pattern is hard to find in the tangle of specialized tasks. In Chan Kom it stands clear in the yearly calendar of any able-bodied citizen. Communal labor falls on every male member of the community as soon as he leaves school, and lasts until he is forty-five. It includes policing, road building, repairs to the school and the town hall, water supply, sanitation, and so on. It used to include house building for everybody.

I have analyzed Mr. Redfield's report of the activities of a young married man with two children for the year 1931. Collective tasks for the town government or for neighbors aggregated 128 days, against 133 for

*Robert Redfield: *Chan Kom—A Maya Village*. Carnegie Institution, Washington, 1934.

strictly private activities—almost an equal division. The ratio of total manpower in a high energy community would undoubtedly show a larger figure for private business, but aggregates for both public and semi-public are very great, especially since the depression. In Russia, of course, the public business ratio must be from 80 to 90 percent.

Semi-public business

In America, we find four classes of business:

1. Private business for survival as in Chan Kom, still practiced by many small farmers and handicraftsmen.
2. Private business for pecuniary profit.
3. Public business in the form of government service.
4. Semi-public business in the form of voluntary non-profit associations.

The first classification steadily diminishes under modern technological conditions; the last is frequently overlooked in the rhetorical warfare between collectivism and individualism, but its extent is enormous. It includes cooperative associations of both consumers and producers, foundations and charities, clubs, fraternal organizations, athletic associations, libraries and museums other than public, churches and religious organizations. A vast amount of manpower and materials is consumed in these activities. Like government business, the total has been gaining relatively at the expense of private enterprise. In 1914, "productive" wealth devoted to profit making was estimated at 62 percent of all American wealth; in 1921, at 57 percent; in 1932, at 52 percent.* If the criterion of pri-

* Robert R. Doane: *The Measurement of American Wealth.* Harpers, 1933.

vate business as against public be the risk of capital with hope of profit, group collectivism belongs on the public side. Cooperative associations strive to eliminate profit from the goods their members buy. When retail profits are squeezed out, these societies frequently go down the industrial ladder into wholesaling, jobbing, manufacturing, transport and even into the production of raw materials. They urge the general public to become members of their societies. Their motto is to substitute the cooperative commonwealth for private business. Foundations, charities, churches seek to serve the general public without pecuniary profit. Clubs and associations are more snobbish, but profit is not in them—except in such examples as the real estate country clubs of the New Era.

I belong to a large university club. We do not welcome the general public except on rare occasions. We wish a quiet and comfortable refuge from the roar of New York; a place to play games, read, converse, eat and drink with some peace of mind. We wish to have this at the lowest possible cost, with the best possible business management. We wish a full record of every department in the club and information as to whether it is paying its way or not. Our accounting system is one of the finest extant, but the only profit is our satisfaction. Sometimes one wishes the whole economic system could be operated on the principles of a good club—fellowship, convenience and comfort, a competent administration, good manners, service at cost.

It is safe to say that public and private business have complemented each other ever since the stone age. A pattern like that of Chan Kom obtains in more complicated societies, but is harder to detect. Public business hitherto has reached its zenith in war, where both primitive societies and modern mechanized cultures must turn a common, regimented face against the enemy. A community without public business is a contradiction in terms.

Public business was alive and flourishing for ten thousand years, more or less, before the word "socialism" was ever heard. To increase it today would not necessarily mean any more socialism than it meant in Chichen Itza when a new temple was to be built by public labor. Socialism, narrowly defined, means the community ownership of the means of production. There is reason to believe, as we shall see, that public business under power age conditions can often be accomplished through control-without-ownership. Public business may undoubtedly involve collectivism and socialization. It does involve socialism, if you want to interpret the word broadly enough to include the communal labor of Chan Kom, and the New York Fire Department. If I avoid the term, it is in an effort to get away from the tyranny of purely emotional reactions to certain words and slogans.

Down the ages, the function of community labor has been to protect, conserve, and where possible to develop and expand the community. The proof of the value of such labor lies in the health of the community. If it is vigorous, the division between public business and private, whether or not it meets the test of impartial justice, is meeting the larger test of adequate survival. In the United States up to the turn of the century, healthy survival and vigorous expansion were manifest. Public business concerned itself largely with protection, courts of law, the guarantee of the medium of exchange, and a growingly complicated series of municipal services. Private business had almost all the

WHAT IS PUBLIC BUSINESS? 13

rest of the field. The semi-public zone was comparatively narrow. For a nation with a frontier to conquer and develop, the division was a workable one.

In the last analysis, public business is the communal draft of manpower and materials necessary to keep a community vigorous. It is now clear that the extent of the draft in a mature community is different from that in a frontier community; different in high energy conditions from low energy conditions. Emotional advocates of private business as a kind of religion cling to the frontier line of 1850. But the march of events has overruled them. Emotional advocates of public business as monopolizing all business have not yet presented conclusive evidence that industrial changes demand such heroic measures. Somewhere between these extremes, the modern community will draw up its Agenda.

Varieties of public business

In preparing its plan, the community may choose from four general types of government activity. These types are apart from the permanent functions of national defense, the safeguarding of property and persons, and the guarantee of the medium of exchange.

1. *Petty regulation* of private business. Legislation covering factory inspection, sanitary conditions and the like. This is an old story and does not concern us in the following analysis.

2. *Major regulation* of business. The concept of utilities as "affected with a public interest" and the regulation thereof. Anti-trust legislation, tariffs, minimum wages, maximum hours, child labor provisions, price fixing, profits and income taxes, the enforcement

of quality standards—as in the Pure Food and Drug Act, and the like.

3. The *control* of private business without ownership of the underlying property. In this case key administrative decisions pass to the State. The War Industries Board assumed such functions in 1917 and 1918. Business continued to own and operate its plants, but the government told business what to make, how much to make, when to deliver it, and sometimes what to charge for it. Policy making, planning, the control of new investment, passed from private hands to public. Large sections of German industry today, most of Italian industry, are under this form of control-without-ownership.

4. Outright *government ownership*. This in turn may take various forms which we shall later examine in detail.

The criterion of profit

Major regulation and control-without-ownership may vitally affect the profits of private enterprise. Either can be applied to socialize profits, but to date this has happened rarely. The War control by and large resulted in an abnormally high rate of profits. The threat, however, remains. A government which has invaded private territory to this extent can sequester profit if it chooses. State ownership automatically socializes the profit of the enterprise. Sometimes cooperating private capital, as in the case of the Swedish Alcohol Trust, is granted a limited dividend, but usually the government socializes the surplus either by selling at cost, or by taking the profit into the national treasury.

Here is one important distinction between the two sectors, a distinction which our planetary traveler with his merely physical telescope could hardly see. A given activity becomes public business when the public takes, or has the specific power to take, its profit. Its function then is no longer to make profitable deals and sales for private owners, but to render useful service for the community. The State may of course fulfill the skeptic's predictions by bungling the job. The community may be worse served by the State seeking serviceability, than by private business seeking vendibility. Such failures as may occur do not, however, affect the function. When the Steel Corporation fires up its furnaces under traditional conditions, it hopes to earn dividends; when the War Industries Board directed the furnaces to be fired, it hoped to obtain steel for specified war purposes. The function had altogether changed, although the temperature in the furnaces was the same.

It should be noted that public business seldom invades the private zone because too much profit is being made. Large profits normally coincide with their reinvestment in new enterprises, which make for a high level of employment and an industrial boom. In booms, private business takes care of itself. Far more frequently, the State is forced in because of the *absence* of profits, because of the wholesale retreat of private enterprise.

Many business men look on the New Deal as a tyrannical machine bent on the destruction of their net income. President Roosevelt is urged to declare that he has no designs on the profit system. Radicals, on the other hand, condemn him roundly because he is not uprooting production for profit. Both contentions are beside the point. The New Deal is primarily concerned with losses. It was inaugurated because private business could not keep the banks open, was losing billions of dollars annually, and had abandoned all support for some 15 million workers. Industry as a whole in 1935 is still showing a net loss. Certain large corporations are making money again, probably too much money, but what they earn is offset by losses in little business, and in many of the heavy industries.

Profit is the reward of risk. The private profit maker is essentially a gambler. He puts down a sum of money which he hopes will be increased by the venture, but which frequently is decreased, if not wiped out entirely. This is a zestful game, even as the races are zestful.

Public business dispenses with profit except for administrative purposes, as in the case of my club. It eliminates the risk—and the zest if you please. It does necessary jobs which otherwise nobody would do, such as public education and street cleaning, or jobs which private business is abandoning because losses exceed profits, like farming, or jobs which private business is disastrously bungling, like the conservation of lumber and petroleum. In brief, it mops up, after the risk-takers have had their excitement. The mopping up after the excitement of the big bull market and the big bank credit boom has been a very extensive and expensive public enterprise. The question remains whether the community can indefinitely stand such a bill for excitement, with consequent disruption to its service of supply, or whether public business, in its pedestrian, matter-of-fact way, may not have to step in and guarantee the service.

CHAPTER TWO

The Trend towards Collectivism

PUBLIC business in colonial America did not differ greatly from that found in Chan Kom today. The small agricultural communities, largely self-sufficient, devoted a substantial part of their total man days to improving the roads, building the church and school house, manning the blockhouse against the Indians if the village lay on the frontier, maintaining order. Semi-public business was done in barn raisings, at which all the neighbors participated, in mutual aid at harvest, for house building, transport, water supply, and in times of sickness.

As the agricultural pattern gave way to the industrial after the introduction of steam, a curious philosophy of private enterprise took root. In America it gained strength from the sturdy independence of the agricultural pioneer, but it operated in a milieu which was rapidly destroying the independent farmer, as markets widened and financial transactions replaced barter. The doctrine proclaimed that to put collective restraints upon private enterprise, as it swung westward over a continent, was unjust if not downright impious.*
A theory of automaticity was invoked, as rounded, log-

* In Europe, the same sanctity was laid upon conquest of foreign markets.

ically beautiful and dubious as most systems of pure metaphysics. Let the government keep out, and private business would automatically provide the community with all it desired. Without plan, without taking thought, without conscious direction, everything would fall in order *as if* it had been consciously planned; nay, far better. Conscious planning opened the door to the devil in the form of bureaucracy.

There was sound reason for this extraordinary credo. A frontier community was not interested in security, public order, and four percent. It was interested in making a killing like Jim Hill, and 400 percent. Industry was a field for adventure. Killings were not compatible with extensive government regulation and control. Meanwhile the wealth of the unrolling continent provided a kind of natural antidote to the wastes and excesses of private exploitation. Not until the shores of the Pacific were reached, was there much to be gained by challenging this doctrine of the main chance.

Dirty business

Public business, save in its skeleton functions of war, law, and legal tender—and, we might add, in the distribution of public land to railroads, speculators and homesteaders—was heaped with moral obloquy. "I go upon the facts," said the Reverend John McVickar at Columbia in the 1830's, "and finding from them all that tends to exalt, refine and give comfort to man, growing up under the patronage of commerce, I cannot but reverence the claims of commerce as something holy." This is a straight transference of the divine right of kings to the divine right of private business.

In a text book by A. L. Chapin, popular in the '70's, it appears that state provision for the unemployed "is the most subversive of all social order"; Ruskin's claim that equal labors are entitled to equal rewards is roundly damned as the suppression of "commercial law which is God's method"; Henry George's proposal to secure to society its own land value increment, was a "wild scheme of iniquity and folly." *

According to Charles A. Beard, the State received another drubbing on animistic grounds. When the classical economists were forced to notice that their laws did not prevent business cycles, they "introduced an extraneous force, the State, to help explain the faulty functioning and periodical collapses of their perfect machine. All would be well if the State would not interfere with domestic or international economy." The State interfered very little in those days, but disappointed prophets require a scapegoat. Today the scapegoat is still being beaten briskly around the bush in the persons of President Roosevelt's brain trust. If only they would go back where they came from, natural laws would reassert themselves and business would recover.

J. M. Keynes has called the nineteenth century an accountant's nightmare. No work could be done unless it "paid"; every activity was subordinated to financial calculations. We built slums because they paid better than decent houses; we disfigured the countryside, wasted our great river basins, razed our forests, partly from ignorance but mostly because it paid—for the moment. We would not put the unemployed to work on public improvements because it did not pay. "We

* For a full length portrait, see R. H. Tawney: *Religion and the Rise of Capitalism.*

have to remain poor because it does not 'pay' to be rich. We have to live in hovels not because we cannot build palaces, but because we cannot 'afford' them." This rule of self-destructive financial calculation governed every walk of life.

It is still a governing principle for thousands of American business men who should know better. Daily the New York *Times* and the *Herald Tribune* run their quota of indignant letters from solid citizens, deploring public works because they do not produce a financial profit, damning all forms of public business as inefficient, knavish and immoral. To wit:

> What we need now is common sense, and lots of it, to come in as an old fashioned doctor, to throw away these poisons and let nature have a chance.... Let us stop passing new laws and regulations every minute, so that the successful, industrious man may again prosper, and as soon as our industrious, frugal business man finds that the fundamental theory of hard work without stint, and saving, are again worth while, then and only then will business again become normal. (Letter to the *Times*, February 28, 1935.)

Here is another, April 10, 1935:

> The public service corporations are accused of seeking profits as a main objective. This is the golden secret of their success and their great advantage to the public as compared with the best political management that ever continued to exist for any considerable period of time in the United States.

In this latter specimen, the old metaphysic of automaticity is beautifully preserved. An electric light company leaving no stone unturned for profit will serve the public better than any organization whose object is strictly to serve the public. That is, if you wish to go west you will get there faster by starting for the east.

Dr. Arthur E. Morgan, wrestling with the complicated technical problems of the Tennessee Valley Authority, is constantly hampered by this cultural lag from a pioneer age:

> Our project here is being severely criticized. There is a habit of propaganda, especially among private utilities, to the effect that everything the government does must be corrupt and inefficient. I think such an attitude comes fairly close to national disloyalty. To convince young men and women that their government is of necessity inefficient and corrupt makes them ashamed of it, and unwilling to work for it. It is our business here to prove it is not so.

Public business in the United States has thus developed under a tragic handicap. The task of its advocates has been like trying to prove to hardshell Baptists that hell is a pleasant place in which to live. We have been telling ourselves for a long time that public business is degrading, and that it should not be allowed to mitigate the evils of unemployment, malnutrition, waste of resources, restriction of output, social misery and insecurity. Only yesterday the word "dole" was one of moral opprobrium. Politics was obscene; "dirty" was the adjective most frequently employed. All forms of public business, save possibly the military establishment—which, in action, *is* a genuinely dirty business—have been mired with this slime. Yet fundamentally, as we have seen, public business has always been mandatory in the life of any human community. An individual perfectly free may be a menace to his fellows. Community connotes compulsion, the only question being how much of it is necessary to keep the community functioning. If you had told a Connecticut yankee in 1760 that it was dirty business for him to go out and work on the town road, he would have stared at you as a madman.

Events vs. philosophy

The moral drives of the nineteenth century continued well into the twentieth, and are still embalmed in letters to the *Times*. But public business, its hair full of mud to be sure, began to enter one neglected economic corner after another. It was an untouchable, but its services were accepted by Brahmins with their noses in the air. The fundamental reasons are not far to seek. The frontier was gone, and with it the old landing net for the economically insecure. The automaticity of laissez-faire could function after a fashion so long as the landing net remained, but not after its removal. Capitalism has long since replaced free competition with straight monopoly, and with its cousin administrative competition, over the bulk of the service of supply, further to impair the automatic conception. "In a realistic view of the old capitalism," says Walter Lippmann, "it is not far from the truth to say that free competition existed in so far as men were unable to abolish it."

No matter how earnestly one may *believe* in the sublimities of an undirected, self-balancing method of furnishing food, shelter and clothing, what is one to do when the food, shelter and clothing are not forthcoming? One has to nail his flag to the masthead, cross his arms and wait for the revolution, or enlarge the area of public business to make good the shortage. We cannot fail to admire the blind courage of those who, like Senator Carter Glass, nail their flags to the mast, but most Americans have accepted the inevitable, and let that be done which had to be done.

To my mind the major force which has encouraged collectivism is the pressure of advancing technology.

A swelling stream of inanimate energy, focused by a growing multitude of inventions, has driven in upon accepted institutions like a rotary plow upon a snow drift. If one charts the increase in the consumption of energy per capita, and lays down the line of per capita expenditures for government—federal, state and local—the parallel is clear.

Elsewhere, I have tried to analyze the effects of modern technology.* Specifically, it has bound us into one network of interlocked activities; has hammered down costs of production in terms of man-hours, threatening vested interests in high relative prices; it has shrunk the map by high speed transport and communication; reduced the working population through technological unemployment with a consequent decrease in purchasing power; it has reared the fantastic towers and piled up the fantastic congestion of Megalopolis; it has equipped backward nations with energy systems of their own and thus encouraged economic nationalism; it has speeded up the business cycle; unbalanced the whole price structure to the particular disadvantage of the business of farming; it has created a production plant far in excess of market demand—though not of human needs; upset the moralities of thrift; placed the consumer above the producer in economic importance while "sound" finance knows no way adequately to finance the consumer; and, in some ways most significant of all, it has reduced great blocks of property to impotence failing mass consumption. Of what use is a factory devoted to mass production without masses of consumers, able and willing to spend? These attacks, disruptions, threats to traditional institutions, to traditional ways of doing business, have

* *The Economy of Abundance.* Macmillan, 1934.

torn the economic fabric in many places. The holes must somehow be patched. The community has moved in to patch them.

Mr. Hoover's Committee on Recent Social Trends supports this conclusion. Government has been forced into economic activity because of technological progress; because of the growing tension and unbalance between industry and agriculture; because of the growing helplessness of the individual in a highly specialized society. During this process, no groups of numerical significance in America, according to the Committee, were advocating socialism, communism, syndicalism or fascism. Propaganda has had nothing to do with the change.

A further specific motive force, especially abroad, grew out of the War. Markets closed by blockade did not reopen. The map of 1914 was torn to ribbons. Nations which had suffered from shortages applied state action to become more self-sufficient. The volume, kind and transits of exports and imports altered. The United States shifted from a debtor to a creditor nation, a role she had never known. In each country, there had been inflation, and each government had now to make decisions as to how far it could or must deflate. "The War dislocated affairs so much that they were no longer manageable by the kind of effort which ordinary men, immersed in their own interests, were capable of making." *

From 1912 to 1930

It is possible to measure the trend towards public business in America both quantitatively and qualita-

* Walter Lippmann: *The Method of Freedom*. Macmillan, 1934.

tively. Taxes, government expenditures, the creation of new government agencies, new functions, new controls, all indicate it. In 1912, in the United States, almost the only camel's nose visible under the sturdy tent of private enterprise was government operation of the Panama Canal. The Canal Zone had been made a socialistic unit, with state housing, power, food supply, bakeries, laundries, cold storage plants, department stores, hotels. This result was viewed with alarm in some quarters, but it was admitted that the military aspects of the canal furnished an extenuating circumstance. Other noses there were, to be sure, large and woolly ones, but use and wont had made them invisible. The country had become accustomed to government interference in the form of protective tariffs, the Interstate Commerce Commission's control of the railroads, the growing host of municipal water works, trolley lines and other services.* Few considered the regulation of public utilities, major regulation as in theory it was, as dangerous interference. The disregard on the whole was well founded. The "public" utilities normally regulated the sundry state commissions.

The year 1913, according to Mr. Bassett Jones in his brilliant mathematical study, *Debt and Production,* marked the culmination in the *rate* of industrial expansion in the United States. Thereafter, industry continued to grow, but at a declining rate. The lusty republic had matured. The year 1913, whether by coincidence or not, marked also the beginning of a new growth rate in public business. Let us look first at the

* In 1800, there was one municipally owned water works in the United States. In 1900, there were almost 2,000. In 1927, there were 2,137 private city power plants, and 2,198 public—Los Angeles, Cleveland and Seattle being the largest.

total tax bill. The figures are from *Recent Social Trends:* *

FEDERAL, STATE AND LOCAL TAXES

	1913	1922	1930	Percent increase 1930 over 1913
All taxes (current dollars)	$2,259 million	$7,561 million	$10,277 million	355%
All taxes (1913 dollars)	2,259 "	4,639 "	6,117 "	171%
Taxes per capita (current dollars)	$23.49	$68.96	$83.71	256%
Taxes per capita (1913 dollars)	23.49	42.31	49.83	112%

That unhappy gentleman in a barrel, the average taxpayer, was assessed $23.49 in 1913, and $83.71 in 1930, an increase of 256 percent. Measured in 1913 dollars, however, a fairer index which takes the cost of living into account, the increase in his tax bill was 112 percent. The burden, if you choose to call it that, more than doubled during the period. Measured in taxes, per unit of the population, the State was twice as active at the close of the period.

Now let us look at all government expenditures. *Recent Social Trends* adopts a somewhat different period for this calculation, but the trend is shown clearly enough:

	1915	1929	Percent increase Current $	1915 $
Federal	$ 719.2 million	$2,779.7 million	289%	125%
State	489.5 "	1,954.2 "	299	135
Cities over 30,000	1,048.3 "	3,307.5 "	216	85
Other local	1,122.6 "	3,410.8 "	205	80
Grand total	$3,379.6 million	$11,452.2 million	239%	100%
Grand total per capita	$33.84	$94.37	179%	65%

* "Recent Social Trends in the United States," Monographs. McGraw-Hill, 1933.

THE TREND TOWARDS COLLECTIVISM 27

This table brings into clear relief the large preponderance of expenditures by city and local governments over those by state and federal governments. It was, however, state and federal outlays which showed the largest growth during the period, indicating the trend towards centralization. The New Deal did not centralize public business over night; it had long been on the way. Measured in 1915 dollars, total government expenditures increased 100 percent, again a better index than the increase in current dollars of 239 percent. The per capita increase in expenditure for all government, in 1915 dollars, was 65 percent. This is less than the tax increase shown in the preceding table, primarily because the base year is different.

Where did these increased expenditures go?

Highway construction and maintenance show the largest relative increase.

Education shows the next largest relative increase.

The federal regulation of interstate trade shows a large increase.

Federal aid to the states for purchases of the public domain, for agriculture, public health, education, public improvements, shows a large increase.

Other mounting federal outlays are for aëronautics, radio control, agricultural marketing, merchant marine, and services to private business, both domestic and foreign. The last rose sharply while Mr. Hoover was Secretary of Commerce.

The states were going in for mothers' benefit payments, old age pensions, central purchasing, social and economic statistics, workmen's compensation, mediation in labor disputes, employment agencies, minimum wages for women, forest fire control, sanitation, parks, fish and game control, the licensing and regulation of business and the professions. One state, North Dakota, proceeded after the War to a very comprehensive program of public business, including a state bank, flour mills, grain warehouses, and crop insurance. It is estimated to have saved the people of the state $100,-000,000 to date.

The cities were going in for zoning and planning, clinics, child welfare, playgrounds, parks, traffic control, public health nurses, vocational guidance, the care of mental defectives, golf courses and airports.

It is estimated that one third of all government activities in 1930 were new, unknown in 1915. But education and highways accounted for nearly half of all the public expenditures in 1930; here is where the big money went.

In 1927, the federal government owned and operated 194 million acres of land, exclusive of Alaska, equal to the combined area of Maine, New Hampshire, Vermont, Massachusetts, Connecticut, Virginia, West Virginia and North Carolina. It also owned 135 million acres more, leased out to private operators. The whole area was valued by the Secretary of the Interior at 26 billion dollars, not including mineral deposits. Meanwhile, at Washington was to be found the largest printing plant in the world, grinding out 50 million books and documents a year to a total of 4 billion pages—the Government Printing Office.

The ratio of government outlays to the national income was 9.17 percent in 1915, 12.8 percent in 1923, 12.44 percent in 1928, and by way of contrast, 20 percent in 1933.

Observe the new federal institutions founded since 1912. The list is not complete, and does not include the War Boards of 1917 and 1918:

THE TREND TOWARDS COLLECTIVISM 29

1913 The Federal Income Tax
1914 Federal Reserve Board
     Federal Trade Commission
     The Alaska Railroad
1915 Bureau of Efficiency
1916 U. S. Shipping Board and Merchant Fleet Corporation
     Federal Farm Loan Bureau
     U. S. Tariff Commission
1917 Inland Waterways Corporation (government barge line on the Mississippi)
     U. S. Employment Service
     Federal Board for Vocational Education
1920 Federal Power Commission
1921 Bureau of the Budget
1922 Grain Futures Administration
1923 Personnel Classification Board
1924 Federal Oil Conservation Board
1926 Aëronautics Branch, Department of Commerce
1927 Federal Radio Commission
1928 Federal Farm Board

The above findings make it clear that at the time when private business reached its zenith, under Harding and Coolidge, public business too was steadily expanding. The President of the Chamber of Commerce might piously say that: "The best public servant is the worst one ... he eats holes in our liberties ... the better he is and the longer he stays, the greater the danger." * But public servants continued to multiply, and to improve slowly but steadily their administrative techniques. Mr. Ferguson's criticism was a moral one. "In practice," says Dr. Merriam, "this position was sharply challenged by the insistent demand for legislation and appropriation to serve various social and class purposes. Paradoxically, the general attitude was that of hostility to governmental expansion as such ...

* Homer Ferguson in the *Nation's Business*, November, 1928.

while in fact, the demand for governmental action went on at a rapid rate at the very urgent insistence of business, labor, agriculture, the professions and the general public. Each might be theoretically opposed to the extension of governmental functions, except in his particular instance." *

Again, while we find little change in the form of government, either national or local, functions were rapidly changing. The traditional checks and balances remained as laid down by the Constitution, but the actual job of governing was being revolutionized. Counties were losing their function as the use of the motor car widened districts; Megalopolis was arrogantly challenging the sovereign state in which theoretically it lay. New York City was prepared to do battle with Connecticut and New Jersey, as well as with Albany. Studying these new functions, we can see the old political forms visibly cracking under forces which the Founding Fathers never conceived. Much of the inefficiency of public business was caused by the attempt to operate large scale economic enterprises within a century old form, designed for a government devoted only to war, law and legal tender. The traditional function of government as protection, and so more or less negative, had shifted to the positive function of *Wirtschaft,* local and national housekeeping on a grand scale. But little provision had been made for giving these positive functions a workable constitutional frame. President Roosevelt was acutely aware of this when, after the Supreme Court's NRA decision, he declared the interstate commerce clause a "horse and buggy" statute, inapplicable to modern conditions.

Here and there a few cities gave up their mayor,

* Charles E. Merriam: *Political Power.* McGraw-Hill, 1934.

who was a little president, and their Board of Aldermen, which was a little senate, and their councilmen, who were a little House of Representatives, and elected a city manager—a step as revolutionary as it was sensible. The public affairs of a modern city constitute a great business, with tens of thousands on the payroll, technical engineering problems galore, cost accounting, budgets, banking, and often subways, power plants, gas plants, ferries, docks, markets, to operate. A little president and a little congress, forever baiting each other, are no more use here than in General Motors or the Telephone Company.

We cannot fail to note that most of the new agencies and expenditures listed above were not "frills and furbelows," but answers to real demands. Nearly every activity has a direct bearing on the developing power age—highways, radio and airplane control, the federal power commission, conservation, aids to agriculture, education, and the rest. Here is no wanton extravagance such as keeps the economy leagues awake at night, but public business of the most urgent kind. That there was waste, graft, and extravagance in detail, goes without saying, but the big, overhead expansion was caused by the community's effort to keep level with an expanding technology.

The dourest spot in the whole catalog was undoubtedly the attempt to enforce Prohibition. This precious legislation was drafted in answer to no genuine social need. It is an outstanding example of an area where public business grossly exceeds its jurisdiction. State control of alcohol is, of course, another matter, in the sense that the public may share in the profits of its own tippling. This is economic regulation. Prohibition was a disastrous attempt at moral regulation.

The single camel's nose of 1912 had multiplied, by the end of the New Era, into a whole circle of noses. The tent was beginning to shake. For the first three years of the depression, the most substantial addition was Mr. Hoover's Reconstruction Finance Corporation. How substantial it proved, we shall see presently. With the advent of the New Deal, the intruders multiplied. Today, most of the camels are bodily in the tent.

CHAPTER THREE

New Deal Collectivism

Mr. Hoover's New Deal

MR. HOOVER, as Walter Lippmann has pointed out, is an unhappy example of the triumph of fact over theory. He acted on a doctrine which he professed to reject. The depression knocked his nineteenth century economic moralities into a cocked hat, and as the official leader of a stricken community he had to turn collectivist. It did not occur to him to follow Cleveland in the depression of the 1890's, Grant in the '70's, Buchanan in the '50's, Van Buren in the '30's, or Monroe in the 1820's. These leaders conceived it no part of their duty to take charge of the nation's economy and direct it through the storm. They had the frontier as safety valve, and allowed nature to take her course. Mr. Hoover regarded it as his duty to interfere, and it was. His attempts were reluctant and not very effectual, but he made them. This is how he defied natural forces:

He spent vast sums for maintaining the prices of wheat and cotton.
He spent large amounts for public works.
He called conference after conference in an attempt to maintain wages and purchasing power artificially.

He tried to inflate credit through open market operations, the buying and selling of government securities.

He put unemployment relief on a federal basis—an unheard-of thing in America.

He organized the Reconstruction Finance Corporation, which promptly poured billions into the tottering financial structures of banks, railroads, insurance companies. In prior depressions, tottering organizations had been allowed to totter into the grave as a part of the so-called cleansing process.*

Mr. Roosevelt's New Deal

Mr. Hoover opened the tent door; Mr. Roosevelt pushed it wider. The camels came trooping in. Mr. Hoover moved against deep emotional convictions; Mr. Roosevelt professed himself an experimentalist. It is safe to assume that when two men so utterly different in temperament follow an almost identical pattern, the pattern is more important than the men; and that whoever, short of a mad fanatic, might have been President of the United States from 1929 to 1935, the curve of public business would have risen at least as rapidly, though the legal forms might have been different.

The Roosevelt New Deal has released novel types of major regulation, new varieties of control-without-ownership, new publicly owned corporations of assorted types, a Tennessee Valley Authority, which acts like a corporation but has no capital stock, and an amazing dromedary known as a "partnership" between government and private business, called the National Recovery Administration. Classification and interpre-

* In one or two earlier depressions, as in 1907, the government gave temporary aid to the banks.

tation of this menagerie presents its difficulties. How far do these agencies actually transfer control to the State; how far has potential control gone; to what degree is the government now responsible for economic policy for the nation at large; how far have profits—or losses—been socialized actually or potentially; how permanent is the mold?

The RFC

The Reconstruction Finance Corporation is at once the oldest agency inspired by the depression, the most massive financially, and a government-owned corporation which, like the German railroads, maintains a degree of independence and initiative on its own account. In three years (February 1932 to January 1935) it spent or allocated just short of 9 billion dollars, a sum which makes it the largest financial corporation ever heard of. Its capital stock of 500 millions was contributed by the United States Treasury; the rest of its capital has come from the sale of its own notes to the government to a total of almost 4 billions. The loans, investments and allocations to December 31, 1934, were:

Under Mr. Hoover	$2,788,000,000
Under Mr. Roosevelt	6,177,000,000
Total	$8,965,000,000

Its profits on operations have been:

Gross earnings (chiefly interest)	$199,000,000
Operating expenses	134,000,000
Excess of earnings	$ 65,000,000

Its balance sheet on December 31, 1934:

Assets		Liabilities & Capital	
Cash	$ 6,000,000	Notes payable	$3,834,000,000
Loans receivable	1,546,000,000	Interest payable, etc.	34,000,000
Preferred stocks held	846,000,000	Capital stock	500,000,000
Accrued interest, etc.	48,000,000	Earnings, as above	65,000,000
Advances for relief to other government units	1,987,000,000		
Total assets	$4,433,000,000	Total	$4,433,000,000

Who was credited with the 9 billions?

Banks—loans, aid to depositors, preferred stocks purchased, etc.	$3,629,000,000
Farmers—crop loans, mortgage help, land banks, etc.	2,127,000,000
Unemployed—advances or allocations for relief	1,300,000,000
Railroads—loans	465,000,000
Mortgage companies—loans	360,000,000
Home owners—advances to home loan banks	325,000,000
Public works—self-liquidating projects	258,000,000
Building and loan associations—loans	143,000,000
Insurance companies—loans and preferred stocks purchased	139,000,000
Drainage and irrigation companies—loans	82,000,000
Securities purchased from the PWA	44,000,000
Business men—direct loans to general business	35,000,000
U. S. Housing Corporation—capital advanced	25,000,000
Chicago teachers—loans to pay accrued salaries	23,000,000
Federal credit banks	9,000,000
Credit unions	1,000,000
Total, as above	$8,965,000,000

This classification is mine, built up in round numbers from the more detailed figures of the official report. Banks, farmers and the unemployed are the three major beneficiaries. Then come railroads, mortgage companies and home owners. The cash actually paid out to December 31, 1934, amounting to $7,502,000,000, was less than the total allocated. Of the total loans made during the three years, $2,465,000,000 has been repaid, which explains why the "loans receivable" on the balance sheet are smaller than the total loans shown in the above table.

In April, 1935, Mr. Jesse H. Jones, chairman of the RFC, remarked: "It looks like we are in the utility business whether we want to be or not." * He had just taken an overdue note, secured by stock of the Utilities Securities Corporation. As a result, he had authority to assume control of about 2,000 public utility plants in the Middle West. At the same time he announced that the RFC owns outright or controls:

> *Three* insurance companies
> *Scores* of national banks
> *Four million* bales of cotton
> *One* railroad
> *One* real estate mortgage loan company

Is this a business or a community chest? It has a balance sheet and a profit and loss account which look like those of a private corporation, but it has a remarkable assortment of financial traffic—drainage companies, insolvent farmers, insolvent banks, home owners, railroads, Chicago teachers, insurance companies. A safe and sane banker, one fears, would retire to his sanctum and shoot himself when the examiners arrived, if they were to find such loans and advances in his portfolio. And yet we all know that little of this stupendous outlay could have been avoided, without bankrupting more companies and more individuals than the nation could afford to lose.

If the banks and the farmers and mortgage companies could never repay, they could never repay. The years 1932 and 1933 were no time to ponder over good and bad financial risks; they were a time to keep our

* New York *Times,* April 7, 1935.

system of production from cracking up; $9,000,000,000 of collectivism helped to mend the crack. One would be foolish to look at the RFC as a traditional business proposition or as an income producing mechanism. It is a field hospital.

Its activities have centered upon relief for capital and relief for the wayfaring man. Capital received first attention under Mr. Hoover, while under Mr. Roosevelt the common man has fared better. But the two are not altogether separate and distinct. In a high energy economy, capital and the common man are tangled up together. Relief to banks and insurance companies has prevented millions of common men from losing their savings. Relief to farmers and home owners has prevented the destruction of creditors who held their mortgages. Capital has undoubtedly had the lion's share, but the price of taking it has been to make the State a partner, silent or vociferous as the case may be, of unnumbered business enterprises. The RFC is deep in the vaults of the banks, deep in agricultural credit, deep in the real estate business, in railroads, insurance companies. It has underwritten the bank accounts of upwards of 90 percent of us who have bank deposits. It is so deep in the economic structure that one wonders whether it can get out.

The RFC's loans, advances and stock purchases put it in the position of a great bank which, in the event of default, may take over the operation of the defaulted properties. It has power to take an active interest in the management of concerns whose paper it holds; to appoint directors in some cases, to dominate the board if need be. Thus the adventure in government ownership of a financial institution may have a secondary effect in more ownership, operation and control.

The RFC is now socializing private losses rather than profits, but it is in a position to control the future profits of many enterprises. Taken together with the growing powers of the Treasury and the Federal Reserve Board, the RFC may eventually provide an alternative to private banking. Nine billion dollars is almost a fifth of the present national income.

Control-without-ownership in agriculture

To my mind, the most significant of the New Deal agencies from the theoretical point of view is control over agriculture. What, basically, has the Agricultural Adjustment Administration done? It is in the process of collectivizing the largest private business in the nation, composed of 6 million farm units. This business has been commercially unprofitable since 1921. Many farmers have made money, but agricultural prices as a whole have not covered costs. Even in such a prosperous year as 1927, *Recent Economic Changes* shows a net loss of $1,717,000,000 to farmers as a class, a loss enormously accelerated by the depression. *Agriculture has failed as a self-sustaining sector of private business.* The farmer feeds the nation, and furnishes many important industrial raw materials, such as cotton and wool. Creditors cannot throw agriculture into bankruptcy as they can a Main Street haberdasher. Finance is important, but food is more important. So farming had to be extricated from the domain of private business and somehow established as public business. The AAA did not buy the farmer out, or set up giant farms and village collectives like the Russians, or incorporate the several crops into huge state trusts, or underwrite a national network of farmers' cooperative associations. It offered to pay farmers for restricting their crops, to the end that their prices might be raised. This was admittedly a retreat to scarcity, but it had the virtue of partially righting the balance between agriculture and industry, a balance which had been going against the farmer for a generation. The method of paying farmers was to tax the millers, canners, cotton manufacturers, cigarette makers, and other processors who used the farmers' raw material. The processors pass the tax on to the public, chiefly the urban public. So in effect the city man subsidizes the farmer. It should be noted that the processors also tend to swing under collective control.

On December 31, 1934, the Federal Land Banks owned outright 20,286 farms, including some in every state but Delaware and Rhode Island, to a value of some $70,000,000. Land acquisitions under emergency appropriations up to January 31, 1935, totaled just over 23 million acres. Outright government ownership is thus making progress too. Forty-one states now have Rural Rehabilitation Corporations, set up by the FERA to aid farm families on relief. By December, 1934, 132,000 families had been "accepted for rural rehabilitation." This means loans and gifts for seed and equipment, assistance with debts, advice from agricultural experts. It is estimated that 440,000 relief families are on such poor land that they must be moved. The Land Program division of the PWA has taken options on 5 million acres and has allotted funds for 13 million more. This vast area is to be turned into parks, playgrounds, wild life sanctuaries, Indian reservations, and so on. There are 42,000 farm families now living on these lands, and 20,000 must be relocated.

More than half the farmers of the republic have already signed contracts with the federal government under the AAA—over 3 million contracts. Ruggedest of individuals, they are perforce becoming component parts of a vast collective machine. As such they will remain, presently to be joined by most of their fellows, until and unless *farming as a private business can show a profit*. In an economy of abundance, with agricultural productivity well in advance of market demand, that profit appears remote. Food is one of those commodities, unfortunate from the commercial point of view, which economists call inelastic. Profits depend on relative scarcity. Probably half the present number of farmers, aided by agro-biology and up-to-date machinery, on well-selected land, could keep the national stomach filled. There is little hope in my opinion for agriculture as a profitable private business. It seems destined to stay indefinitely in the public zone, where, with wise administration, ability and reasonable help from the elements, it may have a great and prosperous future. The AAA has begun the task of socializing agriculture, and there is, for the discernible future, no turning back. Court decisions may alter the form but it is difficult to see how they can check the process in the long run.

"Ask Secretary Wallace or any of his technical advisers," says R. L. Duffus, "and the answer is likely to be two-pronged. They will state that all America's actual needs for food and other farm products can be met, and still leave from 40 million to 100 million acres of fertile land unemployed. This slack can be taken up, they will further contend, only by increase in the population, which is likely to be slow, by increase in domestic uses, which would be relatively small, or by the restoration of the export market." * Which is, we might add, a chimera for years to come if not forever. Too many nations are growing their own crops, assisted by their local AAA's.

It may be objected that erosion, dust storm, drought, are reducing the fertile areas on which the estimate of agricultural excess capacity is founded. This is probably true, but it does nothing to restore agriculture to the arms of private enterprise. Rather the reverse; tens of thousands of families must be moved from barren to fertile soil, or from farm to industrial work. This demands a gigantic adventure in collective planning, an adventure already well under way. The Senate has passed the Bankhead bill, which sets up a billion dollar government corporation to put some millions of share-croppers and tenant farmers on productive land which they may own free of exploitation.

The government is obviously not socializing the profits of the farmers, for there are none. For the moment, as in the case of the RFC, it is socializing their losses, passing part of them on to other sections of the community. Following J. M. Keynes' *Agenda* —the things which the State must do—the government is seeking to do what private business will not and cannot do. It is ominous to find the *Agenda* spreading to the 30 million persons, more or less, who are dependent upon American agriculture. Certain selected and favored crops, such as fruits and vegetables, may remain as profitable private enterprises, but a large, red question mark hangs suspended over the great staples of wheat, corn, cotton, milk, hogs, beef, rye, oats, tobacco, rice.

* New York *Times,* April 7, 1935.

NEW DEAL COLLECTIVISM 43

The control of industry

While the National Recovery Administration permits no such reasonably clear conclusions, it has certain byproducts of significance. It started as an adventure in the collective control of industry, but became lost in the woods. Industry, or at least a large section of it, was still making profits in normal times. Not until the depression did it follow agriculture into default. Then its losses were appalling—probably not less than 8 billion dollars net for all industry in 1932. By 1933, industry, thoroughly frightened, was ready to try anything short of complete nationalization. So the NRA was formulated by the United States Chamber of Commerce.* Business men were to get together with their fellows in the same industry and plan for the good of all; they were to get together with the government and plan for the good of the nation. Charming but impracticable. Nine business men out of ten distrusted their competitors, and ninety-nine out of one hundred distrusted the government. Seeds of cooperation, no matter how thickly showered, could not grow on such stony ground. The business men who had previously got together—like the Steel gentlemen—stayed together, no longer fearful of anti-trust legislation. Those who had previously been asunder presently fell asunder again. The tumult and the shouting died, General Johnson retired to write his memoirs of a very sick blue eagle, and on May 27, 1935, the Supreme Court shot the bird.

The NRA inaugurated three principles of great importance for social control—universal minimum wages, maximum hours, the abolition of child labor. For the

* According to John T. Flynn.

first time the federal government was charged with the safeguarding of workers everywhere from rates of pay below a minimum standard; from excessive and brutal hours of labor. I say "charged," for actual results were disappointing. In principle the State steps into private industry at the bottom and says: Below this line, exploitation shall not go. You must build your business above the prescribed base. If the cost is too great for Company A or Company Z, they must go to the wall. Society cannot tolerate those marginal, ill-managed concerns which cannot afford decent wages and civilized hours.

The Supreme Court has voided the hour and wage standards, but industry is trying to maintain them by voluntary agreement. One fears the attempt will be no more successful than it was under President Hoover. The marginal concerns will chisel, and in due time undermine the voluntary structure. President Roosevelt has directed his attention to a constitutional amendment whereby the federal government may control wages and hours in the national interest. States' rights and the interstate commerce clause were perhaps good doctrine in 1787 when it took as long to go from one county seat to another as it now takes to fly from New York to San Francisco. As I write, New England textile operators are thoroughly alarmed about the effect of the decision on North Carolina textile wage rates. If the latter are cut, New England must cut too, or suffer serious competitive losses. And so it goes, in industry after industry.

We can forego the doubtful blessings of the NRA in delegating law-making authority to private business through the codes, forego the tendency to make monopoly officially legitimate, forego price fixing, restriction of production, "ethical" standards, but maximum hour and minimum wage standards we cannot long forego. By one method or another they must be recaptured, and a constitutional amendment seems the most forthright way.

Relief

Three years ago most business men held that the unemployed could get themselves jobs, and where they could not, worthy cases should be salvaged by private charity. Today, the federal government is keeping more than 20 million Americans alive on a dole and on work relief, at a cost of about 2 billions a year. The President now proposes—and Congress has given him 4 billions—to transform the dole into work relief, for those of the unemployed who are still employable. Socially, the cost of public works is nothing, in that the workers would otherwise be idle. Financially, its cost is comparatively high. Private business, except in the construction industries, now prefers the dole to work relief. The first financial cost is less, and there is less danger of government competition. Nobody in his senses is demanding that relief in one form or another be abandoned. That which was anathema in 1931 is now universally admitted to be urgent public business.

Mr. Harry Hopkins, whose Federal Emergency Relief Administration has been operating the dole, prefers work relief. Up to February 1, 1935, the FERA, through its Federal Surplus Relief Corporation, had obtained 1,190,000,000 pounds of foodstuffs from farmers, mostly surplus stocks, for distribution to the unemployed. The Corporation was a short circuit for the so-called paradox of plenty. Although it seems merely common sense to take surplus crops before they rot and deliver them to hungry men, such common sense under the old division between public business and private had been proscribed. This billion pounds, incidentally, should be chalked up as a credit against the destruction of potential stocks under the AAA.

The FERA is also putting the unemployed to work producing commodities for barter among themselves—mattresses, canned foods, overalls, and the like. It is reported that more than 300,000 persons were so employed in 1935, using idle shops and factories. This is a cheap and sensible way to preserve morale while raising relief standards, but it admits the State into areas heretofore sacred to private business and so is regarded as a very dangerous entering wedge.

One trade association protested violently against the government production of mattresses. While its business was not immediately harmed—because if the unemployed had not made the mattresses they would have slept on bare boards—the association indignantly pointed out that real cotton was going into these mattresses which would therefore last twenty years. The trade normally uses linters, which give a far brisker turnover. Some day, these long-lived mattresses would take profit away from private enterprise. One does not know whether to laugh or to cry. Certainly if private business cannot defend its zone with a better argument than this, we may expect a rapid expansion in the other direction. Adam Smith and the classicists would never have tolerated such nonsense. Their thesis was that private enterprise could lay down an identical article more expeditiously and more cheaply than could the State.

Broadly speaking, relief is negative rather than posi-

NEW DEAL COLLECTIVISM

tive public business. It keeps the community from starving, but does not lead the community forward. When relief steps from the dole, however, to public works, it becomes positive. The unemployed have jobs again; purchasing power is expanded; the community has new school houses, roads, hospitals, forest cover, water systems, and the like. The 400,000 young men in the Civilian Conservation Corps initiated public business which could never have been done by private enterprise. Their number has been raised to 600,000.

Relief has reached astronomical proportions. Methods change so rapidly that it is impossible accurately to assess the gigantic totals, but various estimates have recently been made. The $4,880,000,000 appropriated by Congress in April, 1935, is the largest sum for any similar purpose ever voted by any government. It is equal to all the gold stocks in the world in 1913. It would buy 10 million automobiles, or one for every third family. It means $75 every second, $4,500 every minute, until the date of expiration, June 30, 1937.*

A census made in 1934 of heads of families on urban relief shows that about one third of all were members of the middle class, including skilled workers as middle class.**

```
   65,000 professional persons
  111,000 business men—proprietors, managers, executives
  404,000 clerks and white collar workers
  660,000 skilled workers
1,090,000 semi-skilled
1,374,000 unskilled
          ─────────
3,704,000 total urban relief
```

* New York *Times,* April 7, 1935.
** Aubrey Williams, Assistant Administrator of Relief, in New York *Times,* February 17, 1935.

More than 8 million children are on relief. In South Dakota, 35 percent of the entire population, and in Florida 25 percent, is supported by the State. Eighty percent of all relief households have one or more members able and willing to work. Technological unemployment, Mr. Williams finds, is helping to keep the rolls from diminishing. When business picks up, new machines and processes often do the additional work. Negroes are relatively twice as numerous on relief rolls as whites. One third of all persons on relief are in the four industrial states of New York, Illinois, Pennsylvania and Ohio. The 20 million to 22 million total does not vary very greatly, but the membership varies widely from month to month. Turnover is active. Thousands get jobs, while other thousands lose jobs. Despite some improvement in business, rolls remain high as unemployed family after family comes to the end of its savings. It is estimated that only about half the unemployed are on relief, so this process promises to continue for a long time. It explains why relief costs tend to grow even when business picks up.

A chart prepared early in 1935 by the National Association of Manufacturers, shows that 41 million persons out of a total population of 126 million will receive federal funds, if and when the proposed social security legislation, covering unemployment insurance, old age pensions, and the like, is passed. Nor is this all. The chart does not include farmers' benefits under the AAA, or persons on local relief, or those on the payrolls of state and local governments.

My estimate of the present grand total would be as follows:

Population on federal relief (official)	22,000,000
" on local relief	3,000,000
" supported by regular federal payrolls	3,000,000 *
" " by local government "	6,000,000 *
" " by CCC workers	500,000
" " by PWA workers	1,500,000
Total whose chief support is government	36,000,000
Farm population, partially supported	15,000,000
Grand total	51,000,000

This is about 40 percent of the population of the nation. Old age pensions, soldiers' bonuses, unemployment insurance, will further raise the figure. No allowance has been made for those who have had their homes and their bank balances saved by federal intervention.

Relief on this scale can be only temporary public business. It saves lives and homes in a calamitous depression, *but it does not operate to increase production on the scale required.* Meanwhile the public debt rolls grimly up. In a sense, the program is the same old installment plan of the 1920's on a grander scale, with interest at three percent instead of 15 percent. The installment curve came to a halt when people could no longer afford to mortgage their future earnings, and the same thing will happen to the relief curve if it continues to be financed by mortgaging the future income of the community.

Of the 40 percent of the population, more or less, thus supported within the public sector, a relatively small proportion is paying its way in the sense of producing goods and services in exchange for the goods and services received. Going back to the simple vil-

* In 1934, the Commission of Inquiry on Public Service Personnel estimated 3,250,000 persons on federal and local payrolls. At three to the family, total persons supported would be close to 10 million.

lage pattern, the situation is comparable to an excessive number of man-hours spent by citizens in fiestas, ceremonials, patrolling roads which need no watchmen, and a deficient amount of time spent in the cornfields, with a low standard of living all round as a result. No primitive community could long tolerate such a situation.

In the modern community, when it is proposed to put the unemployed into the cornfields, roars of protest arise from private business, as in the case of the mattresses cited above. This leaves us in an acute dilemma. We need more goods, but powerful pressure groups prevent us from using idle manpower to produce them. So the relief burden and the debt burden mount. The unemployed are literally forbidden to pay their own way.

The acid test of sound public business is a high level of productivity, resulting in high living standards. Work relief is a step in the right direction, but the dole helps very little, while AAA subsidies to farmers tend to decrease production, though they may not lessen net consumption. (In the case of the 1934 peach crop, they operated to increase consumption a little.) This ramshackle, wasteful structure of relief must ultimately be rebuilt from the ground up and the foundation stone must be goods production rather than debt production. We can hardly expect the rebuilding to be done in earnest until the community and its political leaders are convinced that the State must permanently undertake to find useful work, at adequate wages,* for the millions of Americans whom private business can no longer use.

* The wages announced for the new work relief army (May, 1935) appear to be grossly inadequate.

CHAPTER FOUR

More New Deal Collectivism

PUBLIC finance, government direction of agriculture, and public relief—these are the giants in the New Deal's menagerie. The rest of the collection are smaller fry, but warrant mention. One or another of them may presently scramble into the first division. The Tennessee Valley Authority, for instance, is practicing social planning at longer range than any other agency. A decade from now, principles it lays down through experiment may be binding policies of the nation. The integrated use of land, water and power makes a dynamic trinity, strictly in keeping with technological imperatives.

March of the camels

The following list serves to show the impact of the new agencies on various industries. Space does not allow detailed description; even if it did, the description would be out of date before these words are in print. If my publisher would permit, I would insert a few blank pages after the list for the reader to jot down new arrivals. The headlines herald an accouchement nearly every day. From time to time the Supreme Court buries an item. The important thing to indicate here is the mass effect. In 1928, such a march would have been inconceivable. The mere hint of it would have caused editorial apoplexy from coast to coast. You will note some unavoidable duplications, when one agency clearly belongs under two headings.

Overhead controlling, planning and advisory bodies:

The National Emergency Council. Coordinating body for the whole New Deal, headed by the President.

United States Information Service. *Publicity for the New Deal.

Central Statistical Board.

Science Advisory Board. Collaborating with the privately endowed National Research Council to put science to work for the Government.

National Resources Board. (Including the Mississippi Valley Committee.) In the process of becoming the central planning agency of the government. Its recent reports constitute the most comprehensive survey of our national resources ever prepared. Its recommendations will form the backbone of the new public works program, according to the President.

National Labor Relations Board. (Dissolved by NRA decision. The Wagner bill will take its place.)

National Employment Service. It had received applications for 14,545,000 jobs and made 8,523,000 placements in government or private work to December 31, 1934. This is a mobilization of manpower on a par with that in the War.

Agriculture:

The central control of the AAA as described. Up to April 1, 1935, $742,000,000 had been paid out to farmers in benefits, and $777,000,000 taken in through processing taxes.

The huge advances to farmers of the RFC as described.

The Farm Credit Administration.

Federal Farm Mortgage Corporation. To prevent foreclosures.

Commodity Credit Corporation. To advance loans on crops.

MORE NEW DEAL COLLECTIVISM 53

Land Bank Commissioner.
Production Credit Corporations and Associations.
Rural Rehabilitation Corporations as described.
Land Program Division of the PWA as described.
Emergency Crop and Feed Loans.
Soil erosion service.
Federal Surplus Relief Corporation.
Federal Credit Union System.

If the Bankhead bill is passed, a billion dollar government corporation to put share-croppers and farm tenants on their own land.

Alcohol:

Federal Alcohol Control Administration. (Dissolved by NRA decision. Special new legislation being rushed to take its place.)

Aviation:

Federal Aviation Commission. Policies for military and commercial flying.

The subsidy of private air lines through mail contracts. Says President Roosevelt in this connection: "Government aid in this case is legitimate in order to save companies from disastrous loss, but not in order to provide profits."

Banking and credit:

The RFC as described.

The multiform agencies for farm credit as listed above. The Farm Credit Administration has taken over the direction of the widespread credit union movement which provides banking facilities for workers.

The Federal Reserve Board. It is continually tightening its grip on private banking, as in the new Eccles banking legislation.

Federal Savings and Loan System. To aid in home construction. The system works through associations, for which Congress has authorized $100,000,000 for the purchase of shares.

Federal Savings and Loan Insurance Corporation. To insure the above.

Federal Deposit Insurance Corporation. Up to June 30, 1934, it had insured 56 million bank accounts in 13,982 banks to a total of $16,000,000,000.

Home Owners' Loan Corporation. To prevent foreclosure on small homes. Up to June 1, 1935, it had refinanced 861,691 non-farm, owner-occupied homes.

The HOLC, says one of its directors, Dr. Henry E. Hoagland, before it finishes lending will hold $4,750,000,000 in mortgages on 1,500,000 American homes; more than all the mortgages held by building and loan associations, more than by banks, and four times the amount held by all life insurance companies. "The extensive operations of the corporation have made millions of Americans government-finance minded." Citizens, one suspects, will be loath in the future to pay six percent, plus bonuses for second mortgages at 20 to 30 percent, when they know the State can do it at a far more modest rate.

Coal:

Bituminous coal was regulated by an NRA code authority, voided by the Supreme Court. This code, however, like that of petroleum and of alcohol, was of exceptional importance, due to the disorganization of the industry. Like agriculture, soft coal has been in the dumps since shortly after the War. Special legislation is now being considered to take the place of the defunct code, and both operators and workers are demanding government leadership. The Guffey coal bill has been placed on the President's "must" legislation (June, 1935). It provides for a national commission of five members, two representing employers, two labor, one the government. It legalizes collective bargaining, permits price agreements, provides for maximum hours and minimum wages, and gives the commission power to allocate production by districts. The government is empowered to buy up sub-marginal coal lands, and $300,000,000 is authorized for the purpose.

MORE NEW DEAL COLLECTIVISM 55

Communication:

Federal Communications Commission. To regulate telephone, telegraph and radio industries.

Construction, public works, housing:

Public Works Administration. 19,000 projects, of which 11,500 were completed and in use in April, 1935. One hundred and ten million man-hours of work had been provided. Total cost, $2,506,000,000.

The new work relief legislation with its $4,000,000,000.

Works Progress Administration.

Resettlement Administration.

The Federal Housing Administration. Cooperation with private business in house repair and construction.

Division of Subsistence Homesteads, and Federal Subsistence Homesteads Corporation. Building new towns.

Federal Savings and Loan Associations.

Foreign trade:

The legislation which took the United States off the gold standard. The consequent gold "profit" to the government of two billions, and the foreign exchange stabilization fund.

The AAA control of certain imports, such as sugar.

Foreign Trade Zones Board.

Interdepartmental Committee on Trade Agreements.

The Export-Import Bank of Washington.

If one may hazard a guess, based on the record, foreign trade appears to be moving in the direction of an ultimate state control of exports and imports, thus following the common pattern of many other nations at the present time.

Forests and lumber:

The Civilian Conservation Corps. (Emergency Conservation Work.)

The large purchases by the government of marginal land for the protection of the future lumber supply.

The forest shelter belt from Canada to the Gulf. This work is well under way.

Insurance:

RFC loans to insurance companies.

Underwriting of farm and home mortgages on a vast scale by the Federal Farm Mortgage Corporation, and the Home Owners' Loan Corporation.

Federal Deposit Insurance Corporation.

Federal Savings and Loan Insurance Corporation.

The great legislative program of social insurance and security, including unemployment insurance, old age pensions, mother pensions, health insurance.

Committee on Economic Security. (Dissolved after rendering report.)

Oil:

Petroleum Administration. To administer codes and eliminate waste. It has attempted to control physical production by state quotas, until checked by the Supreme Court's "hot oil" decision. The attempt is now being resumed, from a new legal direction, under Federal Tender Board No. 1. More special legislation is proposed.

Power:

Federal Power Commission.

The Tennessee Valley Authority. Appropriation—$75,000,000; staff—12,000. Authorized further to issue $50,000,000 in three and one-half percent bonds having a fifty year maturity for power projects. Receives income from sale of power, fertilizers, electrical appliances, etc.

The National Resources Board. To prepare plans for physical, social and economic development of land, water and other natural resources.

Electric Home and Farm Authority. To distribute electric

MORE NEW DEAL COLLECTIVISM

appliances. Functions like an installment finance company, except that the rates are lower. (Dissolved by NRA decision. Special legislation proposed to continue it.)

National Power Policy Committee.

The Rural Electrification Administration, under Morris L. Cooke.

Boulder Dam, the Grand Coulee Dam, the Passamaquoddy tidal project for power and navigation, etc. It was recently estimated that the value of projects already adopted or definitely under construction will involve a government investment of $3,000,000,000.

The proposed legislation drastically to modify utility holding companies. It is on the President's "must" list, but the power gentlemen have not been idle.

Shipping:

U. S. Shipping Board. Here the government is socializing the losses of the merchant marine through mail contracts, precisely as in the case of aviation. The proprietary interest of the Treasury in the Shipping Board is given as $196,000,000. (This is not a New Deal project, but a holdover from War collectivism.)

Stock exchanges:

The Securities and Exchange Commission. Regulating the exchanges of the nation, a critical function. A good old bull market inflation will now be exceedingly difficult to start.

The Securities Act. Legislation controlling the terms under which new financing may be permitted. The broad principle of state control of new investment is thus laid down.

Transportation:

The Interstate Commerce Commission. Granted new powers under Air Mail Act of 1934.

Federal Coordinator of Transportation. Mr. Joseph B. Eastman has prepared blue prints for coordinating all forms of transport into one organism—including railways, waterways, highways, airways, pipe lines, transmission lines. His possible alternatives are federal major regulation, federal control, government ownership. The Senate has just passed a bill based on his findings to regulate trucks and buses (April, 1935).

RFC loans to railroads.

PWA loans to railroads for new equipment—rails, streamlined trains, electrification, etc.

Government corporations:

A specific list of new government corporations belongs in our inventory despite certain duplications. The information was checked in May, 1935.

Reconstruction Finance Corporation—capital stock, $500,000,000.

RFC Mortgage Company—capital stock, $10,000,000, subscribed by the RFC.

Federal Deposit Insurance Corporation—*A* stock, $150,000,000; *B* stock, $139,000,000; debentures authorized, $250,000,000.

Home Owners' Loan Corporation—capital stock, $200,000,000. May issue bonds in aggregate not to exceed $3,000,000,000.

Federal Savings and Loan Insurance Corporation—capital stock, $100,000,000; subscribed by the Home Owners' Loan Corporation.

Federal Farm Mortgage Corporation—capital stock, $200,000,000; bonds authorized, $2,000,000,000.

Federal Surplus Relief Corporation—allocated, $77,000,000.

Emergency Housing Corporation—allocated, $135,000,000.

Federal Subsistence Homesteads Corporation—allocated, $25,000,000.

Commodity Credit Corporation—capital stock, $3,000,000; has advanced $271,000,000.

Export-Import Bank of Washington—capital stock, $11,000,000.

Tennessee Valley Associated Cooperatives, Inc.—allocated $300,000 by FERA.

Regional Agricultural Credit Corporations.

MORE NEW DEAL COLLECTIVISM

Production Credit Corporations.
Rural Rehabilitation Corporations. (Forty-one of them.)
Banks for cooperatives.
Federal Prison Industries, Inc.—created December, 1934.

It is obvious that the corporate form, so assiduously cultivated and elaborated by private enterprise, is being rapidly adopted for public business.*

The Treasury as an investment trust

The Treasury, among other things, appears to be turning into a vast investment trust, with portfolio already heavy with common stocks, preferred stocks, Class A stocks, Class B, debentures, and bonds of all varieties. We speak of the Treasury now, not the RFC which has its own amazing portfolio. Proprietary interests of the United States in government corporations and credit agencies were $5,529,000,000 on March 1, 1935, according to official Treasury figures, of which $4,439,000,000 were in agencies wholly financed by the State, and $1,090,000,000 in agencies where private capital also participated.

As of October, 1934, the National Industrial Conference Board announced that the federal government was the largest owner of securities in the world, and presented the following tabulation:

Foreign securities, chiefly war debts	$12,015,000,000
RFC, stock and notes, net	2,962,000,000
Securities of other government corporations	1,207,000,000
Miscellaneous securities	655,000,000
Capital stock of war emergency corporations, etc.	116,000,000
Total	$16,955,000,000

* For a detailed consideration of this important point, see Chapter XIV.

Eliminating the war debts—you can take both meanings—the balance is not out of line with the Treasury figures shown above.

If the government is holding corporation paper, the corporations known as banks are brimming over with government paper. According to the Controller of the Currency, national banks in March, 1935, held $7,120,000,000 of government securities, comprising almost 40 percent of all their loans and investments. Forty percent public, 60 percent private. This ratio, curiously enough, is not far from the relief figures cited earlier, in which it was estimated that some 40 percent of the American population was dependent on the State for its support.

Barron's Weekly calculates that between February, 1932, and June, 1935, the federal government will have expended on account of the emergency the sum of $16,837,000,000. Of this, $6,557,000,000 will have gone for purposes upon which private capital would not normally embark—relief, conservation and public works; and the far greater balance, $10,280,-000,000, for purposes upon which private capital *would* normally embark—loans to banks, railroads, mortgage companies, farmers, home owners, power development, etc. Of this latter amount, no less than $9,722,000,-000 is in long term financing. In effect, the government has superseded the investment banker in the capital market. In effect, it had to, for excess capacity had all but destroyed the traditional capital market. The private investment reservoir, which had been some 10 billions in 1928 and 1929, fell to $644,000,000 in 1932 and to $381,000,000 in 1933. In these figures we find the chief reason for the staggering relief totals. Manpower streamed out of the heavy industries, and upon the community payroll. When one side of the balance went down, the other had to go up.

The executive arm

Along with the specific penetration in industry after industry, as catalogued above, has gone a general penetration over the whole economic front. The NRA codes gave pause to every business man in the country, forcing him to take action—compliance or evasion as the case might be. Economic power has been flowing from private business, from local governments, from the state governments, from the courts, to Washington. In Washington it has flowed from Congress to the President. For the emergency at least the initiative for spending money vests in the President, contrary to American practice in the past. In a pecuniary civilization, power of the purse is the most important function. The principle of the Executive Budget has been pretty well established. Public business on a large scale is inconceivable without centralization of financial authority. Congressional initiative means a compromise among the claims—often pork barrel claims—of local districts. Each man for himself. Never is the nation seen steadily and as a whole. Only the executive can grasp the whole picture.

When I was a junior accountant, my seniors taught me that in handling every set of books and records you had to trust somebody. No system could be made burglar proof. Always at the end of the checks and double checks of the paper trail, was a man. If he wanted to steal, he could steal. In public business, too, you have to trust somebody—and it would better be one man in the glare of the headlines, than a group of assorted local wire pullers, or even a group of Solons, each with a different philosophy.

It is probably not too much to say that at the present time, and for the past two years, the executive arm, including Mr. Roosevelt and his administrative staff, has had direct responsibility for all business, whether nominally public or private. When in March, 1933, it was almost unanimously agreed that "natural forces" could not be permitted to continue deflation to the bitter end as they had in all earlier depressions, the State became the official receiver of the system. The nation in effect transferred power to the President. If there was a pump to prime, he must do the priming; if conditions were beyond pumping back to normalcy, his was the responsibility for finding new economic forms.

Broadly speaking, the executive arm of the federal government has been formulating the policies and making the decisions which have bound all American industry during the recent past. True, this work has been done more by default than by positive intention. True, it has not been done very well. It has often been opposed by Congress and courts. The American government had hardly more enthusiasm for collectivism than the American people. Both were pitched into it. In a state of despair which overcame their suspicious reluctance, the leaders of private business were pitched in, too. Even when the NRA was voided by the Supreme Court, thousands of business men wired the President to find a substitute, and find it quickly.

Local business

While the searchlight of news has been focused on Washington, the forty-eight states and their munici-

MORE NEW DEAL COLLECTIVISM 63

palities have been extending the area of public business with unprecedented rapidity. If the federal government had given us time to turn our eyes homeward, we should have stood amazed at the activities of our local authorities. The budget for relief in New York City alone is $20,000,000 a month; a quarter of a billion a year. In most districts, federal funds cannot be obtained unless a local quota is assured.

New York State under Governor Lehman and the New York Power Authority has been rapidly extending its control over the power industry. The governor has submitted a bill for the extension of electricity to farmers. The State has penetrated deeply into the business of guaranteed mortgages, even to the point of operating a series of large apartment houses in New York City which were in default; the new Mortgage Commission has nearly a billion dollars' worth of frozen assets to handle. It has made large purchases of land for reforesting and recreation. It is now entering the insurance business, covering workmen's compensation. It is proposing to set up a huge corporation (note the corporate form again) for rural rehabilitation, to take citizens off the dole and help them to earn subsistence on the land. It is proposing a system of State Regional Markets to aid in distribution of foodstuffs, and is particularly concerned with government control of the milk supply.

In the spring of 1935, forty-three states were wrestling with some 300 bills covering proposals for social security—old age pensions, unemployment insurance, and the like. Many of the bills had been introduced by the governor. "That the issue is no longer a political one is indicated by the fact that many of the governors are Republicans."

Local "Authorities" are sprouting like Tom Thumb golf courses in 1930, inspired by the Tennessee Valley model. The State of Alabama is proposing a whole series of economic Authorities. The Merrimac Valley Authority, the Connecticut Valley Authority, the Blackstone Valley Authority, have all made formal application to the President for an allotment of public works funds, for the purposes of stream control, anti-pollution measures, erosion work, etc. Mayor La Guardia proposes a New York Municipal Authority to spend $1,000,000,000 on public works; a corporation to sell its securities to the PWA at one eighth of one percent interest.

Finally, if you can spare a few side glances from Washington, I advise you to keep your eye on Wisconsin. It has received $100,000,000 from the public works fund and is incorporating a Wisconsin Finance Authority with a new and startling program. A laboratory experiment in social security is being here developed which may one day be a model for all local communities to follow.

Cooperatives

As pointed out earlier, public business is not necessarily carried on by the State alone. Cooperative enterprises are semi-public and not to be confused with private industry. Profits are socialized. Sales by such societies in 1934 in the United States were estimated at $365,000,000, or about one and one fifth percent of the total retail business of $30,000,000,-000. A larger amount is looked for in 1935. The movement has been gaining steadily throughout the depression. There are now 1500 oil and petroleum units in the Middle West—cooperative gas stations. This type of public business has not yet reached great proportions, but it may become very important in the future. It offers one solution for the complicated problems of distribution in the power age. In Europe, as we shall see concretely in the next chapter, the importance of the cooperative movement is profound.

Summary of the New Deal

It is obvious that there has been a tumultuous advance in public business under the New Deal, an advance which dwarfs the very considerable march from 1912 to 1930. Government has stepped into all kinds of activities neglected during the depression by private business—like the capital market, agriculture, housing; it has invaded other activities in an attempt to stabilize them and prevent further deflation—like banks and railroads; it has been forced to assume responsibility, in default of jobs in private business, for some 40 percent of the whole population.

Today, the State is responsible for the economic mechanism, and the executive arm has developed beyond all peace-time precedent in an attempt to wield that control. No major undertakings in construction, housing, mining, transportation, agriculture, manufacturing, communications, power, shipping, are being made without the permission or the encouragement of the government. It is highly probable, though not accurately demonstrable, that without the 16 billions, more or less, which the State has poured out, private business would be at a standstill or even in actual recession. In 1934, steel-rail production was 1,008,000 tons against 408,000 in 1933. This looks like a brave advance for the steel companies. But of the 600,000 ton increase, the government loaned the railroads the cash with which to buy 425,000 tons. Of the 150,000 ton increase in angle bars in 1934 over 1933, 71 percent was bought by federal funds. And so it goes.

"The steel industry, the automobile industry, every industry that has been boasting about its better business in 1934, got that better business out of federal funds paid out to its customers. These industries are on the dole. Their employees are on the dole . . . the stockholders who have been getting the rising dividends and the bondholders who have been getting their continuing interest are therefore also on the dole." Mr. John T. Flynn puts the case dramatically, but it contains a large measure of truth. Indeed, Mr. Eugene G. Grace, president of Bethlehem Steel, supports Mr. Flynn. Departing from Pittsburgh for New York after testifying in the Mellon tax case, Mr. Grace said: "I see nothing to indicate any vital improvement in the steel industry in the next few months, at least from within itself. When the government expends its $4,500,-000,000 as planned, it will be reflected in the steel trade, for such a sum cannot be spent without us getting our share." * Thus, we might add, keeping alive a fine old tradition. In the steel business, us does not normally overlook our share.

The New Deal has socialized many losses like those of the farmers and the railroads, but it has not socialized profits to any marked degree. Industries have not been taken over bodily, income and profit taxes have not been severely applied, interest rates have not been

* New York *Times,* April 24, 1935.

arbitrarily set except in a few cases.* (It is interesting to note, however, that the interest rate is falling like a plummet. Short term government loans have been gobbled up at one eighth of one percent, and the long term rate is now less than three percent.) The power to socialize profits is an obvious corollary of the undertaking to socialize losses. Machinery has been created to socialize either.

The net impression, however, is that of a gigantic wrecking car, hastily assembled, painfully lifting the economic mechanism out of a ditch into which, at eighty miles an hour, it had fallen. The mechanism is no longer mired, but it is still badly damaged. The wrecking crew have got it out but they have not got it going. If they retire while it moves off under its own power, collectivism will be postponed. At present, it seems more likely that a long towing job is in prospect.

In 1926, J. A. Hobson said: "Apart from all theories of socialism and individualism, a general tendency is seen in civilized countries toward the assertion of public ownership, operation and control of land [natural resources and agriculture], power, transport, money, insurance, education and hygiene, regarded as necessary prerequisites of liberty and opportunity." The stoppage of these services "inflicts intolerable injuries upon the community," and the State is bound to intervene. Such intervention, Hobson believed, must be permanent. Under the clutter of hastily improvised controls, we find this pattern strongly marked in the New Deal, thus giving it some sense and direction. If you review the agencies one by one, you will find that they tend to cluster about the functions Hobson men-

* New income and inheritance tax legislation is now before Congress. (July, 1935.)

tions, of which land use, money and credit, social insurance, power, transport, are the most immediately important. This fact argues with some force for the permanence of the function, if not for the form adopted.

The revolutionary significance of the security program

The New Deal has repudiated the idea that the misery of the unemployed is due to their own improvidence. This, for America, is a genuinely revolutionary conception. The State has underwritten the livelihood of every citizen, a totally unprecedented thing. Heretofore, the frontier has underwritten our livelihood. The last family can eat, if not too proud to ask for relief. Beyond this base of security—humble in amount, important in principle—the administration proposes that the State shall find everybody who can work a job, if not in the private sector, then in the public. This has been done in part through the NRA, in part through the Civilian Conservation Corps, in part through the Public Works Administration, in part through the barter industries and work relief of Mr. Hopkins' organization. The President now has 4 billions with which to carry the principle further. Beyond this, the administration proposes a universal program of economic security by means of unemployment, old age and other forms of social insurance. The specific program will probably be on the statute books before the year is out.

It is impossible to overemphasize the ultimate significance of collectivism in this form. If economic security for all becomes the objective of the State, private business will have to fight for its profit-über-alles, or clear the track. It will be a difficult fight to win, for the mass of the people is militantly aroused to demand security. Whatever vested interests block, obstruct, or delay the program must show cause why they should exist; traditional property rights, especially of intangibles, may not be good enough. The Supreme Court in the gold decision has already given traditional property rights a body blow.

Here, in embryo, is a new test for every economic activity, private and public: Is this business consistent with general economic security, or is it not? No such yardstick has ever appeared in America before. Not even in the War was collectivism in this sense contemplated. Yet in a high energy culture, the underwriting of the last family is not only feasible technologically,* but it is the only means yet discovered of supplying adequate purchasing power to keep the plant operating at something near capacity.

One would be rash to hold that the New Deal will carry the principle through to its logical conclusion. But one can say that an impressive beginning has been made in the specific actions and policies above recited. And one can say that the private citizens of America, probably close to 100 millions of them, are massed in favor of an extension of that beginning.

* The National Survey of Potential Product Capacity computes a possible living standard of $4,400 per family in 1929, based on the physical plant in that year.

CHAPTER FIVE

Public Business Abroad

IF PUBLIC business were a disease, as many conservative students regard it, and private competition the only healthy economy, where should we place the line of quarantine? There is evidence to show not only that it is too late for a quarantine today, but that the plague was widespread in foreign countries even before the War.

In 1914 Mr. Sidney Webb and his associates in the Fabian Society of London published a comprehensive study of public business the world around. Control by regulation and by taxation, and the work of cooperative societies, were excluded from the definition. In Western countries, they found no fewer than 12 million workers and managers actively engaged in manufacturing commodities or rendering economic services on the payroll of the State.

Telephones and telegraphs were owned in whole or in part by every nation except the United States, Brazil and Spain—an incongruous trinity. Out of seventy national railroad systems, fifty were prevailingly state owned and operated; other nations owned their lines and leased the operation to private interests. Only in the United States and England were the systems privately owned and operated. The municipal ownership of light, power, water, gas was increasingly common. Superpower developments were to be found in Switzerland, Norway, Sweden, Italy, Japan and Canada. Large scale public housing projects were under way in Great Britain, Germany, Italy, France, Australia and the Argentine. In 1814, such education as was offered was private business; by 1914 the State had everywhere taken it over and made it compulsory and universal. "Governments have become quite the largest producers in the world of books and other educational printed matter." As for health, "literally a majority of the medical practitioners in Western Europe were brought by 1913 into government pay in one form or another."

Australia, Switzerland, Russia and Prussia operated government banks. New Zealand did half as much insurance business as all private companies combined, and produced 12 percent of the country's coal. Government mines were to be found in Russia, Austria, Hungary, Sweden, Serbia, Holland; tin mines in the Dutch East Indies; emerald mines in Colombia. Forests were publicly administered in Germany, France, Russia, India, and Japan. In Australia, the government was "collectively grading, branding, storing, packing, shipping and selling the agricultural produce of individual farmers." State monopolies of matches, cigars, porcelain, salt, potash, and agricultural implements were in evidence in a number of nations. Governments, federal or local, were operating quarries, brick works, iron and steel mills, tin and copper smelters, flour mills, bakeries, shoe factories, slaughter houses, distilleries, breweries, clothing factories, furniture mills, scientific instrument shops; indeed, "manufacturing in one place or another every conceivable commodity for the use of the consumer." West Australia was even producing sleeping cars for all the Australian railroads. The City of Glasgow, tired of the wiles of trolley car contractors, had undertaken the manufacture of this equipment for the municipal trolley lines.

"In these days," said Mr. Lewis Harcourt, Secretary of State for the British Colonies, "the Colonial Office has more the attributes of an immense trading and administrative concern than those of earlier days when it was a mere machine of government. My days and nights are spent in the study of medicine, in the details of railway construction, with a desire that the smallest sum of money may lay the largest number of miles of track in the fewest possible days. I am a coal and tin miner in Nigeria; a gold miner in Guiana. I seek timber in one colony, oil and nuts in another, cocoa in a third—copra and *copal,* sisal and hemp, cotton, coffee, tobacco are common objects of my daily care." *

With the evidence in, Mr. Webb proceeds to a summary:

In face of the widespread incursion of state and municipal governments over the world into so many different departments of industry—continued for a whole century and steadily increasing in volume with growing experience of the results—it is, we think, only of academic interest to discuss the question of whether or not government enterprise as such can be deemed "successful." No such abstract question can be properly put or answered. Whether any particular forward step shall be taken is in fact decided whether or not we should have it so, not on general principles by the academic economist, or by the partisans of either individualism or collectivism, but on the actual experience lying behind each case, by the practical administrator

* London *Times,* July 1, 1914.

and the citizen elector. The general trend of these decisions is unmistakably shown in the great development of state enterprise in all the civilized countries of the world, in practically all the departments of life.

The War

During the World War, the rate of growth accelerated to the point where the Supreme Economic Council of the Allied Nations was administering the industrial activity of half the planet—the nearest approach yet reached to a World State. Prices were fixed, supplies rationed, labor conscripted, production directed, cross hauling eliminated, capital allocated, excess profits confiscated. Practically all business became public business. Yet the standard of living hardly declined. In certain countries, including the United States, it actually increased, despite the huge subversion of manpower to the military establishment. In England at the close of the War, the government held complete control—although not the ownership—of the railways, the mines, the metal trades, the food supply, wool, leather, the import trade, shipping, as well as all materials entering into munitions.

The War made it clear that business is business without a great deal of difference who owns it or administers it, provided those in control are interested in delivering specified goods to specified places at specified times. The physical work in all cases is done by inanimate energy and human labor, guided by the findings of modern technology. To nations faced with the danger of conquest, state control proved superior to private, in delivering the goods at the times and places demanded.

Russia

After demobilization, all nations to a greater or lesser degree demobilized their economic controls—with one exception. Russia maintained public business without a break; indeed, she increased its area. She continued to control credit, fix prices, conscript labor, direct production, ration supplies, allocate capital, monopolize exports and imports. During the interval of the NEP, from 1922 to 1927, when private enterprise was permitted a certain scope in retail and wholesale trading, Russia may have had a slightly less collectivized economy than had England at the close of the War. Today, of course, she holds the all-time record for public business.

The civil wars ceased in 1921, leaving Russia economically exhausted; her fields fought over, her cities burned or dilapidated, her scanty industrial equipment depreciated and obsolete if not destroyed. In 1922, Lenin's Gosplan began to function, planning for a supernetwork of electric power to transform Russia from a vegetable culture into a metallic one. The task looked utterly hopeless, but thirteen years later, it is all but done. Russia is now the third industrial nation of the world. In 1935, it is probable that her iron and steel output will exceed that of Germany, making her, on the metal scale, the second industrial nation. If our domestic metal industries continue indefinitely depressed, Russia may pass the United States by 1940. While the rest of the world sags up and down, and mostly down, Russian industry since 1926 has been compounding at the incredible rate of 20 percent per annum. This figure is greater than any national advance known to history. It is so great and so unprecedented that observers in the West simply do not perceive it. Like Mr. Roosevelt's budget, the figures are beyond their comprehension. While they shake their heads with disapproval over the plight of political prisoners, the hardships of the kulaks, or the condition of plumbing in Moscow hotels, Russia with her army, her air force, her organization, discipline, immense natural resources and leaping industrial output, is on the threshold of becoming the most powerful nation on earth. Ask any competent diplomat. Ask the Japanese General Staff.

You may or may not like Russia, her methods, her laws of property, her movies, her ballet or her political murders, but it behooves you to respect her naked military and industrial power. Witness the recent scramble of France and Great Britain to her side. If private business had been the rule since 1921, would that power be in evidence to command respect? It would not. Russian business men would have restricted production when the depression began its attack on prices like big business men everywhere else. Rather than a 1934 production 250 percent that of 1929, it is safe to say that it would have been appreciably less than 100 percent. Russia would have mattered hardly more today than Rumania or Yugoslavia.

Industry in Russia is largely in the hands of gigantic corporations or trusts, owned by the State, but maintaining a considerable degree of independence. Trade is in the hands of consumers' cooperatives plus chains of government stores. Agriculture is largely in the hands of village collectives, plus a series of huge mechanized state farms for staples like wheat. The railroads and certain other services are government departments. Credit, money and banking are government monopolies, as are exports and imports. Private business is still to be found in a minority of agriculture, in some handicraft production, and, with a microscope, in petty trade and personal services.

Few individual industrial units in Russia are as efficient as many privately owned industrial units in the West—when the latter are operating at capacity. This is, however, only a minor part of the efficiency of a national economy. The major aspect is found in operating the whole plant at capacity without duplication; in building no more woolen mills than can supply the demand for wool; in constructing no parallel lines of competing railroad track and terminals; in drilling no more wells into a pool of oil than the best geological practice permits. From this point of view, Russia's industrial system is markedly more efficient than that of other countries. That it more than compensates for inefficiencies of unit factory operation the increases in production make evident. By virtue of her natural resources and her intensive collectivism, Russia has largely immunized herself against the ravages of the business cycle.

Sweden

Russia is a dictatorship. Sweden, in spite of her venerable king, is administered by an elected parliament on democratic principles. Her collectivism is not so harsh as that of Russia, but it is sufficiently impressive. It has been developing for thirty years and more. The State owns and operates 33 percent of all mines in the nation; 25 percent of the forest area. It owns and operates all railroads, telephone and telegraph systems. It generates 34 percent of all electric power, and furnishes householders with 80 percent of their current. The Royal Board of Waterfalls has now electrified 60 percent of all farms—as against ten percent in the United States. Power and light are vital in Sweden because of the long northern winters, and the State early took steps to keep rates down by public yardsticks. In 1929, the government's investment in all business was $613,000,000, on which it secured a six percent return. The State maintains a monopoly of tobacco, liquor and radio broadcasting, and is now instituting monopolies for the wholesale drug trade, coffee, and combustible liquids.

The cooperative societies of Sweden own and operate ten percent of all industry and handle some 50 percent of all retail trade in such essentials as food, clothing, shoes. Cooperatives and municipal government together operate a quarter of the housing in Stockholm and Gothenburg. "Prices of the principal commodities, rentals, utility rates, have been forced downward, often with dramatic suddenness, by the aggressive competition of the State and the cooperatives." * The cooperatives broke the margarine trust, the flour trust, the shoe trust, the electric lamp cartel. They break one private monopoly after another by threatening to organize their own supply. This has proved far more effective than anti-trust laws. The price of lamps was driven down from thirty-seven cents to twenty.

Sweden has obviously mastered the yardstick technique with which Mr. Roosevelt is now struggling. She has the highest standard of living in Europe, higher even than for the mass of Americans. She is now about 50 percent collectivized—including the cooperatives as public business. Private capital has re-

* Marquis W. Childs in *Harper's Magazine*.

signed itself to the inevitable, and from time to time actively cooperates in some aspect of state enterprise. The collapse of Ivar Kreuger hurt more Americans than Swedes. You are taxed for the State's broadcasting programs, but not if you are blind, sick or old. Artists of the highest ability are designing the output of mass production factories. Public business has obviously not prevented Sweden from becoming one of the most civilized nations on earth. There is reason to believe it has helped.

Italy

The collectivism of Sweden, Denmark, Finland and Norway is indigenous and long in the making. That of Italy and Nazi Germany was inevitable, if you will, but its form was thrust suddenly down from the top. The form may some day dissolve as suddenly as it came, but it is extremely unlikely to be replaced by a regime of private business.

Fascism [says Charles A. Beard], may be regarded as an effort to organize industry, agriculture and labor, thus serving as a preliminary to socialism. From no point of view can it be considered as opening the way for a return to laissez-faire. But how it will ever seek to meet the issue presented by the productive potentials of technology is nowhere evident in its program or performances. And yet, since its inner logic is war, it must make full use of them or incur the risk of inviting defeat at the hands of nations employing their technology at high tempo. It therefore has a fateful contradiction in the rationale of its own working policy.

The Fascist State seeks to freeze the status quo, but in the process, it tends to destroy the free market, private business and traditional capitalism. Capitalism, depending as it does on a compound interest curve of reinvestment, cannot survive a protracted freezing.

Fascism has no established body of philosophical or political doctrine behind it, certainly nothing to compare with Marxism and its century of exegesis and counter exegesis. Its outstanding metaphysic is a militant nationalism which makes the State greater than the sum of its citizens, a proposition as dubious in politics as in Euclid. Those who hold that Fascism is the last stand of capitalism had better read Mussolini on this point.* He tells us that capitalism was dynamic from 1830 to 1870, static to the World War, degenerate thereafter. It became soft with its trusts and monopolies. He says:

> When does capitalistic enterprise cease to be an economic factor? When its size compels it to be a social factor . . . it is the moment when the intervention of the State begins rendering itself more necessary. We are at this point. Now there is no economic field in which the State is not called upon to intervene. Today we bury economic liberalism. Corporationism is disciplined economy, and from that comes control, because we cannot imagine a discipline without a director. Corporationism is above socialism, and above liberalism. A new synthesis has been created. It is a symptomatic fact that the decadence of capitalism coincides with the decadence of socialism. We take the vitality from both and march on. . . . Italy is not a capitalistic nation.

It certainly is not. All economic activity is divided into nine syndicates; four of employees, four of employers, one of professional people. The four include: (1) agriculture, (2) commerce, (3) banking and finance, (4) manufacturing and general industry. The syndicates are supposed to run their own affairs, but the State has the power to veto their decisions, to arbi-

* New York *Times,* December 3, 1933.

trate all disputes, to fix wages, to prevent strikes and lockouts. "From the local syndicates whose task it is to stipulate labor contracts and watch over their correct observance, up to the confederations, to the Council of Corporations, to the Ministry of Corporations, to the labor courts, every part of the vast and complicated machinery is composed of government organs or is subject to State supervision and control." * The State can expropriate lands, it can force corporations to cease building new factories; it is a tremendous shareholder—a veritable RFC—in private enterprise through the Credito Mobiliare. "The corporative system on the one hand, and specific legislative measures on the other, which empower the State to control the industrial activities of the nation, have placed the Fascist government in a position to guide and direct Italian production in a manner which finds no parallel in any other country with the exception of Soviet Russia. The government has been enabled to embark on a policy of economic planning which, although it has not received the wide publicity of the Five Year Plan, may prove the deciding factor in shaping the future destinies of Italy as an industrial nation."

The announced principle is to interfere as little as possible, but the State has the power, unchecked by the courts, to interfere anywhere in the industrial structure, at any time, and that power is constantly used. In short, the Italian Corporative State appears to be a vast system of control-without-ownership, though many activities, like the railroads, are owned outright. It offers no solace to rugged individualists. Operating nearly as long as the Russian system, it has, however, produced no such dramatic results in industrial recon-

* Arnoldo S. Cortesi. New York *Times,* May 14, 1933.

struction. This is due in part to the fact that Italy has very limited natural resources, but also to the policy of freezing the status quo instead of discarding it altogether as did Russia. Wages have fallen during the Fascist regime, unemployment is still acute, social security has increased a little, but there is no comfort budget in sight; no economic basis for a permanent and prosperous civilization. Russia has done far better in one way, and Sweden far better in another. Italy's war move in Ethiopia gives strong indication that domestic conditions are highly unsatisfactory.

Germany *

The German pattern of collectivism was not greatly different from the Swedish up to the Hitler coup. One found a hardy crop of cooperative societies, municipal utilities, state mines, forests, railroads, quasi-public cartels, superpower developments. Without the disorganization of the war and the treaty, Germany might resemble Sweden today, instead of which it has turned sharply in the Italian direction. Old provincial areas, such as Bavaria, are being recut into twenty-two standardized administrative districts, each with about 3 million population. Cities, towns, villages have been deprived of their ancient autonomy and subordinated to the "principle of leadership." A member of the Nazi party dominates the mayor of every city. The Ministry of the Interior is empowered to supervise the budgets and economic conditions of each local community. In large cities the ministry may veto any appointment. The Hitler cabinet is supreme, subject to

* Data chiefly from Fritz Ermarth. *Plan Age,* January, 1935.

no check by legislature or courts. Extreme centralization has become the rule.

The Reichsminister of Agriculture can empower the Federal Food Guild to regulate the production, distribution and prices of all products. No peasant is allowed to sell any of the goods so regulated directly to the consumer. Milk, grain, eggs, cattle, feed, are among the regulated commodities. In 1934, prices were fixed for almost every agricultural crop. The producer has the *duty* to deliver certain amounts of certain products at a fixed price.

The Ministry of Industry controls cartels and big business units. It can abrogate their agreements; restrict new machinery, factories and investment; organize new cartels, or establish compulsory cartels. The latter have been set up for paper, radio sets, cigarettes. All industrial prices are subject to control except in the case of luxury goods. A line is thus drawn between necessities and superfluities. Stores are frequently closed as reprisal against price boosting. Straight line distribution methods can be enforced to keep down costs and prices. Industry has been organized into thirteen compulsory groups—such as iron and steel, chemicals, energy. The government controls 70 percent of the stock of the German banking system. New banks are forbidden. Profits are strictly subordinated to political considerations. When made, they are limited to six percent, sometimes eight. "Business is regimented under a vast and unprecedented bureaucracy. The bare principle of private enterprise and private ownership is preserved, but for the present it seems to mean only private responsibility without freedom of action." * If the American business man hesi-

* F. T. Burchall. New York *Times*, January 27, 1935.

tates because he lacks confidence in what the government may do next, consider the state of the nerves of German business men today. In April, 1935, business was officially warned that export sales must be forced on a profitless basis, losses to be taken from profits, if any, on domestic sales.

The citizen becomes in effect a soldier in the industrial army of the State:

If he is under twenty-five, he may be ordered to turn his job over to an older man, and go into the labor service or the military forces.
If he is unemployed he may be sent to a labor camp.
If he is a farm hand he cannot go to the city to seek work.
If he is a peasant, his farm becomes an "hereditary manor" which he cannot sell, but must hold intact for his eldest son.
If he is a shopkeeper, he is liable to arrest for raising prices, even if his costs go up.
If he is a manufacturer, he must employ as many workers as the State commands, whether he needs them or not. He must consult with his workers, organized into Nazi unions, and be responsible for their welfare.
If he is a professor, artist, writer, clergyman, he must conform to the Nazi dogma or lose his livelihood if not his citizenship.

All mines have been taken over by the Reich and given in charge to Dr. Hjalmar Schacht, who is also the czar of exports and imports. By his dictum, exports must balance the daily income from foreign exchange. Ten percent of all foreign trade is now in the form of straight barter. "No government in any capitalist society has had larger power to interfere with private business and has made greater use of this power by regulating production and distribution."

Nazi Germany, like fascist Italy, is not a capitalist society in the accepted sense. To call it so would make

Adam Smith turn in his grave. It is a reasonably ruthless collectivism on the post-war fascist model. The extent and completeness of the centralized control are demonstrated by the manner in which, secretly, and contrary to solemn treaty obligations, Germany rearmed, to challenge the rest of the world with a *fait accompli*, in March, 1935. The extraordinary fascist paradox, pointed out by Beard, remains. Modern mechanized warfare and the vast industrial efficiency which it demands, are hardly consistent with a retreat to the sub-vegetable culture of tribal Nordic gods.

England

England has been repeatedly held up by American editorial writers as the nation which met the depression with good old-fashioned methods and conquered it. The hallelujahs are premature. In the first place, while England has arrested a descent to the lower depths, she rests on a shelf in the wall of a precipice. She cannot feed herself; many of her most essential raw materials must come from overseas from nations raising new trade barriers. Japan has seriously undermined her cotton trade. This is no position in which to become overcomplacent about "recovery."

In the second place, the aforesaid Anglophiles show a fine disregard for the extent of collectivism in Britain. The shelf has indeed been won, but at some considerable cost to the accredited principles of private enterprise. The State has seized few businesses, but it has tended to meet the depression as it did the War, by a wide extension of control-without-ownership. "The truth is," says Gustav Stolper, "that no government in England has ever interfered more fundamentally with the economic and social structure of England than the seemingly inactive National Government. England's abandonment of the gold standard, and England's shift from free trade to protection, have had a thoroughly revolutionary effect. The 19th of September, 1931, was a financial earthquake. . . . England's transition to protection has affected world trade many times more than any tariff policy of the United States was ever able to do, and it has achieved more in reshaping English industry than all the 700 codes of the NRA in American industry."

We must remember that England is thirty years ahead of the United States in social security legislation. Lloyd George forced through the Old Age Pension Act in 1908. Unemployment insurance followed in 1911, compulsory health insurance in 1912. She has maintained a vast army of unemployed on the dole since the War. Between 1919–1929, she built 1,275,000 houses, one third by lump sum subsidies from the State, one third by private enterprise with State assistance, one third by straight private business. In January, 1935, the government launched a nationwide housing and slum clearance measure. Whole areas in London and other big cities will be transformed. It will be a punishable offense for more than two persons to occupy a single room. The number of houses to be replaced is expected to run into hundreds of thousands. Housing is not the only measure of large scale public enterprise financed by the British government. It has nationalized the superpower network, rigidly controlling both the generation and the distribution of power. It has nationalized radio broadcasting. It has set up a series of agricultural controls more far reaching and more effective than those of the

AAA. The financiers of the City carry on, as is the way with Englishmen, but business in 1935 is a very different kettle of fish from business in 1913—or in 1930.

Let those who believe in Britain's cheery recovery read J. B. Priestley's *English Journey,* published in 1934.* Let them follow him from the Black Country to the West Riding to the Potteries to Lancashire to the Tyne to East Durham and the Tees—steel, machine building, wool, ceramics, cotton weaving, coal, shipbuilding—from one grim desolation to another:

> My guidebook devotes one short sentence to Jarrow: "A busy town (35,590 inhabitants), has large iron works and shipbuilding yards." It is time this was amended into "an idle and ruined town (35,590 inhabitants, wondering what is to become of them), had large ironworks and can still show what is left of shipbuilding yards." . . . One out of every two shops appeared to be permanently closed. Wherever we went there were men hanging about, not scores of them but hundreds and thousands of them. The whole town looked as if it had entered a perpetual penniless bleak Sabbath. The men wore the drawn masks of prisoners of war. . . .
> After a glimpse of the river-front, that is of tumbledown sheds, rotting piles, coal dust and mud, we landed in Hebburn. . . . It appeared to be even poorer than its neighbor. You felt there was nothing in the whole place worth a five pound note. . . . Here again, idle men—and not unemployed casual laborers but skilled men—hung about the streets, waiting for Doomsday. . . . There was one ship in the yards where there used to be twenty. Down the Tyne we could see the idle ships lying up, a melancholy and familiar sight now in every estuary around the coast. . . . We have these vessels doing nothing; we have coal for their bunkers; our ports are filled with ships' officers and men out of work; we have goods that other people need, and across every stretch of ocean are goods that we need; and still the ships are there, chained and empty, rusting in the rain, groaning in idleness night and day.

* Published by Harper & Bros.

Canada

Here is a country with some frontier remaining. Vast resources. Progressive, vigorous people. She should weather the tidal wave of public business. But has she? Alas, no. To begin with, the Canadian National Railways and the Ontario Hydroelectric have been operating for many years, taking two huge sections away from private business. The former, with assets of $2,345,000,000, is the largest corporation in the Dominion, the latter is the fourth largest. Now comes Prime Minister Bennett to offer a Canadian New Deal, comprising: *

A National Economic Council for centralized planning.
A Federal Department of Communications.
The extension of federal farm credit.
Civil Service reform.
The prevention of mergers and stock watering.
Control by the Bank of Canada "of currency and credit for social ends."
Unemployment insurance.
A National Products Marketing Act.
Federal aid to Alberta and Saskatchewan for the administration of natural resources.
Maximum hour legislation for industry.
The reclamation of 11 million acres of drought stricken prairie land.

On February 28, 1935, the Prime Minister introduced a resolution into Parliament to take over the whole grain trade of the Dominion. The state grain board shall "have power to purchase, receive and take delivery of wheat, oats, barley, rye and flaxseed, or any one or more such grains for marketing and to sell, store, transport such grains." The new legislation

* J. Bartlett Brebner in *Current History*, March, 1935.

will create a national compulsory board along the lines operated by the Dominion during the War, but with additional power to organize western farming on a more efficient basis, and to direct the course of production. It will, if confirmed, control exports as well. With this announcement a shiver ran through Wall Street at the prospect of the government's closing the Winnipeg exchange, the only surviving free market for wheat.

Here and there

Almost simultaneously, Wall Street shivered at Argentina's new central bank. "The development follows closely the action taken by Canada, and coincides with the fight now on in Washington to replace the Federal Reserve System with a strong central banking system to control money and credit." Indeed Wall Street must tremble incessantly as blow after blow falls from all quarters of the globe, upsetting established methods. Mexico has embarked on a Six Year Plan with socialistic trimmings unpalatable to foreign concessions. Uruguay's new president, Gabriel Terra, is building a "Third Republic" complete with state packing plants, banks, insurance companies, telephone and telegraph lines, munitions manufacturing, the monopoly of foreign trade on a quota basis, compulsory cultivation of lands to relieve unemployment.

France has instituted sickness, maternity and old age insurance programs. The latter was made compulsory in 1928. She subsidizes housing projects by financing second mortgages at two to three percent. Czechoslovakia has maintained Austrian property taken over after the Treaty as public property. She operates her railways, telephone and telegraph systems, as well as mines, smelting works, tobacco factories, spas. The Japanese government operates the largest steel plant in the country, accounting for 60 percent of all production. New Zealand has instituted compulsory control of agriculture, confiscated the gold reserves of banks, forced the investing class to submit to a conversion loan at lower interest, and arbitrarily raised the foreign exchange rate.*

Cooperative business

We have defined the cooperative movement as semi-public business, and never to be confused with private enterprise. In 1933, a survey by the United States Department of Labor, covering 400,000 societies in forty-three countries, disclosed a total membership of 106 million. More than half of these, however, were in Russia, with 59 million members. (In 1935, the number is reported to exceed 70 million.) Other large memberships were:

Germany	9,714,000	
Great Britain	6,908,000	
India	4,429,000	
United States	3,790,000	(mostly agricultural societies)
France	3,354,000	
Czechoslovakia	2,150,000	
Poland	1,896,000	
Italy	1,715,000	
Rumania	1,641,000	
Hungary	1,477,000	
Finland	1,099,000	

A much better index of the strength of the cooperatives in any given nation is found in the figures showing

* New York *Times*, June 9, 1935.

the ratio of members in consumers' societies to total population:

Russia	44.5 %
Great Britain	14.6
Finland	13.2
Denmark	11.2
Switzerland	9.8
Hungary	9.3
Sweden	8.4
Germany	8.0
Iceland	7.4
Austria, Belgium, Esthonia, France, Czechoslovakia	5.0 % each (approximately)

In Russia, the total sales of consumers' societies are nearly $11,000,000,000; in Great Britain, over $1,000,000,000. Many of these societies combine into wholesale buying groups, and even into manufacturing units. The main types include:

Consumers' societies	69,595,000	members
Agricultural "	21,898,000	"
Credit "	9,658,000	"
Workers' productive societies	2,281,000	"
Housing societies	934,000	"
Other "	1,086,000	"

Cooperatives have grown steadily through the depression, contrary to private business. In 1932, the cooperatives of Holland reached an all-time peak.

Denmark founded her first cooperative dairy in 1882, when life for the peasants was hard. The soil was indifferent, natural resources almost non-existent. Today, Denmark is a cooperative State which has grown out of experience step by step. The population, due to an admirable system of public education, agricultural schools, people's high schools, is exceptionally intelligent. Intensive cultivation, scientific agriculture, is the rule. All but 400,000 citizens live on the land. The big estates have been broken up, giving way to small farms, 90 percent owned by those who work them. The output is handled by cooperative societies, superbly administered. A great export trade has been developed, especially with England, where Danish pork, butter, eggs and cheese are standard. "Denmark is the only State which has succeeded in making a society of peasant farmers effectively self-governing." She has given them one of the highest standards of living in the world.

The inventory might be indefinitely prolonged. Australia, New Zealand, Tasmania are great laboratories of public business and have been so for many years. We shall look at the Australian sugar control in some detail at a later point. Items come from South Africa, Latin America, the Dutch East Indies, from all points of the compass. If Sidney Webb estimated 12 million engaged in strictly public business in 1913, we should probably be safe in estimating 50 million today, so rapid has been the growth, especially since the depression. If regulation, taxation, and cooperative societies were included, the public payroll might well double again.

The forms are manifold and perplexing, but at least five great patterns are discernible:

1. The dictatorial state socialism of Russia.
2. The dictatorial state control-without-ownership of Italy and Germany.
3. The democratic collectivism of Sweden.
4. The agricultural cooperative State of Denmark, and to a lesser extent of Finland.
5. The assorted, experimental New Deals of the United States, England, Canada, Mexico, Uruguay, and other nations.

Public business is on the march the world around. Who shall run it? Take your choice, gentlemen. Dictators leaning to the left; dictators leaning to the right; dictators leaning down the middle of the road; parliamentary States slowly forcing back the claims of private property; cooperative States widening their scope of economic action; confused States hoping for a revival of private business, but in its absence experimenting with collectivism in many forms.

CHAPTER SIX

Six Studies of Capitalist Decay

WE HAVE seen public business expanding on every continent. The map of the world groans with it. To deny its omnipresence and importance is like denying oxygen in the atmosphere.

The American business man, however, tends to remain unimpressed. Mr. Charles R. Gay, president of the New York Stock Exchange, gives a typical reaction.* "A gigantic jam of accumulated wants and buying power waits to be released. The only way in which it can be accomplished is by satisfying the conditions under which private business can afford to take risks." Three conditions are necessary: "freedom for management, a greater sense of security, and an abatement of the hostility toward profits." Estimates show a capital goods deficit for the depression of $27,000,000,-000 to $85,000,000,000, with the National Industrial Conference Board standing between these extremes at $69,000,000,000. "These figures indicate an assured pathway out of the depression. There is no substitute which can replace the natural action of private enterprise. Two facts are obvious: First, that the task is too great for the government and, second, that business

* Before the Chamber of Commerce of the State of New York, June 6, 1935.

has the power to recover if granted a reasonable opportunity to do so free from uncertainties."

This is what business men want to believe. In a pathetic way, it is what nearly all Americans want to believe. For a hundred years we were going somewhere, although the precise location had never been defined, and going at a grand gallop. The recession since 1929 has been frustrating, boring, intolerable. The old road may have had its ruts and bumps, but one moved on it. Faster and faster. Ah, to be off on it again!

What is capitalism?

The good old road has been roughly identified as capitalism. The typical business man is not a capitalist, for he works rather than invests for a living, but he professes a strong belief in the regime. He has from time to time made good money under it. He hopes to make good money again.

There has been much loose talk about the demise of capitalism, with little attempt to define its meaning. The word itself constitutes what Alfred Korzybski calls a high order abstraction. Such abstractions are useful to the processes of human thought and action, provided the user does not forget the chain of sub-abstractions from which they are built up, down to the primary events in space and time. Back of "capitalism" stand such abstractions as "profit," "the free market," "labor," "credit," "contract," "property"; and back of them a series of local abstractions dealing with personal "income," "savings," "costs"; and back of them uncounted millions of symbolic acts by millions of individuals involving marks upon pieces of paper called checks, account books, invoices; and back of them the movement of machines and materials by human direction or effort through time, which constitutes the final reality.

Without some conception of this chain, the word capitalism remains pure metaphysics, a creature of the brain only, and so a sort of god or demon, depending upon the point of view of the individual using it. A fighting word, full of emotional content and nothing else. "Democracy," "freedom," "fascism," are kindred terms.

Suppose we break down capitalism into abstractions of a somewhat lower order. It can be defined in various ways:

1. The total of human acts and behavior involved in the process of providing for the physical wants of Western societies under the economic system recently prevailing.
2. That part of the system devoted to private enterprise.
3. That part of private enterprise devoted to free competition. The area of rugged individualism.
4. The private ownership of income-producing property, and the resulting production for pecuniary profit rather than for specific human use.
5. The exploitation of the working class by the owning class.
6. A productive mechanism depending for its stability upon a flywheel of reinvestment in so-called capital goods. This results in something close to a mathematical formula, governed by the laws of compound interest. The division of income between owners and workers being a constant (running about 30 percent for owner to 70 percent for worker, including farmer, year in year out) the owner must either spend or reinvest his share to maintain equilibrium in the system. The spending and reinvesting both put men to work and thus provide purchasing power, again to be divided 30-70, in an endless spiral. As the owners can spend but a fraction of their share, they must constantly be on the lookout for profitable investment. The new investment results in more plant capacity which demands an

expanding market. Any prolonged interruption of reinvestment reduces jobs for capital goods workers, cuts back upon the total income distributed to the whole community, and sets up a condition of accelerating degeneration, unless checked by other forces.

When one holds that capitalism has collapsed or is collapsing, which definition has he in mind? Or is he just indulging in wishful thinking about something he does not like? Going down the line, we can make certain definite statements about each of the above:

1. The prevailing economic system as a whole is visibly undergoing more or less violent transformation.

2. The area devoted to private business is everywhere shrinking relatively to the area devoted to public business, and has been shrinking for decades.

3. The area within private business devoted to free competition is shrinking relatively to the area devoted to monopoly, and the "administrative" competition of Big Business. This process has been cumulative for fifty years.

4. The private ownership of income-producing property is still general, but two important qualifications are in order: first, the property is producing more losses than profits in many industries; second, the legal owners are increasingly surrendering control of their property to corporate managements. When Mr. Charles Schwab of Bethlehem Steel was lately taken to task for the huge bonuses voted to himself and Mr. Grace, he said to newspaper men that he supposed he had not realized "that the damned old company didn't belong to him." *

5. The exploitation of workers by owners, or by management control, is still very general in the sense that no significant change in the ratio between earned and unearned income has taken place. Both classes, however, have been forced to accept during the depression a total distribution 40 to 50 percent below normal. This has driven millions of workers out of the arena of private exploitation altogether and upon relief rolls. It has ruined thousands of small investors, and even seriously damaged many substantial capitalists.

* Quoted by John T. Flynn.

SIX STUDIES OF CAPITALIST DECAY 97

6. The mechanism of reinvestment at a compound rate of interest has had six years of hiatus. The ground now to be made up, so that prosperity may roll forward again on the old formula, is fantastic in extent. Capital goods production has shrunk to a contemptible fraction of its 1928–1929 volume in the United States, and obstinately remains at low levels except as stimulated by public works.

When I speak of the crisis in capitalism, I have in mind primarily the last definition. I cannot see how private investment can be revived on the scale required in the face of such stubborn obstacles as the decline in foreign trade due to economic nationalism, the decline in population growth rates, the chronic menace of overproduction in both agriculture and industry. This does not prove that capitalism differently defined is passing from the scene, although, as we have noted, it is undergoing transformation in terms of all six definitions. The private ownership of the means of production, and the exploitation of one class by another are not disappearing very rapidly. These things, however, were common under feudalism, where nobles owned the land and took the surplus above subsistence from peasant and serf. Feudalism had a slow moving base in agriculture, with stability not dependent on high speed methods of production. Exploitation is an ancient human institution, and for this reason I prefer the last definition as more rigorous, giving to capitalism its characteristic modern connotation. Capitalism in this sense ceases to function when capital becomes a drug on the market. Current interest rates, as we have seen, are the lowest ever known.

In support of the view that capitalism as an investing machine is entering the twilight, I shall now present seven witnesses. Each has prepared a thesis in quantitative terms which commands attention, and with which the average business man must sooner or later reckon. The cumulative effect I find very sobering for those who are sure that only a little confidence is needed to replace us upon the good old road. Of necessity I have tried to summarize in a few paragraphs material which is contained in a whole book or monograph, and has taken years of preparation. You are urged to consult the original source for further detail.

Buying power

Mr. Arthur H. Adams * is a consulting engineer, who has managed industrial plants, and had no little part in the introduction of labor-saving machinery in the years before the depression. I introduce him first because he is what is generally known as a practical business man, and a devout believer in the superiority of private enterprise to public. Some years of painstaking research have convinced him that there is a key ratio in economic activity as it has been conducted in the past. When the ratio is at par, say 100, the system is in balance. When it slips to 90, danger threatens, when it sinks to 75, the system is unworkable. In no former depression has it ever dropped so low. Assuming the ratio as 100, or normal, in 1922, it dipped to 73 in 1929, and in 1934 still stood at 75. "Insofar as our ratio defines a condition, that condition is now practically not improved since 1929. Also it seems to be heading downward with no reason to look for a reversal."

The key ratio is a fraction with *real wages of con-*

* "Key Ratio to Balance." *The American Federationist*, November, 1934.

sumer goods workers as the numerator, and *output per man-hour* as the denominator. If productivity increases more rapidly than real wages, the ratio drops. To keep it at par, real wages must rise as fast as productivity.

It has long been common knowledge that buying power must keep up with output, or overproduction results. It is now common knowledge that output per man-hour has increased phenomenally since 1920, and has increased throughout the depression. Mr. Adams is the first so far as I know to reduce this general knowledge to the terms of a mathematical formula which acts as an index of the health of capitalism. He has checked and rechecked but cannot escape the gloomy import of his own calculations. "The unbalance we have reached this time is so big that natural or automatic restoration of balance, or recovery, cannot occur. The buying power of all consumer goods workers in the United States *needs to be raised about 35 percent on the average,* and with *no* increase in their producing power, before an intelligent man should even hope for business to become self-sustaining at normal levels." The government can bring about an appearance of improvement by mortgaging the future, but there is no real health in this remedy.

Mr. Adams' monograph is long, and highly technical, and only its outstanding conclusions can be reproduced here. It involves a theory of the business cycle which most economists would recognize as the work of a genuine student; a careful distinction between capital goods and consumer goods; a study of the distribution of man-hours in the total economy; and an estimate of the ratio between work income and ownership income.

How is private business to increase real wages 35 percent, which means raising payrolls 35 percent with no increase in prices? Mr. Adams admits that a business man who embarked on such a policy would be a maniac. It has to be done by all business men, simultaneously, and without chiseling. With the experience of the NRA behind us, such a step is equally fantastic.

Mr. Adams has a plan based on intervention by the State, but he does not hope much from it. His faith in the implacable nature of his ratio is, however, profound.

Liquidity

Mr. A. A. Berle, Jr.,* cooperating with Miss V. J. Pederson, has dug for capitalism a less conventional grave than has Mr. Adams—who has only had the audacity to measure what many economists have noted as a dangerous drift. Not one economist in a thousand, and certainly no banker, has ever seen the end of capitalism through a rise in liquid capital—as though it would drown itself in its own fluidity. Mr. Berle has measured this phenomenon as carefully as Mr. Adams has measured his critical ratio. The results are equally appalling, but from a different angle. It is probable, however, that there is a pretty broad subway between inadequate wages and the activities of the stock market.

The thesis is this: In 1880, of the total wealth of the United States, 16 percent was in liquid form. Liquid wealth means money, or something that can be turned into money without delay. All shares listed on the stock market are liquid, for you have but to pick up your telephone to get cash for them within a few

* *Liquid Claims and National Wealth.* Macmillan, 1934.

minutes. So are listed bonds. So are bank deposits, and the cash surrender value of insurance policies.

By 1912, the ratio had crept up to 20 percent—not much of a change. Then something began to simmer inside the economic caldron. Liquidity increased in waves. By 1926, the ratio was 28 percent; by 1929, 38 percent; by 1930, 40 percent. The depression thrust it back a little, but in 1933 it still held at 34 percent—a third of all national wealth. Within a decade, one sixth of American wealth had shifted from the hands of responsible owners, into the hands of managerial or manipulatory groups.

Liquid property is always irresponsible property, it has no strings upon the owner. "It appears to be a fact that the increase in the demand for liquidity almost of necessity weakens a civilization based on individualism and individual property." The great bankers, the great promoters, the great architects of super-mergers, all hastened this landslide away from the ownership of physical to that of liquid assets.

On a 15 percent ratio, the system can weather a panic or a depression without great difficulty. The amount of wealth which can be thrown on the market is small compared with total wealth. At 20 percent the danger increases. The depression of 1921 was a taste of blood. At 38 percent, as in 1929, the market is shattered by millions of citizens rushing to present their liquid claims—runs on commercial and savings banks, stocks and bonds dumped on the stock markets, loans demanded on life insurance policies. "The mechanism of liquidity is like a detonating cap in a stick of dynamite. Particularly if the mercantile and the investment processes are tied up together in one banking system, an explosion in either will wreck both."

It was stampede for liquidity which closed every bank in 1933, a phenomenon unheard of in any former depression.

The whole trend of modern corporate and capitalistic finance is in the direction of greater liquidity. Big man and little man want their property where, in an uncertain world, they can cash it in. In the depression of 1942, with liquidity at 50 percent, we may face the plain fact that no financial structure, no matter how attentively nursed by a solicitous government, can stand the simultaneous presentation of so many liquid claims. The banks must snap, the insurance companies crack wide open, the stock markets close their doors. In such circumstances there is no appeal to "natural" laws, no chance to let weak banks and companies go down the drain in a wholesome purge. When a few go, the whole body begins to dissolve. Liquid property is dangerous property. "It was certainly not perversity that led substantially every major government in the world between 1929 and 1934 to interpose artificial measures rather than pay the price of letting the cycle work itself out."

The problem is hardly conceived of in the United States, still less in the rest of the world. It constitutes perhaps the most violent threat extant to personal property, in its modern form. No solution has been offered, or can be offered without reversing nearly everything that American business men mean by "recovery." Of course we want bigger bank deposits, more life insurance, more stocks and bonds instantly negotiable on the exchanges. Of course we do not want a sanitary cordon between investment finance and mercantile finance.

So if we heave ourselves out of this depression, and

get back on the good old road, what is going to happen in the next one?

Overhead

Mr. Rautenstrauch * is Professor of Industrial Engineering at Columbia University. He invites us to consider all American industry as one great factory. The sales of the factory correspond with the national income. The costs of the factory are the wages and salaries paid to producers, or direct labor, plus the wages and salaries paid to the non-productive, overhead workers, or indirect labor. It is the object of every factory manager to keep his overhead down. If it soars too high, it wrecks the business. How has our national factory fared in this connection in recent years? It has fared in a way likely to give any good manager insomnia.

If we take 1917 as a year in which the national factory was a stable business enterprise, with production and consumption in reasonable balance, we find that producers constituted 63 percent of the employed population. This direct labor included farmers, miners, factory workers, railroad and power plant workers, and all others engaged in the primary processes of production. These producers received about half the national income. Despite a steady increase in physical production through the 1920's—though the *rate* of increase was tapering off—by 1932 the number of producers had declined to half the employed population, and their income to a third of the national total. In 1917 and 1932, the national income, or the money spent on the plant, was substantially the same, about

* Walter Rautenstrauch: *Who Gets the Money?* Harpers, 1934.

48 billion dollars. Today the overhead group receives two thirds of all money spent, and constitutes half the working population.

"In other words, in 1917, when producers got one dollar for making goods, overhead people got another dollar for the various services leading up to the sale of goods to the consumer. But in 1932, when producers got one dollar, overheaders got $2.30. In 1929, they got $1.60. Overhead costs marched rapidly forward during the 1920's, and broke into a run with the coming of the depression. Business on the downgrade; overhead on the upgrade—here is abundant evidence of shocking management."

If the ratios between direct and indirect labor were about right in 1917, to recapture them, we should now need to:

1. Shift 12,300,000 more workers to the producers' group.
2. Increase producers' income about 56 percent.
3. Increase farmers' income about 216 percent—as their proportionate share in the producers' group.

These figures measure an enormous displacement in fifteen years. The national factory is losing its producers at the benches, while the office is swarming with clerks, salesmen, and financial experts. It is too much to say that more overhead necessarily means more waste. The problem is not so simple as that. As the power age develops, services must tend to displace much manual labor and other forms of productive work. We have seen how government service expanded from 1912 in response to an authentic demand. The question however remains: Is not a 130 percent increase in overhead in fifteen years an intolerably high ratio of displacement, and more than the national factory can absorb?

The new overhead armies are not all engaged in useful community service. Perhaps the majority are parasites on the financial and credit organism. "In 1918, the managers and workers of your national plant learned a new technique of operation. They discovered how to divert people's free money and savings into stocks and bonds and first mortgages and similar securities. In that year, we began to create a nation not of consumers, but of investors and speculators." Or, as Mr. Berle would say, we began to go in for liquidity in a big way. Mr. Rautenstrauch has prepared a chart which shows strong correlation between the rise of the overhead and the rise of loans and investments. We employed new millions of workers to assist us in piling up debts.

Obsolescence

David Cushman Coyle * is another engineer. He used to calculate wind resistances for skyscrapers, but the skyscraper business not being what it was, he turned to the study of resistances in financial pyramids. In common with many others, he looks at capital goods as the cardinal element in the maintenance of traditional capitalism. For a time he thought that if a fire could be built under the stock market and a speculative boom engendered, capital goods might be revived in the ensuing era of good fellowship. The length of the revival, and the basic health of the system so vivified was, of course, another matter. With the passage of the Securities Exchange legislation, and the restrictions

* "The Capital Goods Fallacy." *Harper's Magazine,* December, 1934.

upon wash sales and pools, he became doubtful about this method. He sees no way to stimulate capital goods to the huge proportions necessary; he finds that the business men themselves under the NRA codes were organizing to prevent such expansion.

The business man reads his *Business Week* and sighs to himself that nothing is done for the heavy industries. That, he agrees, is the great failure of the New Deal. If the Administration would just give up all its radical experiments and get out of the way of the capital market, unemployment would soon disappear and business would be prosperous. Sighing deeply, he rises and goes across the street to his code authority, where he shoulders a musket and stands embattled at the gate lest any bond salesman get in and stimulate the capital goods industries at his expense. Capital investment is great stuff everywhere except in any particular place.

The textile people may want a revival of the heavy industries in general, but do they want a string of new, efficient textile factories in the hands of competitors? A thousand times, no. In an expanding country, investment can roll into new geographical areas, new industries, new construction work, without greatly harming industries already established. In a matured country, new investment tends constantly towards improvement in existing industries, and so accelerates the problems of competition, technological unemployment, and inadequate purchasing power. Even monopolies are in constant fear of a new technical process which, financed by upstarts beyond their control, may loosen their grip on the market.

Mr. Coyle has worked out a general formula for the optimum rate at which to invest new productive capital. "In the system as a whole the optimum rate of replacement is proportional to the square root of the rate of technical invention divided by the square root of the cost of machinery. Or, in English, if technical invention were four times as fast, the rate of replacement might justifiably be doubled; if the cost of machinery for a given production schedule were cut to one quarter, the rate of replacement ought to be doubled again." This formula, of course, cannot be expressed in numbers, because the rate of invention is not precisely measurable. In the nineteenth century, the demands of growth used up so much capital that the rate of replacement was within the margin of safety and all was well. Thrift and savings were a virtue and helped, by encouraging new production, to improve the standard of living. But as productivity increased, there came a time when the spontaneous rate of capital accumulation overtook and passed the optimum. "From then on the optimum rate is less than the existing rate, and all the moral standards and institutions set up to encourage thrift become means for lowering the standard of living." The paradox of plenty appears in many forms to indicate "that the long established axioms of common sense no longer make sense of any kind." In the 1920's, the United States ran far over the optimum rate. Any stable condition must now be predicated on a capital investment relatively less than it has been in the past. This means a far larger proportion of the national income devoted to spending for consumers' goods; which demands, in turn, relatively more for wages and salaries and less for property owners; which means a break in the 30 percent ratio for property discovered by Mr. Rautenstrauch and others as a constant. "Sound finance" cannot tolerate such a break. It is built on the principle of expansion through investment. Deadlock. Mr. Coyle believes that only a wholly new type of financing, where production and distribution are not based on the accumulation of invested capital, can restore health to the economic mechanism.

The business man, typified by Mr. Gay of the Stock Exchange, quoted at the beginning of the chapter, casts up his glittering total of 69 billions for replacements, more or less. But if Mr. Coyle is right the figure is a statistical heaven, and not of the earth, earthy. It is based on the assumption that we shall continue to outrage the optimum obsolescence rate. Furthermore, we might inquire what the outlook for employment would be, if and when 69 billions were spent on modernizing American industry. Mr. Ford has just modernized a new steel mill, which is automatic to the point of permitting 500 men to make as much steel as 2,500 used to make a few years ago.

Debt and time

Mr. Bassett Jones * is a practical engineer, hitherto engaged in applying the laws of mathematical probability to the operation of high speed elevators in tall buildings. Without such applied mathematics, the elevators would run through the roof. Like Mr. Coyle, he has turned his attention in recent years to a study of the economic mechanism. He has applied higher mathematics, especially the differential calculus, to the growth of physical production and of debt claims over the past fifty or sixty years in the United States. The curves of growth have been charted, with some devastating conclusions. For many decades, both physical production and debt (including corporation equities)

* *Debt and Production.* John Day, 1934.

expanded at a roughly similar rate. The lines resembled a five percent compound interest curve, or thereabouts. Shortly after 1910, physical production began to taper off; it grew, but at a declining rate. It had to. There was not enough iron ore in the world to supply the steel required, if the growth characteristic of the steel industry in the '60's and '70's had been maintained to 1950. And so with coal, oil, cotton, wheat, copper, lead, almost anything you please.

But finance had become habituated to a compounding advance in capital claims. Its rate of expansion after 1910, instead of diminishing, actually increased. By the late 1920's, it was bowling along on an eight percent basis. So the curve of production levels off, while the curve of debt goes upward still more steeply. In the last analysis, the validity of any debt depends on tangible wealth. By 1929, the jaws which separated the two curves were open in a terrible yawn. Something had to be engulfed and it was. During the depression, production has actually declined in amount, let alone in rate, while capital claims, especially long term interest bearing debt, continue at high levels. No healthy correlation has been established. The RFC, for one thing, would not permit it.

Mr. Jones is unable to see how capitalism can continue to function, until debt has been driven down to a workable relationship with physical production. Such liquidation would ruin large sections of the present capitalist class, however much it might open opportunities for new capitalists in the future. The present incumbents naturally object to large personal sacrifice on behalf of a high abstraction. Again a deadlock. To revive capitalism on the old formula would require a wiping out of $100,000,000,000, more or less, of vested claims.

Mr. Frederick L. Ackerman, a co-worker of Mr. Jones' and a distinguished architect, amplifies the debt theory. He is particularly concerned with the time factor in economic dynamics—a factor generally neglected by the faculty. Indeed, this whole approach of the engineers, with their concepts of rates, and rates of change, is, to my mind, of first importance. We really live in a dynamic process, rather than a series of fixed institutions. In a recent letter, Mr. Ackerman remarked:

> Credit is an item that has meaning only in the time dimension. Our wealth is an item of the time dimensional world and has no real meaning in terms of the present. It is, in fact, an item of a conjectural world—a world of our imagination—which does not rest for such meaning as we temporarily attach to it at a given point in time, upon carefully worked out probabilities of the future. Instead, it rests upon assumptions which, upon mere inspection, turn out to be no more than a description of a highly improbable if not impossible run of events.
>
> The effort now being made to give both validity and liquidity [vide Mr. Berle] to our mountainous debt claims is merely an attempt to get out from under the jurisdiction of the time dimension—that is to say, to escape from the certainty that "we live in the most probable world." A debt economy such as ours can operate only under the auspices of a hedonistic point of view; and optimism is as essential to its working as is gas to an internal combustion engine. So one comes to the question: How is such an economy going to work when, by reason of a decline in the growth rate, the future fails to hold the prospects which have hitherto served to animate the system? The answer seems fairly clear—it isn't.

One pictures Mr. Ackerman and Mr. Average Business Man in spirited discussion. Mr. Ackerman understands his hedonist, but the business man does not know what Mr. Ackerman is talking about, and so calls him an impractical visionary. Time dimensions indeed! Yet the business man's note runs for six months, and the bonds on his plant are due in 1945. He will have to reckon with Mr. Ackerman's conclusions, whether he understands them or not, before he can have a secure world in which to do business.

Prices

In a sense, the findings of Dr. Gardner C. Means * are the most alarming of all from the point of view of reestablishing our traditional economy. They do not deal with debts and finance directly, but rather with prices and physical production itself. Dr. Means is a professor of economics and co-author with Mr. Berle of that twentieth century classic, *The Modern Corporation and Private Property*. The findings now to be given are embodied in a special report recently made to Secretary Wallace:

	Percent drop from 1919 to 1933	
	In prices	In production
Agricultural implements	6 %	80 %
Motor vehicles	16	80
Cement	18	65
Iron and steel products	20	83
Tires	33	70
Textiles	45	30
Food products	49	14
Leather	50	20
Petroleum	56	20
Agricultural commodities	63	6

The implications of this little table are profound. During the depression one group of commodities acted

* *Industrial Prices and Their Relative Inflexibility.* Senate document 13, 74th Congress.

in a totally different way from another group, suggesting that we have not one economic system, but two. Agricultural implements, motor vehicles, cement, steel, tires (and many others) show a drop in production far in excess of the reduction in price. The blows of the depression were taken on the production end, rather than on the price end. But textiles, food products, leather, petroleum and agricultural commodities—especially the latter—took the depression on the price end, and did not restrict production to any such degree. The first group is a place where monopoly or "administrative competition" obtains; the second group is a place where free competition still obtains. When a depression hits the free market, down go prices but not production. Indeed, during the early period of the depression, agricultural production actually increased, despite the drop in prices. Each farmer tried to hold his cash income by larger crops at a lower price. When depression hits the controlled market, output is restricted and prices held.

Dr. Means finds that the controlled market is roughly coincident with Big Business units. It is the picnic ground of the 200 great corporations which chiefly provide the service of supply to the American people. It is *the* dominating system. The free market is devoted to small fry—farmers, canners, creameries, food processors, textile mills, oil drillers, the handicraft trades. In bulk and in kinds of products, it is still important but is constantly losing ground to the administrative market.

Prices are set in the free market by supply and demand; the interaction of buyer and seller. Wheat and cotton prices are so made. Classical economics and all its laws are founded thereon. Prices are beyond the control of any individual, who takes perforce what the market offers. In the controlled or administrative market, prices are made by individual fiat. General Motors posts the price for Chevrolets, f.o.b. Detroit, six months in advance. Take it or leave it. Demand has no effect upon it—though it may have some effect on the next six months' price. The administrative market is not necessarily a monopoly market in the accepted sense, but it is a market where a few big corporations dominate the field and tend, with or without formal agreement, to behave in the same way. Thus General Motors and Ford are mighty competitors, but they set their administrative prices within a few notches of one another, and there is little real price competition between them in the free market sense. They know—within a few moments of each other, apparently—when to stop; when to halt price declines, when to check production.

These rigid prices are now dominant in our economy. In the depression the whole price structure has pivoted about them. The depression indeed might be defined as a general slashing of prices at the flexible end of the scale, and a slashing of production at the rigid end. "The shift from free market to administrative prices is the development which has destroyed the effective functioning of the American economy and produced the pressures which culminated in the new economic agencies of the government." The farmer could not stand the pressure, hence the AAA.

Under laissez-faire, individuals made policy for their own businesses, but industrial policy for the economy at large was beyond them. Under administrative competition, individuals in great corporations now make industrial decisions. For six years their decision has been to restrict production and so depress the standard of living for the whole people. "When the business man has the power to affect industrial policy, he almost necessarily makes wrong industrial decisions." His training forces him to. He may be the finest fellow in the world, but he is bound to go wrong for the economy as a whole. In order to maximize profit, he *must* hold prices and curtail production, in nine cases out of ten, for the amount he can count on through lowering prices is usually so small that the whole balance of his interest as a business man swings the other way. A "price chiseler" is a term of opprobrium applied to the business man who does not play the administrative game.

The net effect of this control over industrial policy is to aggravate fluctuations in economic activity and to prevent necessary readjustments. A slight drop in demand may be transmitted into a full sized recession. Only if the business man acts counter to his profit interest can this tendency be overcome. Which is absurd. "Thus administrative coordination—the very thing that has made modern technique and a high standard of living possible—has destroyed the effectiveness of the market as an overall coordinator by the inflexible administrative prices which are inherent in the reduction of competing units it has produced."

This inflexibility has been a major cause in breaking up foreign trade, in disrupting monetary policy, in wrecking banks, obstructing the full use of capacity and resources, disorganizing the flow of savings, unbalancing the national budget, increasing economic insecurity.

The more we leave industrial policy to Big Business, to those lords of practicality, the more administrative prices we shall have, the more rigidities, the less possibility of making essential readjustments. Here lies a cardinal difference from earlier economies. The community may surrender control to a system where the free market is dominant, and survive, as it did in the nineteenth century. If it surrenders control to Big Business, it is faced with an eventual breakdown, which *includes Big Business itself*. The kind of decisions which Big Business is bound to make in the interest of workaday profit, or avoidance of loss, lead to a destruction of that mass market which is its life blood.

It is too late to resurrect the free market, as every intelligent man knows. We cannot pulverize these great units without disaster—Senator Borah to the contrary notwithstanding. So the community must sooner or later remove from Big Business these fatal industrial decisions. The NRA codes, according to Dr. Means, were useless in this connection because initiative was left to business men, who promptly made the wrong decisions—restriction of output and high prices.

Review of the parade

Here are seven able gentlemen with six avenues of approach, converging on the one conclusion that traditional capitalism is inoperable. Mr. Adams finds a critical index, the ratio between real wages and productivity, that should be 100 but is now 75, with no prospect of improvement by natural law. Mr. Berle notes a tremendous increase in the percentage of liquid assets to total national wealth, which promises to drown any economy when a downswing precipitates these liquid billions on the market. Professor Rautenstrauch has calculated an increase of 130 percent in the overhead costs of the economic system in the past fifteen years, and concludes that the system cannot endure a mounting overhead indefinitely, any more than a single plant could endure it. Mr. Coyle has determined a law of replacement in capital goods which was disobeyed during the 1920's by excessive additions to plant, and which prevents a revival of the heavy industries to their accustomed levels. He finds further that while business men desire the stimulation of capital goods in general, they oppose stimulation in their own industries. Messrs. Jones and Ackerman have introduced the time factor into economics; they conclude that the debt structure is fantastically out of line with physical production, and can never be validated. This conclusion acts again to discourage new debts for new capital goods. If the present debt is in jeopardy, why contract more? Dr. Means finds that the free market has been largely replaced by a market of administrative prices, arbitrarily determined by giant corporations. The profit motive on which prices are administered leads inevitably to restriction of output. The give and take is removed from the structure, and it becomes rigid, vulnerable, and presently unworkable.

One may quarrel with a detail here and there in this cumulative indictment. I am skeptical of the exactness of Mr. Adams' ratio because of the statistical difficulties in obtaining his numerator and denominator, but I have no doubts about the principle involved. Mr. Berle's liquidity is so new and startling that it arouses a defensive reflex. But the more one studies it, the more persuasive the logic becomes. Professor Rautenstrauch's nightmare of overhead is apparently an authentic spook, but nobody knows exactly how much waste capitalism can stand without going under.

Doubts may be raised as to the accuracy of the data from which Mr. Jones derived the curve of the rate of physical production; indeed, in a subsequent monograph he raised a certain doubt himself. In a more recent study, as yet unpublished, he has reached the same conclusions by a more rigorous route. An industry mechanized to the extreme of automaticity has not a wide margin for the rigid high prices found by Dr. Means. Few whole industries are so completely mechanized, however, and his figures represent the actual condition.

Our business man, sighing for happy days again, has seven heads to cut off—and when they are severed, I can supply more. (Mr. Lawrence Dennis, for instance, and Signor Mussolini, and Professor M. J. Bonn.) What is he going to do about overhead, liquidity, the debt burden, the distorted obsolescence rate, the ratio of productivity to real wages, the rigid price structure —to say nothing of declining population rates and frozen foreign markets? Admittedly he is a stout fellow, but is his sword sharp enough?

I do not believe that it is. Capitalism in the sense of my sixth definition is passing, and must continue to pass from the scene. The ends of the curves are clearly visible. I leave our business man to devise an arrangement for private property and enterprise which will work better. With prevailing trends to reckon with, he has a man-sized job. For my part, I prefer to swim with the stream and admit public business as the dominating factor in the future service of supply.

CHAPTER SEVEN

Agenda of the State

MANY new activities have been forced upon the State by technological pressure; many more have been forced by the depression. If even one of the somber prophecies as to the future of capitalism just recorded is substantially accurate, collectivism of some kind is here to stay. Where is the long term line between public business and private? If nothing so fine as a line can be discovered, what activities are demonstrably public, what private, and what are left in the zone between? We come now to the heart of our inquiry. Upon what principles shall the Agenda of the State be based?

As Keynes has pointed out, the matter is one of paramount importance. Here are governments the world around, staggering and swaying under vast new functions. There are more than 20 million unemployed in America and Europe at this moment. Perhaps the load is overgreat; perhaps private enterprise should be coaxed back to resume part of the burden. Which part? One difficulty is that nothing coaxes private business except the hope of profit, and profits in worldwide depressions do not grow on every bush.

The gravity of the problem demands the utmost objectivity in approach. A battery of photoelectric cells geared to record the facts and innocent of emotion, opinion, dogma, traditions, mental habits, would be more than welcome. No brief would be held for the State or for the business man, for socialism or capitalism, for regimentation or rugged individualism. Those fighting words would mean nothing, touch off no psychic responses to obstruct a clear appraisal. Only the facts would register. Unfortunately, no mere human brain can be so dispassionate.

Theories of public business

The theory of the Incas of Peru was that all economic activity should be dominated by a benevolent dictatorship, personified in the god-emperor. The theory of modern Russia is that the principal means of production and distribution—perhaps 90 percent of all—should be vested in the State or in cooperative societies. The theory of the United States Chamber of Commerce seems to be that no productive activity should be public business—"the best public servant is the worst one."

Adam Smith, founder of the philosophy of laissez-faire, was almost as strict. The business man "neither intends to promote the public interest nor knows how much he is promoting it.... He intends only his own gain, and he is in this led by an invisible hand to promote the end which was no part of his intention." The hand, which later commentators piously took for the finger of God, automatically insured the community through the operation of supply and demand in the free market. Smith placed upon the Agenda, however, state subsidies for shipping under the Navigation Acts, as well as the army, navy, police power and courts. Foreign shippers were to be penalized, foreign imports in effect taxed. This at once stained the unblemished front of pure laissez-faire. Even the father of individualism was prepared to make exceptions.

The line of public business in the United States has been a shifting one. In the Revolution and all subsequent wars it has moved rapidly to the left. In times of peace, the ideals of Adam Smith have been in the foreground, as exemplified in the annual conventions of the Chamber of Commerce to this day. The duty of the State was neither to plan nor to execute, but to referee through the courts of law; to maintain order, property rights and contracts. In practice this simple conception has been corrupted at many points. As property became more liquid and intangible, the courts were forced to render economic decisions, and so put the State in business. The impartial referee began to carry the ball down the field. Meanwhile a growing series of industries were declared "affected with a public interest," and the State—federal or local—moved to their regulation and control; the phrase, however, as we shall see later, was loosely interpreted. Meanwhile special lobbies secured the intervention of the government for the promotion of their particular interests, such as "infant" industries wailing for tariff protection. Taxation powers grew, and with the income tax, the State was given a mighty bludgeon of interference. Ideals and theories have repeatedly been set on one side by the march of tangible events, but certainly the aim has been to let the free market rather than the State direct the flow of goods to the community. If the community could be fed by an invisible hand, it was argued, why bother with conscious controls? The trouble now is that the invisible hand has lost its grip.

The courts and the Agenda

A brief glance at the law, and its difficulties in maintaining the Agenda, is instructive. Even the sacredness of private property had to be qualified. Property at law, however, is more a bundle of rights than a concrete object.* I own a walking stick. I can carry it or not, prevent others from taking it, paint it sky blue, or burn it in the fireplace. But I cannot hit other citizens over the head with it. The State protects me in the right to use my property. Good. But it throws me in jail, indeed, it may hang me by the neck until I am dead, if I make certain uses of my property. There is no such thing as unrestricted private property.

The Supreme Court many years ago decided that the hatters of Danbury, Connecticut, could not boycott their employer. It was deemed an infringement of his property. But every competing business man is destroying, or trying to destroy, his competitor's property by taking business away from him. This put the learned bench on a tough spot. Nothing daunted, the Court evolved the famous "rule of reason." The injury permitted to a business man is such injury as "reasonably" arises, in a "reasonable" pursuit of "reasonable" purposes. The metaphysic is an excellent example of a high order abstraction which can mean anything or nothing. What is a reasonable profit, a reasonable damage, a reasonable business purpose? The answer may depend on the state of the court's digestion. Speaking as a professional accountant I know something of the hopelessness of the attempt to determine what constitutes a reasonable profit on any set of basic

* I am following in this section the admirable legal summary in *Economic Behavior*, by Atkins and others. Published by Houghton Mifflin Company.

principles, although one can arrive at an approximation in a given case. In the sense of constant economic interference through the courts, the government cannot stay out of business no matter how hard it tries.

Congress has been given the power to interfere with private enterprise in taxation and in interstate and foreign commerce. Other interference is legally permissible only by stretching the interpretation of "police power"—namely, the right of the State to promote public safety, health and morals. The New Deal has undoubtedly done considerable stretching. The State has long had the right to *prohibit* business in the public interest—traffic in dangerous drugs, opium, alcohol, white slavery, gambling, blue sky stocks. The Volstead Act destroyed a vast industry over night without compensation. Not only were the liquor interests hurt, but workers, grape growers, grain farmers, bottle manufacturers as well.

Here is a list of those industries hitherto subject to regulation by virtue of being "affected with a public interest":

Steam railroads	Heating companies
Trolley lines	(in large cities)
Carriers by water	Water companies
Wharf and dock companies	Sewage companies
Terminal companies	Ice companies
Express companies	Telephone and telegraph companies
Bus and taxicab companies	
Toll bridges	Radio broadcasting
Ferries	Messenger service
Canals	Market ticker service
Booming and rafting companies	Produce exchanges
	Stockyards
Gas companies	Gristmills
Power companies	Grain elevators

Creameries	Cotton gins
Commission merchants	Laundries
Hotels	Irrigation companies
Insurance companies	

Why these particular industries? Granted that nearly all furnish an important commodity or service to the public, why are ferries included, and filling stations neglected; why is a cotton gin more affected with a public interest than a shoe factory; or a laundry more than a bakery? True, some listed industries are natural monopolies, like the water supply, but hotels and taxis are notoriously competitive. The only pattern discernible is the general inclusion of transportation, communication, and municipal utilities. The rest seemed to have wandered out of private enterprise haphazard. Anthracite coal is a monopoly, but it is not included; neither is Mr. Mellon's airtight aluminum combine. Monopoly per se has obviously not been the criterion.

The industries are "affected" either because of custom—the common carrier and the innkeeper have been "public callings" since feudal times; or because of insistent pressure in the direction of public safety and convenience, as in the case of municipal utilities; or because of occasional local clamor due to exorbitant profiteering. There is obviously no consistent body of theory here at all. What was deemed the public interest in feudal times, under a low energy culture, is no test for a high energy culture.

Logic being absent, the Supreme Court has had the unhappy duty of supplying it. The results have been remarkable.

The power of the State to fix prices was first used in the case of Chicago grain elevator rates in 1877.

It was promptly challenged as a violation of the Fourteenth Amendment. In *Munn v. Illinois,* a divided Supreme Court upheld the state, but Chief Justice Waite in rendering the majority opinion implied that such price fixing could only be exercised over the comparatively narrow circle of business affected with a public interest. Subsequent interpretations further narrowed the doctrine of regulation to rates which were not "confiscatory." As Robert L. Hale points out, interference was thus made horizontal by applying it to specified businesses, and vertical by applying it to rates which must be reasonable and not confiscatory.*

The Chicago grain elevator case was decided on the ground that land was dear in the city and the elevator, "standing at the gateway of commerce," possessed a virtual monopoly. In *Brass v. Stoeser* in 1894, a grain elevator in North Dakota was involved. There was no question of monopoly in this case, as land was cheap and anyone might have set up an elevator. Nevertheless, the Supreme Court upheld price fixing again, not because of monopoly, but because grain elevators had been admitted to the sacred precincts in *Munn v. Illinois.* "The curious result would seem to be that where the peculiar circumstances of a business in one case place it in the class of those affected with a public interest, that same business must remain in that class even when the supporting circumstances are lacking." The Court was growing dizzy. Four justices dissented.

The next important case was *German Alliance Insurance Company v. Kansas* in 1914. The Court sustained the power of Kansas to regulate rates of fire insurance companies. There was no monopoly, and fire

* In the *Columbia Law Review,* March, 1934.

insurance had hitherto been outside the affected zone. Mr. Justice Lamar dissented vigorously: "It is evident that the decision is not a mere entering wedge, but reaches the end from the beginning and announces a principle which points inevitably to the conclusion that the price of every service offered can be regulated by statute." Fire insurance, he said, was not a prime necessity of life.

Mr. Chief Justice Taft did not help the cause of clarity by declaring in the Wolff Packing Co. case in 1923 that "the owner by devoting his business to public use, in effect grants an 'interest' in that use, and subjects himself to public regulation to the extent of these interests.... The thing which gave the public interest was the indispensable nature of the service and the exorbitant charges and arbitrary control to which the public might be subjected without regulation." Is there a single essential industry which at one time or another has not indulged in exorbitant charges or arbitrary control? Consider the whole phenomenon of prices set by administrative fiat rather than by the higgling of the market, as documented by Gardner Means, and cited in the last chapter. Food, fuel, clothing, housing —all are indispensable, and so logically affected with a public interest. But Mr. Taft did not contemplate any such landslide.

In the Tyson case in 1927, the Court sought to unscramble theatre ticket brokers from brokers in general. Says Mr. Hale of this decision: "The theatre is not affected with a public interest, therefore a theatre ticket broker, since he is a mere appendage of the theatre, is not so affected; therefore, no broker, even if not an appendage of the theatre, is so affected. A more perfect non-sequitur it would be difficult to devise." It was the word "broker" which seemed to paralyze the Court's reasoning faculties, not what the broker actually does. The decision was philological rather than economic. The Tyson case was celebrated for a dissenting opinion in which Mr. Justice Holmes rose above the legal word juggling of a generation: "The notion that a business is clothed with a public interest and has been devoted to the public use is little more than a fiction intended to beautify what is disagreeable to the sufferers. The truth seems to me to be that, subject to compensation when compensation is due, the legislature may forbid or restrict any business which has a sufficient force of public opinion behind it."

In the New State Ice case, Mr. Justice Brandeis provided another brilliant dissent along the same line. "The notion of a distinct category of business 'affected with a public interest,' employing property 'devoted to a public use,' rests upon historical error. . . . In my opinion, the true principle is that the State's power extends to every regulation of any business reasonably required and appropriate for the public protection. I find in the due process clause no other limitation upon the character or the scope of regulation permissible."

Finally in *Nebbia v. New York* in 1934, concerned with regulation of the milk industry, the Court in a majority decision drew level with Holmes and Brandeis. As expressed by Justice Roberts: "It is clear that there is no closed class or category of businesses affected with a public interest, and the function of courts in the application of the Fifth or Fourteenth Amendments is to determine in each case whether circumstances vindicate the challenged regulation as a reasonable extension of governmental authority or condemn it as arbitrary or discriminating."

The horizontal fences are knocked down. The State can regulate any business anywhere which needs regulating. The test is public need, and each case is to be decided on its merits. The word "reasonable" is still with us, but when applied to a specific case, it is not so obfuscating as when erected into a "rule of reason" doctrine. If we took over the railroads, there probably is, at any given date, a specific sum of dollars which reflects a reasonable compensation to the owners, within a margin of say plus or minus ten percent. If a given industry is so mismanaged that the community suffers, the community when it has suffered enough can, through its representatives, transfer it to the public zone by regulation, control or ownership, and the law will offer no objection in the long run, however thickly the suits and counter suits may fly at first. On the vertical front the Supreme Court will undoubtedly insist on reasonable compensation, which is fair enough. It is, however, somewhat dismaying to find that it takes the Supreme Court fifty-seven years from 1877 to 1934 to get its mental processes in tune with economic facts. We cannot afford any such time lag in the years immediately before us.

Under the NRA decision, the Supreme Court will not allow law-making authority to be delegated to a "partnership" of the government and private business —a ruling full of wisdom. It will not allow a blanket economic control of all industry, for under the Court's interpretation of the interstate commerce clause, wages and hours cannot be nationally regulated. The forces of modern technology are battering realities. The hour and wage controls of the NRA were in line with those forces, while the rest of the NRA probably was not. Either the Constitution or the battering realities must give ground. Fortunately the Constitution has provided a way to give ground gracefully by its own quite legitimate amendment.

Recently the *New Yorker* ran a cartoon showing a huge cement power dam nearing completion, with gigantic abutments and vast sluiceways. In the foreground are two engineers, one waving a telegram: "My God, Joe, the whole thing has been declared unconstitutional!" It is true that the courts can hamper and deflect the attempts of the American community to provide for its own survival. But in the long run, if the case is sufficiently urgent, the courts can no more set aside what has to be done than they could set aside the War legislation of 1917—which was shockingly unconstitutional—or set aside a million cubic yards of cement. It is extremely probable that future historians will regard the interpretation of the American Constitution in the twentieth century on all fours with the learned debates in the tenth century as to how many angels could dance on the point of a needle.

Survival as a basis for theory

A human community, whether it be a Yucatecan village like Chan Kom, or a great interlocked, mechanized society like the United States, demands in the last analysis two things: survival and progress. The second is of course less essential than the first. But that community has obviously lost its vigor which is without ambition for a better and a fuller life. In an old document which describes the founding of Harvard University, I find the following:

After God had carried us safe to New England and we had built our houses, provided necessaries for our livelihood, reared convenient places for God's worship, and settled the civil government, one of the next things we longed for, and looked after, was to advance Learning and perpetuate it to posterity . . .

Western nations at the present time are facing a problem of survival. Their populations are undergoing progressive degeneration through unemployment, malnutrition and hopelessness. They will not be blotted from the face of the planet—except possibly in the event of a sufficiently mechanized and extensive war—but they cannot maintain themselves as healthy communities unless and until their economic arrangements are vastly bettered. They have tragically bungled the application of that abundance which science has thrust into their hands. A flare-up of credit inflation, or a speculative boom here and there, for a few months or a few years, will not save them. The maladjustment lies deeper.

The State has not kept out of business in the past, despite the theory of laissez-faire. Its interference, however, has been largely at the instigation of groups of producers—tariff-protected industries, farmers, business men, occasionally organized labor. In an age when production was a dominant consideration, this was to be expected. As we shift to an age where distribution becomes dominant, the direction of public business must also shift. All citizens are consumers, and it is upon the problems of adequate consumption that the Agenda must now be based.

I think we should admit freely, with no quibbling, no qualifications, that the function of public business today is to do whatever must be done to assure the healthy survival of the whole community.* The com-

* For a spirited defense of these Agenda, see *The Open Door at Home,* by Charles A. Beard, especially the last chapter.

munity should move to its own protection with the swift reflex of a swarm of bees whose hive is attacked. If you grant that it is actually in danger, the necessity is not arguable. But the premise is hard to accept because of the difficulty of an objective view, and because of the soothing effect of habit, modified so slowly that we think we are still living as we have always lived.

Is the danger real? You have had my answer and the answer of seven able investigators. You have the answer in your own heart when you think of the future of your children, or of your old age.

So long as private enterprise assures community survival, public business need not advance except in the peripheries. But when survival is threatened, when old margins of safety shrink and disappear, the community must act. As we have seen in some detail, it has already begun to act, and failing a miraculous revival, it must so continue.

CHAPTER EIGHT

A Budget

The herculean task of the United States government today is to take care that its citizens have the necessities of life. We are seeking honestly and honorably to do this, irrespective of class or group.

PRESIDENT ROOSEVELT, in his message to Congress vetoing the veterans' bonus, thus defined the *Agenda* of the State in the broadest terms, and expressed the aim which I believe should dominate every public decision and all economic activity. In this study, however, we shall confine ourselves to a somewhat narrower and more concrete definition. Into what industries and enterprises must the State move as a first step towards providing the necessities of life? What specific goods and services do citizens need to maintain a normal existence? They must have a decent minimum of food, shelter, clothing, health service, education. They must have these material things in the present, and their prospect in the future—in other words, a measure of economic security for themselves and their children. Finally they must have work, not only to exchange for the first five items on the list, but as a psychological necessity without which men may lose their reason.*

* By a neurosis technically known as "unemployment shock," akin to shell shock.

"One sometimes wonders," says Dr. E. S. Robinson of Yale, in an excellent monograph on the law, "whether we should not be better off one hundred years from now if we could set out with the single objective of bodily health for the population of the world. War could not be tolerated because it brings death and disease, economic uncertainty could not be tolerated because worry, besides being a disease itself, brings other diseases in its train." I confess those philosophers who are forever proclaiming that man does not live by bread alone; that a sound body is useless without noble thoughts furnished by the said philosophers; that poverty may be a blessing in disguise; and that security is a cowards' prison—arouse my indignation. These gentlemen should spend a few days getting their food from the garbage dumps back of the Yards in Chicago—as hundreds of Americans have done in this depression.*

If we can name the commodities and industries necessary for community survival, we have a rough inventory of the possible field of public business today. The community must take steps either to insure the supply, through the operation of private enterprise, or to control the service itself. Per contra, those businesses which are not in the category of survival requirements are of secondary interest to the community, and tend to fall in the zone of private enterprise.

If this criterion is accepted, it will appear that a few activities which are now in the public zone do not belong there, and should be transferred. It will appear, further, that the area for individual enterprise is large, and once security is won, may grow faster than the public area.

* See studies made by the University of Chicago. Illustrated.

The modern flow of supply is almost intolerably complicated. A lump of iron ore, hacked from its bed in Minnesota, may travel as widely and swiftly as Will Rogers before it finds a resting place in the steel beams which hold your house together. Even then, if your house is some day torn down, the beams may go back into the scrap iron market, and start their travels through furnace and mill over again. "Food" and "shelter" are high order abstractions. Each is composed of a whole series of sub-abstractions—like the meat supply, cereals, vegetables, fruits; these in turn are composed of many processing industries, and below the latter stand millions of individual farms. When we say that public business must insure the food supply, we have a long series of events to reckon with. Since, however, the food supply is fortunately already organized and delivering output to the community, the task of public business becomes not that of operating the food complex from top to bottom, but rather of bringing the supply to the required standard. After that comes the larger problem of seeing to it that the supply comes through. This will be found far easier, and in some cases virtually solved, if the supply is considered public business, and made adequate in quantity. It is the margin of deficiency which needs first attention.

The food requirements of the community must be known, based on some dietetic standard; the available facilities must be known. Surpluses must be discouraged and shortages made up. Storage facilities must be extended—a type of public business as old as Pharaoh; wanton destruction of needed crops and supplies prohibited. Distribution facilities must be canvassed, and made to function effectively. Such is the approach indicated for public business. In working to Budget, the State in effect takes pecuniary speculation out of the food supply, precisely as it has already taken it out of the water supply in most cities.

The very process of making such a national Budget in terms of commodities furnishes information of great collateral value. The community learns how many additional farmers are wanted, and where; how many canneries, packing establishments, storage plants. Light is thrown on requirements for trucks and freight cars. The survey instantly illumines the question of employment and work. Thus a beginning is made towards organizing the opportunity to work, which, as we noted, is one of the six cardinal demands.

The following List A indicates major processes and commodities so essential to the consumer as to be legitimate public business. It will be followed by List B, which indicates the underlying industries and services which make List A possible. In the next chapter appears List C, the indicated domain for private enterprise.

List A

Survival Necessities
Consumers' Goods

Food and water

Raw farm products: fresh vegetables, fruits, eggs, poultry, cattle, etc.
Fresh fish.
Processed products: meat packing, milk products, canned goods, cereals and breads, sugar, etc.
Imports: coffee, tea, spices, fruits.
Water supply, individual and urban, including protection of the watershed.

A BUDGET

Shelter

Residential construction and materials.
Fuel and light: coal, oil, wood, gas, electric power.
Equipment: furnaces, ranges, refrigerators, electric appliances, furniture, utensils and tools, textiles, plumbing, ceramics, glassware; spare parts and repairs.
Hotels, clubs and boarding houses—in default of homes.
Laundry and cleaning services and supplies.

Clothing

Textile and leather production, and certain intermediate industries like the manufacture of buttons.
Suits, coats, dresses, shirts, underwear, boots and shoes, hosiery, gloves, hats, sweaters, work clothes. Estimates should calculate these for protection and decency only.
Repair services for garments and shoes.

Education

Public school construction and maintenance.
Instruction service.
Furnishings, text books, supplies.
Libraries, museums, adult education, information service.

Health and primary recreation

Sanitation services, hospitals, institutions, clinics, doctors, dentists and nurses.
Drugs.
Parks, playgrounds, sports and games.
Motor cars.

This list deals with the primary services of supply upon which every member of the modern community depends.* Not every citizen will consume equal

---

* All lists have been prepared by reference to Harold Loeb's *Chart of Plenty*, where every economic activity of moment in the United States appears. I have of necessity condensed the titles, but I doubt if many important functions have slipped through the dragnet. The lists come close to giving the broad outline of the total American economic scene.

amounts, nor will all need and desire identical products. But a balanced diet, decent shelter, elementary education and the rest, are mandatory if the community is to maintain its vitality. Very few luxuries are included here; very little which specifically stimulates cultural progress.

The question may legitimately be raised whether motor cars do not belong in the luxury list. A generation ago they did. Now they have become the outstanding symbol of American mass demand. This nation without a motor car for the majority of its families not only would be hard to imagine, but would demand a vast uprooting of institutions now based on the automobile. It is a recreation agent, but also a necessity for commuting to work, carrying children to school, transporting supplies. Literally millions of families could not live where they now live without the aid of a motor car. Libraries and museums are in part luxuries; I consider them also necessities, but admit that the point is open to debate.

This Budget can be met only by the operation of a host of underlying economic activities, which in all logic must also be affected with a public interest.

List B

Materials and Underlying Economic Activities Essential for the Survival Budget

Natural resources

Soils: for agriculture and grazing.
Water: fisheries, navigation, irrigation, power sites, reservoirs.
Forest cover and wild life.
Energy materials: coal, oil, natural gas.
Ferrous metals.

Non-ferrous metals: copper, lead, bauxite, zinc, chromium and others.
Clay, sand, gravel, building stone, lime, etc.
Chemical deposits such as phosphates, nitrates, sulphur, potash.

Capital goods

Construction industries for factories, commercial buildings, railroads, highways, utilities, etc. Dockyards.
Iron and steel mining and manufacturing. Coke production.
Non-ferrous mining and refining: copper, aluminum.
Lumber production.
Cement production.
Chemical production other than for consumers' goods: sulphuric acid, rubber, etc.
Brick and tile making.
Quarrying and stone cutting.
Machine making: for agriculture, factories, office, construction work, mining, hydraulic work. Locomotives, trucks, engines, lathes, presses, etc.

Services

Transportation: railway, highway, waterway, airway, trolley, pipe line, transmission line, terminals.
Communication: mails, telephone, telegraph, cable, radio, messenger.
Distribution: wholesaling, retailing, warehousing, public markets, the export and import traffic.
Banking, insurance, stock exchanges, investment service.
Government service: defense, police protection, municipal services, the courts and the law.
Scientific research, to maintain the technological structure.

It is better to set down the items one by one than to argue about public and private zones in the abstract. Merely to set them down, however, is to realize once and for all that the modern world is too complicated to offer anything so fine as a single line, on the one side of which fall pure public, and on the other pure private activities. The shuttle weaves back and forth. The steel industry furnishes the municipal bridge and the millionaire's yacht; the telephone summons the fire department, as well as the blonde to her admirer's little dinner. What one drinks is one's own business, although the case of government control in Sweden makes it evident that the public can drink more safely and comfortably when the traffic has both the poison and the profit taken out of it.

Faced with this complexity, it is perhaps natural that business men should want a unified pattern with the State all out, and the radicals should clamor for a unified pattern with the State all in. Unified patterns are easier for the mind to grasp. Public business, however, as we have seen, has been with us since the stone age, and the field has always been divided *de facto*. History will doubtless continue to divide it, despite all unified field theories.

List A indicates a broad zone of essential consumers' goods in which the community has a vital interest. Here public business should be dominant at least to the extent of restraining private enterprise from twisting or checking the flow. Much private business can probably remain. The same conclusion holds in List B, the zone of the underlying services which make the essentials possible. In a third sector, private enterprise and individual initiative should be dominant, tempered by public regulation in the interest of health, safety, wage and hour standards. If we want survival and security, we can thus determine where to concentrate legislative and administrative effort, and where to save our energies and let nature take her course. The New Deal has been galloping over the whole economic front, paying little attention to certain yawning omissions in the consumers' budget, while soldering and patching activities in the non-essential domain which would better be left alone. Witness many of the NRA codes which died before the Supreme Court killed them. The lists as prepared seek to show what is important and what is not. Better lists can undoubtedly be made, but I believe the theory behind them must stand.

Let us go down the line and mark the state penetration already in evidence, together with an indication of the shortages and surpluses now obtaining.

Food

Here penetration is heavy. The AAA, as we have seen, has virtually adopted the farms and their owners, and interfered drastically in the private control of food processing. Before long an amended Pure Food and Drugs Act will undoubtedly be passed, to give the consumer a measure of protection in his eating and dosing. The grading of canned goods to government standards is promised, even in chain grocery stores. Subsistence homesteads are gathering new farmers and old under the government's wing. The protection of soils from erosion is on the calendar for a great public works undertaking in the near future. Everyone who has seen newsreels of farmers abandoning their dust-buried homes will applaud the project.

The community is obviously groping its way to the protection of its food supply, but the aim has not been clarified. A good part of the effort to date has been deflected in attempts to subsidize farmers' losses. In public programs, at least, nobody seems to have thought steadily of the national food supply as such. We know that malnutrition—especially among children, some 8 million of whom are on relief—is widespread and growing. We know that against a balanced national diet we have surpluses of cereals, sugar and lard, and huge shortages of fresh fruits, vegetables and milk. Public business is attempting to cope with certain financial problems in this department, but not effectively with physical problems. Unfortunately we cannot eat mortgages. That this business is genuinely affected with a public interest, however, has been amply demonstrated, not only in the United States, but in government controls springing up all over the world. Here public distribution has in fact been inaugurated, in school lunches as well as in breadlines; and the surplus wheat, cabbages, pigs, bought by the government for the unemployed. Public business is consumers' business.

Shelter

This division, so long the happy hunting ground of those who buy by the acre and sell by the front foot, is hovering on a wholesale plunge into public business—with a splash which will reverberate. Mass housing abroad long ago left the domain of private enterprise. Even Wall Street talks about housing as the next great industry which is to pull us out of the depression, as the automobile pulled us out of 1921; and Wall Street, if anybody, knows that private capital is not interested in thirty-year amortizations at two percent. If mass housing is to be constructed, the State must finance it, though not necessarily do the actual building. Slum clearance and construction projects are now under way in Cleveland and elsewhere. Some $300,000,000 has been appropriated out of the new work relief fund.

Large sections of the farm population are to be moved and rehoused as their soils dissolve into dust storms. Dr. Tugwell is preparing the plans. Some 200,000 coal mining families can no longer go to the pits for their livelihood. They must find shelter as well as occupation in other regions. The State, through the farm and home owners' loan services, has already saved at least a million families from the agonies of foreclosure and eviction. Elaborate plans are being drawn to coordinate housing with industrial decentralization. As in the case of the food supply, these projects are more financial than physical, and occasionally conflict with each other; but the penetration grows day by day.

"Just as society," says A. H. Hansen, "may in its own interest require its citizens to meet certain minimum standards of education, so also it may require its citizens to measure up to certain standards of housing decency." We know that a full half of our population fails to meet even a low standard. Slums, both urban and rural, are breeding places for crime, disease and degeneracy. In some respects the results are worse than that illiteracy which it is the duty of education to liquidate. Public schools are compulsory, universal and free. Some day, when the prefabricated house becomes a roaring industry, shelter may move into the same category as education and the water supply. If pictures of public shelter in the Tennessee Valley are a good sample, no one need scorn a government house. With this sort of work undertaken on a substantial scale, the net saving would be very large. The bill we now pay for rotten, jerry built, insanitary shelter is perhaps the largest bill for waste in the nation.

Clothing

Here conditions are less acute than in food and shelter. Minimum requirements for warmth, protection and decency can readily be turned out in factories already standing, and are now distributed to the majority of the population. Above this minimum line, clothing is a matter of individual taste, conspicuous consumption, fashion and display. As such, it belongs to good tailors, designers, and other private enterprisers. The penetration by the State so far is found in the FERA production of clothing by the unemployed for their own use; in the AAA cotton, wool and leather controls. Minimum clothing requirements must be safeguarded, and of course labor conditions, but the public business here involved is not very great. Science, furthermore, has a few surprises for us in the form of cheap synthetic textiles, which may make the problem of physical supply even simpler in the future.

Education

This department is already 90 percent in the public zone. Some extensions are badly needed in rural areas, and in the general field of adult education. Heaven knows that the art of teaching, as well as the great media of mass information—newspapers, magazines, radio—could be improved. Broadly speaking, however, the community, both here and abroad, has taken the essential steps to assure the literacy if not the superior intelligence of its citizens. Recent developments in the United States have been in the direction of centralization. The federal government, already deeply involved, may become permanently responsible for a considerable part of the whole educational program.

Health and recreation

In Western Europe, the medical profession is a close ally, if not a subject, of the State. This has come about through the development of health insurance and socialized medicine. In the United States, agitation has begun for similar institutions, with vigorous opposition from the old guard in the American Medical Association. The gentlemen would be well advised to save their breath, for they have a powerful world trend against them. If the doctors would cooperate to speed the transition, and determine the best forms for socialized medicine to take, they could do the public, their own profession, and incidentally themselves a great service.

The old dispensation has failed to provide some 40 percent of the population with medical care. The survival Budget demands that these people receive attention, not only for their own sake, but for the sake of the rest of us. The only apparent way to provide this attention is through public medicine. This means the services of thousands of additional physicians, surgeons and dentists, tens of thousands of nurses, hundreds of thousands of hospital beds. In brief, more work for trained people. City health departments and sanitation measures have already afforded a precedent, and part of the necessary organization.

Recreation is a survival item in respect to public parks and playgrounds, without which Megalopolis could not breathe. To keep a community healthy in the power age requires a large extension of such facilities. A program to this end is being actively pushed by the CCC, and by other federal and local agencies. The case of the motor car we have already touched upon. As toil and hours of labor decline, recreation in one form or another must mount. Conservative critics complain at the ironic implications, and indeed it is something like feeding cake to the breadless. But would the conservative taxpayer rather enlarge a jail than a playground? Recreation is no longer a question of uplift or charity, but of the implacable demands of power age productive methods.

Natural resources

The safeguarding of soils, waters, forests, mineral deposits, from excessive exploitation and waste has long been included in official theories of public business. Theodore Roosevelt first raised the issue in a dramatic way in the United States. Even such a proponent of private enterprise as Mark Sullivan recently said: "Coal, oil and natural gas are, in the legal phrase, affected with a public interest. These natural resource industries should be set apart in law, as nature has set them apart in fact. They should be given a status and treated in a manner analogous to the status we have already given public utilities."

Various European nations have been conserving their soils, forests, power supply, ores, under state direction for many years. With the New Deal, the movement has gained headway in the United States: witness 2,000 CCC camps, the petroleum legislation which provides for a rationing of output, the Tennessee Valley Authority, and the vast proposals outlined in the reports of the National Resources Board.

Before the New Deal, in the early part of 1933, the Geological Survey drew up an impressive exhibit of government-owned natural resources. Public lands are estimated to contain 30 million acres of coal land, half a million acres of phosphate land, a large acreage of potash deposits, 4 million acres of oil shales. Sixty-five oil fields are now in operation on government property, yielding more than 30 million barrels annually. Of the 15 million horsepower now developed from falling water, 5 million are on government lands.

The division of natural resources is so important that we shall look into it further in a later chapter.

Capital goods industries

Opinion is general that capital goods or the heavy industries are the balance wheel of the whole business system. The government has been eager to revive them. To date, however, beyond the stimulation received from public works, loans to railroads for equipment and rails, not much progress has been registered. It is hoped that the housing program will provide a fillip.

Neither the State nor the community at large has yet had the courage to face the critical problem of capital goods. Are we to admit that the zone must be relatively smaller in the future than it has been in the past, due to the deceleration of capitalism; or to expect that somehow the old proportions can be revived, and effort concentrated upon ways and means to restore the ratio? The function of the State will be very different, depending upon the answer to these questions. Shall we prime the pump and then let her go under her own power, or make provision for a permanent area of public works to replace a shrinkage in flow which no priming can ever make good? I agree with Mr. Coyle, Mr. Jones and the rest, that pump priming is a waste of effort, and that the country must face the blunt fact of a capital goods sector different in kind and relatively smaller in size.

Underlying services

Transportation, communication and finance are already widely recognized in theory and in law as affected with a public interest. The railroads seem to be moving steadily towards government control, while Mr. Eastman has brought in his integrated program for all transport, including railways, waterways, highways and airways. An act of Congress is expected to make bus and truck traffic public business, probably in 1935. The new banking legislation will further concentrate the control of credit in the federal government. Mr. Morgenthau asks that the State own the stock of the Federal Reserve Banks.* Radio waves are already licensed and policed. Foreign nations almost without exception are heavily involved in state operation or direction of transport, banking and communication and we may expect to follow them. No pattern is more clearly indicated than the encroachment of public business in these three services.

In retail and wholesale distribution the penetration is small in the United States, but marked in many foreign nations, especially in the form of consumers' cooperative societies. The movement grows here too, as we have seen. The chain store is working out its peculiar variety of big business collectivism, which we

---
* New York *Times,* May 18, 1935.

will examine later. The steady progress both here and abroad towards monopolistic control of exports and imports tends to involve the government in balancing needed supplies against surpluses for export. Foreign trade used to be for profit only; now it is increasingly a question of national requirements.

Summary

When the State goes to war, a line must speedily be drawn between public and private business. Wars today involve the civil population as well as armies, and the bulk of the essential service of supply as well as gunpowder and rifles. The following are now the strategic essentials: *

Food	Tin	Manganese
Power	Potash	Aluminum
Machinery	Chromite	Nitrates
Chemicals	Rubber	Mica
Steel	Cotton	Antimony
Iron ore	Lead	Wool
Petroleum	Mercury	Nickel
Coal	Phosphates	Zinc
Copper	Tungsten	Sulphur

Whatever private enterprise may do or say, no State in 1935 dares allow these materials and industries to be mislaid beyond rapid mobilization in event of war. One might as well surrender without a battle. What is psychologically possible in war is not psychologically possible in peace, when the economy is in reasonable balance. In peace, what is good enough is good enough. But if an economy leans so far out of balance that its survival is threatened, there is no reason why a

* Brooks Emeny: *The Strategy of Raw Materials.* Macmillan, 1935.

division between essentials and non-essentials, possible in one crisis, should not be possible in another. The zones of course will differ, for the object of the one is death, and of the other, life, but the underlying principle remains the same. It is ironical that mankind accepts the wartime division as a matter of course, and has hitherto regarded the other as impractical and visionary, but we have to take mankind as it comes. The point I wish to make in submitting this Budget is that nothing is impractical when economic conditions become sufficiently distorted. A Reconstruction Finance Corporation in 1928 would have been a madman's dream; five years later it became a practical and accepted institution.

It is obvious that the State has already taken long steps in the direction of the Agenda for survival. It is dominant in the divisions of food and education; rapidly becoming dominant in natural resources, in public health, in the underlying services of banking, transportation, communication, exports and imports. It is making deep inroads into shelter, and trying by public works to set up an alternative to private investment in capital goods. Only in the division of clothing is the penetration relatively slight. The Agenda, in a confused way, are already half outlined. What is needed is a conscious realization on the part of statesmen and of the public generally that there is a tangible goal, and that it may be expressed in terms of tangible commodities and services.

We know for the United States what this survival Budget foots up to both in physical quantities and in money. The National Survey of Potential Product Capacity, after a nine months' survey by sixty engineers and technicians, has struck the totals.* In 1929, an ample budget of health and decency for the 30 million families in the country would have cost, in current dollars, something over 135 billion dollars, or about $4,400 per family. The physical plant was in a position to produce the bulk of the required goods. Adequate housing would take a few years to construct. The Survey found that a mass output of consumers' goods much above that figure *could not be used*. Let me say it again, for this is one of the most astounding findings in modern research: *A greater output could not be used*. Four to five thousand dollars' worth of quantity-produced food, sound shelter, good factory clothes, education through high school and the rest, including a motor car, is about all that the average family can consume. Much more is a waste and surfeit. The stomach can hold only so much; the body requires only so many cubic feet of space in which to keep biologically comfortable. Additional goods and services are often eagerly desired and can be readily consumed, but they fall in the province of private business (List C). There they tend to leave the domain of quantity production, and enter that of handicraft, individual design, custom building, personal taste, service trades. Some say there is no ceiling to such wants, but there is, at least for me. I could use perhaps double the survival Budget in books, decoration, travel and the like. Beyond that, the sheer care of things is more trouble than it is worth. Ceilings vary with the individual, like the blood count.

Your ceiling for luxury goods may be higher than mine. You may think that the floor-line I have set for

* Harold Loeb and associates: *The Chart of Plenty*. Viking Press, 1935.

all our fellow-citizens should be lowered. I have called it a budget for *survival,* not for subsistence. Americans could doubtless subsist for a time at the level of Chinese peasants, and many of them, I am afraid, are now trying to do so. But if this should continue for long, the nation as we know it would be transformed into another and lower culture.

From the exhaustive researches of the National Survey it is apparent that if the community can assure an adequate volume of mass produced goods and services, and assure that they will not be dumped, ploughed under or thrown away, distribution tends to take care of itself. When wheat enough for all Americans is grown, Americans must all consume it, because Mr. Mellon can hold no more wheat than one of his workers. If 30 million motor cars were put upon the roads, they must be widely shared because only a small proportion of families have the space or the income to maintain more than one car. On the other hand, production of emeralds or oil paintings can be indefinitely absorbed by a minority of the population, up to whatever ceiling of surfeit may there exist.

We shall refer frequently to the base standard set in this chapter. I shall call it for brevity simply the Budget. Please remember that it is a community budget, subject to some revision upward or downward, but not very far in either direction without changing our definition of the healthy survival of the American community and its standard of living.

If the Budget were met, the problem of security would be well on the road to solution. The problem of work would remain. True, to meet the survival requirements would demand an operation of the quantity production plant at a higher percentage of capacity than it has ever known, and so absorb more manpower. True, to meet requirements in health and education would absorb huge levies of skilled teachers, doctors, dentists, nurses, and attendants. As invention progressed, however, and as preventive medicine gradually lifted the medical burden, employed manpower might be expected to become stationary and then to decline.

Three alternatives are open: (1) To spread work by a general reduction in hours. (2) To absorb labor in the zone of private enterprise by the production of luxury and æsthetic goods and services. (3) To set up a public works division engaged not in survival activities, such as the protection of natural resources, but in progress and cultural activities, such as public architecture, the extension of medical research and recreational facilities, the cleaning up and putting in order of a continent ravaged by two centuries of ruthless exploitation. We shall probably use all three, but in what proportions no one can now tell.

A case study

I know of no better argument for the necessity of work as well as bread, than the account given by Dr. Ansel Franklin Hall, of the National Park Service, concerning certain relief workers recently put under his direction.* The government wanted to find jobs for a number of CCC and CWA people. Could Dr. Hall use them?:

Frankly, I wasn't too enthusiastic, but we needed help and here was a chance to get it. With resignation that rapidly

* *Science News Letter*, May 18, 1935.

changed to astonishment and thanksgiving, we went through the file of applications from the local jobless. I don't know what we expected. Certainly not what we got. Engineers, draftsmen, molders, sculptors, architects, artists, trained librarians, photographers, historians, book reviewers, newspaper men, advertising men, radio technicians, teachers. We employed fifty-two. Of these, eight were Ph.D.'s and eight were candidates for Ph.D.'s. Over 75 percent of the men were university graduates. Fifteen were women. In addition, we had six CCC boys.

How did these intelligent, specially trained professional men and women feel about working for a laborer's wage? That, too, was a surprise. They liked it. This is not saying that they rejoiced at the change from $3,000 or $5,000, and in some instances, more per year, to the CWA scale ranging from forty-five cents to $1.10 an hour. But many of these people had been out of work for a long time. And many of them had never had the opportunity to do the work they really liked. In our shops, our laboratories, and studios, each person did something he enjoyed. There was no commercialism, no rush, no competition. The job was the thing. . . .

After the day's work was over, everybody had to help clean up. This was usually complicated by certain enthusiastic ones unwilling to quit when the whistle blew. Believe it or not, it was harder to get them home when the work was supposed to be over at night than to get them back on the job in the morning. When I went down to the office on Sunday, I looked in at the studio, and almost always found more than half of the men at work. Why? Well, because they liked it, and were accomplishing something.

The projects were frankly a cultural activity, carefully planned by the Museum Headquarters staff. They included models of certain prehistoric animals needed for the museum at Petrified Forest; miniature models of pueblo and pit house dwellings for Grand Canyon National Park; drawings to illustrate the fur trade at Scott's Bluff; and most ambitious of all, a series of relief models of various national parks, to ac-

quaint visitors with what they were to see. The latter were built up from the Geological Survey maps, contour by contour, out of cardboard, and finally cast in plaster. Some of them were eighteen feet long. The lantern slide work was handled by a CCC boy who rapidly became an expert in darkroom technique. The tracing of contour lines with the lantern was handled by an electrical engineer and an architectural draftsman. The cutting of the traced line from cardboard by special machine was done by two CCC boys and a former piano tuner. The building up of the contours into mountain ranges was in charge of a professor of civil engineering and consulting civil engineer. "Under their skillful hands, plateaus and mountains rise as if by magic. They know the names of every tiny river, every little peak as these take form under their hands." The work of assembling the sections was presided over by a professional cabinet maker. The finer modeling and minute details of sculpture were done by a draftsman, a graduate architect, a National Park ranger and two CCC boys. Then came the caster's turn. He was a glutton for work. "That's finished, isn't it? Here, I'll take it."

"Wait a minute. I want to look at this lake again. Needs to be eased off just a little."

The implications of this little story are wide and clear. There is nothing I can add to them.

CHAPTER NINE

The Field for Individual Initiative

IN THE Agenda as developed, the community becomes consciously responsible for the necessities of life at every stage in their production. It follows that all other areas on the economic map belong on the non-Agenda and so in the province of individual enterprise. Let me emphasize again that no hard and fast line can be drawn. The Agenda are dominated by the public interest; the non-Agenda by private interest; but much private business will be found in the former, and a considerable amount of public regulation in the latter.

Before tabulating the private zone, it may be well to turn the question inward, and to ask one's self what specific freedoms he desires. As an individual and an American citizen, I ask myself that question.

I have long been a defender of a functional society, and exceedingly suspicious of the health or continued stability of a culture founded on acquisitiveness. For twenty years I have watched with close attention the gathering forces which demand more conscious control of the economic complex. Yet I am in a way a rampant individualist. I detest most forms of personal regimentation. A pretty paradox. Nor is my case unique. One finds that the majority of those afflicted with visions of a functional society are rampant individualists.

They wear queer clothes, go to queer places and say queer things. Their sense of the eternal fitness of things is alarmingly perverted. One never knows what they will be up to next.

Here am I, a student and a writer whose books would doubtless be burned in Nazi Germany did I live there. I resent any authority dictating what I shall say or think. I resent any authority which would deny me the right to go to this publisher or that with a manuscript. I resent any authority which might dictate where I must live, or, with certain reasonable exceptions, in what kind of house; or what I must wear or buy. I want freedom and plenty of it. No corporation has ever had me on its payroll except as a professional accountant with the right to come and go at my own convenience.

I should not feel my freedom outraged, however, if the State guaranteed me economic security. For that guarantee, furthermore, I should expect to render a *quid pro quo*. As matters now stand, I have not the slightest idea what is going to happen to me and my family when I am old, or what would happen should I be long incapacitated through illness or accident. Since the debacle of 1929, I have lost all faith in the dependable liquidity of savings and private insurance. If the requirements of the Budget of public business should demand some hours of my time in budget work —say the auditing of certain links in the chain of food supply, or assistance in the statistical work of forward planning—I should be cheerfully prepared to do it, at whatever wages were normal. If I were in dire want, I should be willing to accept a fairly assigned task of almost any kind; and let it be task, not dole. If I were a student in doubt about choosing a profession, I should welcome advice and tests of my abilities. But if all my time were demanded at a prescribed task, year after year, I should violently object, and do my best to escape into Mexico.

I am quite willing, furthermore, to buy my mass production supplies and staple foodstuffs from sources where the quality is guaranteed by the government or by a cooperative society. As the bulk of the service of supply is now in the realm of quantity production where individual taste is not particularly important, the lower the price and the higher the standard, the better for me. All that I want from furnace, refrigerator, stove, incandescent lamp, hardware, window frame, paint, washing machine, flour, sugar, butter, milk, canned goods, is dependable quality and reasonable delivery. I do not want to go shopping about for these staples, and my wife does not want to. We prefer to exert our consumers' choices in other fields.

I am willing to pay income tax on a steeply graduated scale, if I know that this helps to balance the national economy by stabilizing the ratio between saving and spending. I should be willing to live in a prefabricated steel house, if I had a choice of models, and would cheerfully pay $4,000 for it with money furnished by a state home owners' mortgage corporation at one or two percent. Or if I were about to build a house in a small community, I should accept reasonable restrictions on its situation and style of architecture. I would cheerfully borrow money when I needed it at a government branch bank at two percent, and it makes no difference to me who clears my checks so long as I have some confidence in the bank. At present I have no confidence in any private bank except as the government and the RFC have thrown their credit under it.

My sense of freedom would not be outraged if I received regular medical advice and attendance through a system of group medicine. I am quite willing to pay a good deal less for hospitalization and operation fees than the rates now current. In the past, I put off a needed operation for years because I could not afford it, a delay which came close to criminal negligence. I have no objection to playing tennis on good municipal courts, or spending my vacation in Glacier National Park.

I am willing to obey all sensible rules and regulations governing the conduct of my automobile on the roads, or myself in trains, elevators, subways or public buildings. I never jump traffic lights and regard those who do as dangerous hoodlums. If it is a demonstrable matter of public health or safety, you can regiment me to the bitter end. Fortunately or unfortunately, I have a lively appreciation of what one billion horsepower of energy loose in the republic means in the way of watching one's step. Many of my fellow-citizens proceed on the assumption that they are still living in the days of oxcarts, until they wake up in the hospital. I always hold my place in queues. I want to do what I please, but not at the cost of painful personal injury, or at the cost of causing my neighbors inconvenience or harm. I do not class slight moral shocks as harm.

I cannot see for Stuart Chase, living as he does, and being the kind of person he is, that the Agenda would necessarily thwart him, or destroy his freedoms. By offering security for his family and his old age, they would, on the contrary, greatly relieve him, and perhaps stimulate him to better work in the sense that he could ignore the commercial demands of publishers and editors. But his work as such, his interest, and certain of his material wants, lie primarily in a field altogether beyond the Agenda.

Turning my eyes inward, therefore, as honestly as I can, I find many items in the zone of private enterprise and personal taste necessary for me, as I suspect they are for you, and for every civilized human being. We must rigorously oppose the domination and meddling of the State over an area which belongs to the individual and his free choices. Here is a categorical indication of that industrial area:

List C

Luxuries and Preferences with Which Public Business Is Not Primarily Concerned

Food and drink

Alcohol, soft drinks, confectionery, out-of-season foods, vintages, imported delicacies.

Shelter

Domestic servants, hand made furnishings, objets d'art, interior decorating, landscape gardening, country estates, "scarce" goods generally, not susceptible to mass production.

Clothing

Last minute fashions, women's hats, custom made garments, rare fabrics, furs, lace, real silk, some sports clothes.

Education

Colleges, private schools, foreign travel, patronage of the arts, operas, symphony concerts.

Recreation

Country clubs, golf, tennis, sports equipment, races, circuses, prize fights, contests, gambling resorts and equipment, watering places, hunting and fishing, yachting, hobbies and collections, philately, amateur photography, amateur science, much reading material, musical instruments, radio sets, the theatre, including vaudeville and motion pictures.

Health

Split fee operations, smart sanatoria, consulting physicians.

Personal

Jewelry, cosmetics and toilet accessories, barber and beauty shops, churches, clubs and lodges, tobacco, chewing gum, notions and gifts, writing materials, funerals, flowers and home gardens.

It will be noted immediately that collectivism is relatively weak in this department, although we find here non-profit activities like clubs and churches. Many of the industries mentioned were under NRA codes but are no longer. The Food and Drug legislation has its eye on cosmetics, but this falls under the traditional police power concerned with public safety. Many universities are owned and operated by the State. Prohibition of alcoholic beverages was planted here once but it has gone.

Broadly speaking, the interference of the State in this division is confined to the protection of the employees and of public health and safety; to the protection of public morals, as in gambling laws; and to the usual clutter of petty regulation dealing with inspection and licensing. In my state, one must take out a license to go fishing, and wear a badge prominently displayed as he casts his line.

Prohibition was not designed for protection against a dangerous drug—as in opium legislation—but for protection of public morals. From the days of the Puritans, the State has continually tormented its citizens with this kind of public business. Laws and censorships without number have been leveled against card playing, Sunday sports, cigarette smoking, prize fighting, horse racing, novel reading, play acting, "salacious" photography and art, prostitution, the profession of communism or anarchism, ribald poetry, post cards, short skirts, and every variety of gambling except the Wall Street variety. As I write, the New York state legislature is solemnly debating an antinudist bill. Any competent psychologist will tell you that the net effect of all this mountain of meddling has been either to increase the activities proscribed, or to drive them underground into more vicious forms.

Twenty-one hundred years ago, Hanfei, last and greatest of the legalist school of philosophers in China, delivered the final word as to public business of this nature: *"The beginning of political wisdom lies in rejecting all moral platitudes and shunning all efforts at moral reforms."* * The typical American politician has been a geyser of moral platitudes—exceeded only by such spokesmen for business as Mr. Bruce Barton—and the State a perfect rolling mill for the mass manufacture of moral reforms. I confess myself a devoted defender of the non-Agenda according to Hanfei. The State should be taken by the scruff of the neck and thrown out of every domain where it seeks to regulate morals, unless it can be shown by duly qualified experts, armed with competent quantitative data, that public health and safety are actively endangered. In regu-

* Lin Yutang in *Harper's Magazine*, May, 1935.

FIELD FOR INDIVIDUAL INITIATIVE 161

lating prostitution, for instance, there is manifestly an acute question of public health. If the State seriously needs revenue, a case can be made for taxing so-called luxuries like horse racing, cigars, prize fights, but this should be the limit of the interference.

You cannot make people moral by fiat. You can improve behavior about a thousand percent by abolishing poverty. Complete economic security would, I submit, produce more moral improvement in one year than all the moral legislation in all the nations in the 2100 years since Hanfei.

The State, in my opinion, should reduce its jerry-built tax edifice to:

> Income taxes, including levies on corporate surplus
> Inheritance taxes
> Land value taxes
> Taxes on luxuries and nuisances when revenue is urgent
> Taxes in lieu of specific bills for costs, like assessments for improvements, and motor fees for maintaining roads.

The income tax could be collected by the federal government and a part of it divided among the states. The land value tax could be the mainstay of local communities. Assessments on personal property other than land could then be eliminated. Effort could be concentrated on making this simple schedule as fair in principle and as efficient in collection as possible. The plaguing of travelers by spilling the contents of their trunks on dirty wharves might well be abandoned. The tariff could give way to an export-import state monopoly.

With the protection of morals deleted from the Agenda, and taxation reduced to a few simple levies, public business in its most infuriating and obnoxious forms would be obliterated. The area of the non-Agenda would stand relatively free. The interference of the State in this zone would be limited to:

> Simple forms of taxation
> Minimum wage provisions in commercial enterprises
> Maximum hour provisions in commercial enterprises
> The protection of public health and safety
> The promotion, when funds were available, of the arts and sciences, but not the dictation thereof.

The arts and sciences

In addition to the specific items on List C, certain important general considerations are in order. The non-Agenda should be the home, broadly speaking, of the arts and sciences, and of new inventions and industries.

The creative impulse does not submit graciously to organization. Even the Foundations have found this out. You can give an artist a trip to Mexico, a writer a lovely little studio with sharp pencils in a row, a scientist a shiny new laboratory, but heaven knows what will be the result. If you insisted on putting me into a model writer's bungalow full of typewriters and sharp pencils, I should probably burn it down. Per contra, some of the best work I have ever done has been on the New York Central Railroad with the pencil lurching and the car full of tobacco smoke. I should not go so far as to say I prefer to express ideas in this environment, but I go so far as to say that I am a poor man to organize. Max Eastman in his *Artists in Uniform* has shown in painful detail the absurdity of trying to organize Russian artists and writers to a Marxian model. The experiment is being rapidly abandoned. Security of livelihood writers will gladly accept, encouragement also, but dictation reduces them to impotence. It is far better to feed an artist and let him work out his own salvation.

The New Deal is feeding artists and giving them walls to paint murals upon. Mr. George Biddle tells me that this helping hand has given American artists freedom and vitality above anything heretofore known in this country. He looks for an artistic renaissance to come out of it. In the past the American artist has lived as the client of an art dealer who slowly educated millionaires to like his paintings—or if they did not like them, at least to buy them. This has not proved a very satisfactory economic arrangement, especially when whole brigades of millionaires lose their millions, as in 1929, and new brigades must be painfully educated over a long period. Apparently it takes about ten years to indoctrinate a Park Avenue millionaire with the virtues of a given local painter. Of course he will buy Old Masters, sight unseen. It may be that the New Deal is doing more for American art than all the millionaires since George Washington, but it is still a long way from nationalizing artists.

Scientists can stand more organization, but not much more. They require costly equipment, and are always lamenting the lack of a new $10,000 gadget for recording their experiments. A judicious distribution of equipment and laboratories does undoubtedly further the cause of science, but if the State attempts to set the problems and demand results within specified periods, your scientist is likely to find the creative juices oozing out of him, precisely as does the artist. State research in the technology of war has not been very productive.*

* See Frederick Soddy and others: *The Frustration of Science*. Norton, 1935.

Science, as Veblen long ago pointed out, is at bottom idle curiosity. If you put a devotee too rigorously on schedule, his curiosity vanishes.

New inventions and industries

The inventor is a half-brother to the scientist. The entrepreneur who exploits his invention is a pure business man. Both can be exceedingly useful citizens, and should be encouraged to the limit—with greater legal protection for the former against the latter than has obtained in the past. If the Budget were operating, there would be no necessity for absorbing instantly every new process which comes along. Let the inventor and the exploiter make some money out of it, or as more frequently happens, lose their shirts. Let the invention stay in the non-Agenda until it has thoroughly proved its worth. When it has moved into mass production and become a real public necessity, then is the time to consider it as an item of the Agenda. The airplane is still in its development stage. Beyond provisions for safety and the policing of airways, the State would be foolish to try to assure a steady flow of planes to the civilian population. Some day a foolproof model may be put on the market to rival the motor car as a mass necessity. When that day comes, the airplane industry might be transferred to the public zone. Radio is getting ripe; television is still raw and green. A good, but not necessarily conclusive, test of maturity is manufacture by straight line, automatic or semi-automatic methods—unless the item itself—say a steel tennis racket—belongs in the private zone to perpetuity. This admission represents a certain sacrifice from one who has suffered from the inferior rackets of private makers. Generally speaking, quantity production tends to be Budget; hand production, private.

Private business in the public zone

The goods and services on List C, the arts and the sciences, new inventions and industries, by no means exhaust the activities open for private business. Australian sugar farmers, as we shall see later, have submitted to state control of output and prices, but continue to exercise their individual initiative as private owners in reducing costs. It is extremely probable that our future economy will use such procedures, where the State makes the overhead decisions governing requirements for the Budget, and private business strives to increase efficiency and margins within that overall control.

The United States government prepares the blue prints for Boulder Dam. Government engineers supervise and check every step of the construction. But contracts are let to private firms, bound by this supervision. The project is public business, but private enterprise does much of the actual work. This combination has been very general in the past, and may be expected to continue in the future.

Pick up such a publication as *The American City*. A copy lies on the desk before me. It is devoted to municipal administration problems. Here the city manager can keep abreast of the latest in airports, taxation methods, bonds, fire departments, housing, traffic control, street lighting, power plants, zoning, radios for police cars, sewage systems, water supply, relief work. Yet the magazine is bulky with advertisements, nor can I find a bathing beauty in the lot. The advertisements are addressed to hard-boiled municipal purchasing agents, and hence reasonably accurate and informing. Private business is offering to supply public business with aerial surveys, cast iron pipe, wire fencing, valves, landscape architecture, road building machinery, scientific instruments, chlorides for purifying water, tractors, sewer machines, scales, roofing, paving brick, asphalt, cement, street lighting devices and steel bridges. The two divisions seem to get along together fairly well between the covers of *The American City*.

Why the private zone may grow

It was reported several years ago that one plant in Akron could produce all the rubber tires then required for American automobiles. The new straight line, continuous process glass plants and steel plants are powered to make colossal holes in total requirements for glass and steel. The straight line, continuous, largely automatic production of commodities is apparently the road which industry has elected to travel. Dr. W. O. Willcox informs us that the new techniques in agrobiology make it theoretically possible to produce our present output of staple crops on one fifth the present acreage, using one fifth the manpower. The mechanical cotton picker has at last been perfected, and its application will render needless some 75 percent of the hand labor hitherto employed.

Is it too much to expect that in due time the production of items needed for the survival Budget will require but a small fraction of the total effort of the community? Even now it probably requires not more than 50 percent of all man-hours expended. If the Budget were actively functioning, the 50 percent would rise to perhaps 60. Then, as improved methods were introduced, the ratio would begin to fall. What the bottom would be, no man can say. Each new invention, when thoroughly tested out and absorbed, would drive the figure down. If synthetic foods, and the synthetic construction of raw materials eventually come out of the laboratory, as promised, the bottom will be very low indeed.* I should guess that we already have the technical knowledge available to produce the Budget with not more than 33 percent of our manpower, and an ultimate 25 percent does not seem a fantastic figure, considering the march of applied science. Contrast this with China, where at least 90 percent of all human work goes for survival—food, shelter and clothing. List A would shrink faster than List B, for the underlying services of List B furnish supplies for the private zone as well as the public.

Any such ratio means that public business will cover a relatively small part of the total economy. It follows that the area for private enterprise will increase correspondingly. The bulk of our work will be concerned with services, comforts, luxuries, cultural activities, which it may be the function of the State to guide and encourage, but not to dominate and control. But such a shift presupposes an adequate financial mechanism, or Professor Rautenstrauch's objections about overhead will apply.

When I list the items of the Budget today, the reader may stand appalled, if not infuriated, at the prospect of state control over wide areas hitherto sacred to private enterprise. He may conclude that the nation will be choked by an all pervading bureau-

* See *The Frustration of Science.*

cratic control. But ten or twenty years from now, the equivalent items may have shriveled in importance. If the engineers and inventors keep at it, there is no other possible outcome. Survival business must shrink, the area for individual taste, choice, effort, expand. Already the question of leisure is becoming a national problem. The expanding area will include, of course, many non-profit activities, which may grow even faster than commercial business.

What is the outlook for the American business man in the event that the community does elect to insure economic existence for all? At present he is quaking in his shoes at the thought of being scrapped in favor of a vast bureaucracy. So he runs out—or, better, gets some other chap to run out—and breaks up a communist meeting. This tactic, spiritedly pursued, may, true enough, ultimately bring an all-inclusive bureaucracy like that of Russia. Worse fates might befall the country. But the Agenda here set forth will not bring such a bureaucracy. Under them, the business man would find scope for:

1. The operation of activities shown in List C, with a minimum of regulation.
2. The development of all new inventions and processes, except in medicine.
3. The continuation of his business in many departments under Lists A and B, subject to state controls, but not state ownership.

This seems to provide room enough to turn around for business men who enjoy their calling and wish to produce useful goods and services. For those business men interested in speculation only, in the pursuit of something for nothing, the prospect is not so bright.

While profits and good profits are easily defensible as the fair reward of service and invention in the private zone, their reinvestment at a compounding rate, on a large scale, cannot be tolerated. By and large, the profits will have to be spent, or saved on a dollar-for-dollar basis without compounding. Mr. Bassett Jones and certain other mathematicians have demonstrated in great detail why this must be so. Compound interest will probably never again function in any economy, socialistic or capitalistic, on the scale we have known in the past.

Into the distribution of the Budget, once its production is assured, we cannot go very deeply here. But it should be pointed out that there are two and only two broad methods of insuring distribution: The community may seek to control the *financial mechanism,* and by the administration of prices, profits, new investment, and the flow of money, distribute purchasing power to the last family adequate to buy the necessities of life. Or the community may seek to control the *physical mechanism,* and in effect, ration the supply. We shall return to this distinction later, for it is important. Here it is enough to note that in the first case, financial control, the margin for private enterprise is larger than in the second case. The trend, however, seems to be towards a combination of the two.

A community has lost its sense of direction which begins a program of public business by undertaking to do for itself what private citizens are already doing well. Why take on administrative burdens which others are willing and competent to assume? The criterion for stepping over the line is a threatened Budget; a breakdown in survival requirements. If there is no threat, let the State stay on the sidelines.

The division I have tried to draw in the last three chapters may strike the reader as strained and theoretical. If he will turn back to the account of what actually is happening, as set forth in the inventories of trend and current performance, he will find that I have only tried to make conscious a goal towards which communities all over the world are more or less unconsciously moving. There is nothing excessively theoretical about self-preservation.

CHAPTER TEN

Nobody's Business

IT HAS long been the duty of the State to do what private enterprise will not or cannot do. The area has expanded in modern times. England fought the American Revolution with the aid of Hessian soldiers hired from private contractors. Private armies were once common, and a kind of vermiform appendix is still found in the coal and iron police of the steel barons. Prisons have been operated for private profit, highways were frequently toll roads, fire departments have been private companies, and in many small communities are now semi-public enterprises maintained by volunteer organizations in the form of a men's club. I belong to one myself. Of the thirty city water companies in the United States at the beginning of the nineteenth century, only one was municipally owned and operated.

Today armies, navies, police forces, education, highways, prisons, fire departments, water supply, are everywhere accepted as public enterprises. Private business is not greatly tempted, either, by parks, playgrounds, sanitation, sewers, public health service, coast guarding, channel clearing, lighthouse keeping, geodetic surveying, the standardizing of weights and measures, and scores of other essential activities. Part of the apathy is due to custom, part to the fact that there is no quick money in these services.

Said Adam Smith himself: "The third and last duty of the sovereign or commonwealth is that of erecting and maintaining those public institutions and those public works, which, though they may be in the highest degree advantageous to a great society, are, however, of such a nature that the profit could never repay the expense to any individual or small number of individuals." So far this is orthodox enough. But Adam Smith went on to say: "The performance of this duty requires, too, very different degrees of expense in the different periods of society." * This would indicate that, as society evolved, public business would also change or expand its forms.

While great corporations are now vying with the State in respect to longevity, most private businesses were set on foot because a profit was foreseen within the lifetime of one man; hopefully within a few years. An afforestation project may be productive of large profits, but who is going to wait a generation or two while the trees grow to maturity? When I see the square miles of twenty-year-old pine trees, still but saplings, which cover the watershed of New York City's great reservoir at Croton, I realize that only the undying body politic has the patience, and commands the low interest rate, to see the project through.

A careful survey would disclose many other opportunities for useful work which are now nobody's business. I give you in passing:

Comprehensive pest control.
Adequate endowment for research in pure science.

* *The Wealth of Nations*—Book V, Chapter I, Part III.

Research for the protection of the consumer: testing, quality standards, specifications.
Education for civil and public service.
Adequate economic statistics and indices. (We have no reliable current figures on unemployment, and no dependable general indices of prices, production or cost of living.)
A comprehensive system of social insurance.

The last has become public business in Europe, and a beginning is being made in the United States under the New Deal. We note beginnings as well in pest control (the CCC, and certain bureaus of the Department of Agriculture), and in more adequate records and statistics.

Mr. I. M. Rubinow has prepared a comprehensive table showing the field of social insurance. A glance at it will indicate how far we still need to go in this country before adequate security becomes a fact.

Hazard	*Type of Social Insurance*
1. Industrial accidents	Workmen's compensation
2. Industrial or occupational diseases	Workmen's compensation or health insurance
3. Non-industrial accidents	Health insurance
4. General illness	Health insurance
5. Maternity	Health insurance or special maternity insurance
6. Chronic invalidism	Health insurance or old age pensions
7. Old age	Old age pensions or insurance
8. Death	Life insurance; widows' and orphans' pensions
9. Desertion or imprisonment of breadwinner	Mothers' assistance funds
10. Unemployment	Unemployment insurance; home relief; work relief

Workmen's compensation is now fairly general; some states have old age pensions, and a few like Wisconsin have unemployment insurance. Private companies furnish life insurance to working people at high rates. Broadly speaking, however, the great majority of American families are either completely without protection, or inadequately protected against the hazards of modern life.

The greatest vacuum which the State is now trying to fill is relief and work for the unemployed. Private business has no place for some 12 million Americans. This, however, is a part of the whole broad problem of economic breakdown, and somewhat beyond Mr. Keynes' original definition of nobody's business.

Whether the Budget for community survival be accepted or not, certain it is that the State is literally forced to perform many services in which private business, because of custom or uncertainty of profit, has no interest. Some of the items listed above are subject to controversy, but not the function itself.

THE LOSS BATTALIONS

As we have repeatedly noted, capitalism is not a profit system, but a profit-and-loss system. Four retailers out of every five go bankrupt. The economic coast is strewn with far more wrecks than there are brave ships at sea. Free competition was predicated on the survival of the fittest. Not only do countless firms go upon the rocks, but from time to time whole industries all but disappear. Where are the once flourishing trades of wooden ship building, and harness making?

Times change. Carriages give way to what some

of their critics call four-wheeled projectiles. Free competition gives way to monopoly and administered competition. The old flexible structure, specifically designed to absorb the shocks of losses, bankruptcies, obsolescence, is no longer the ruling mode. Yet losses are still being made. Agriculture, bituminous coal and textiles have been in the red since 1920, while the lumber industry has been declining since 1906. In 1932, all American corporations showed a combined net loss of nearly 6 billion dollars, according to official Treasury figures. The gross value of all manufactured products fell from 70 billions in 1929 to 31 billions in 1933, a decline of 55 percent, while no less than 68,000 manufacturing establishments disappeared from the industrial register. The national income, which in the last analysis is industry's sole support, was 83 billions in 1929, 42 billions in 1933, 48 billions in 1934.

The railroads are running swift new streamlined trains, but even more swiftly are they running into insolvency. The sales of the Baldwin Locomotive Works averaged $40,333,000 a year for the decade to 1930. In 1931 they were $8,131,000; in 1932, $4,397,000; in 1933, $2,150,000. In 1934, the railroads as a system failed to meet their fixed charges by $53,000,000 and their net operating income was about half what it was in 1923–1925. Net income for 1935 is still declining. At the end of 1934, 45,000 miles of road were in receivership. The construction industry has seen no black ink on its ledgers for five years; the capital goods industries in the aggregate are making no money.

At the bottom of the depression it is doubtful if one bank out of a hundred was technically solvent. Today the banks have huge reserves and very slender profits. Said the New York *Times'* financial editor in April, 1935:

> Even highly efficient banks cannot make a profit if a large part of their funds is not in use, and another large part is invested or lent out at such low rates of interest as now prevail. Until recently this situation has not occasioned active alarm because it was felt that recovery would bring a rising demand for credit from business which would again permit the profitable employment of bank funds. Now, however, there is a growing doubt whether even a substantial improvement in business can absorb, with profit to the banks, the vast supplies, present and potential, of unused bank credit.

Between 1926 and 1931, the cotton textile industry lost $77,000,000. Sales in the durable goods industries—which include capital goods and long term consumers' goods like furnaces—were in 1934 only about one third the volume of 1929. Their aggregate surplus had declined 45 percent.

A computation of earnings made by Standard Statistics, Inc., for 1933 and 1934, shows the following industries with either net deficits or very low aggregate profits:

Aircraft	Machine manufacturing
Amusements	Metals
Building	Railroads
Coal	Railroad equipment
Iron and steel	Shipping
Textiles	

The condition of aircraft and amusements need not greatly worry us. In the others, the infection lies deeper.

With free competition unable to absorb these losses, tremendous pressure has been brought upon the State to absorb them. The business man, damning the government with one hand, and petitioning a special subsidy with the other, makes a picture as common as it is whimsical. Banks, insurance companies, farms, railroads, steamship companies, aviation concerns, mortgage companies, have all been drinking deep at the public trough, as we saw in Chapter III.

Conservative critics, unless they own stock in the aforesaid companies, cry paternalism. Paternalism it is, on an unprecedented scale. But if the government withdrew its support, one fears that the conservatives would have no breath left to cry with. The subsidizing of industrial losses is now an established function of public business, presently to be blessed by custom and tradition—like the franking of Congressmen's mail. Federal loans to small businesses are being widely agitated, and a few are already being made. A keen executive recently told me that he estimated 75 percent of such loans would go to salvage concerns which would otherwise go under, as marginal firms have always gone hitherto. Such a program appears an expensive way to prolong the agony.

If capitalism recovers, certain of these dole schedules can doubtless be abated. If it cannot again pay its own way, what is to be done with these patients of charity?—beggars would perhaps be too harsh a term. Even if capitalism should revive, the patients would all return, with more at their heels, in the next depression.

We have a delicate question here, only less delicate than the allied question of human employment. Starving capital and starving men. If these industries dealt in diamonds or cigar lighters, it would be easy to cut them off with a shilling and let them disappear. Banks, railroads and capital goods cannot be cut off with a shilling. Most of the industries on the dole are of cardinal economic importance, and must at any cost continue to function. Yet so long as they continue to make losses rather than profits, capital will not be attracted to them, private enterprise will progressively abandon them. Where can one find enthusiastic entrepreneurs now going into banking, lumbering and coal mining? After a sufficient period of losses, the life blood of a private business dries up. But the community may badly need its service.

Once the State has stepped in, how long can it afford to subsidize losses? Perhaps the air-transport industry, a husky infant, can be spoon fed through mail contracts, until ultimately it stands on its own feet. But agriculture and railroading are old industries, weakened by the buffets of a changing technology. If the community must support them indefinitely, they must obviously be reorganized, their costs and wastes reduced. This means far more than financial handouts; it means drastic state control, if not ownership. Opposition may be considerable in theory—but it is likely to be slight in practice. Private business, whatever its moral and philosophical scruples, is not really interested in unprofitable enterprises.

When the New Deal underwrote the banks, they were in a desperate condition with their assets tightly frozen. Some thawing has since taken place, but in general the 200 billion dollar drop in values placed on the national wealth during the depression has fallen largely on the portfolios of the banking institutions, and no amount of superficial liquidity can ultimately hide the fact. This means that the government must keep its credit under the banks indefinitely. It might be cheaper and less troublesome to take them over, particularly if the finance of the future is to concern itself more with consumption than with production. Private bankers do not know how to finance consumption, and they are afraid to try.

The loss battalions are retreating upon the Treasury. Even England is doling out money to ship builders. But an industry replete with duplications, marginal concerns, ancient equipment, technological obsolescence, is a bottomless sink. Stockholders may be charmed, but the Treasury cannot indefinitely stand the drain. If the government is to become financially responsible, it must presently become physically responsible and attempt to put the enterprise on a sound operating basis.

"Panic stricken security holders," says Congressman Sam Rayburn, "have been clamoring to the federal government that the taxpayers relieve them of their losses. When the railroads were prosperous these very security holders resisted every suggestion that the taxpayers should share in the profits, but as soon as the railroads ceased to be prosperous, they became very vocal in their demands. There is now a strong movement on the part of holders of junior bonds of railroads to have the government take over the railroads." *

If this sort of thing becomes vocal enough, I shall be tempted to agitate for the organization of an Anti-Government Ownership League for Junior Securities at Par. Millions for food, but not one cent for watered stocks.

At this point the survival Budget might prove a useful measuring device. A losing industry should be

*Before the Associated Traffic Clubs, May 11, 1935.

salvaged if it contributes directly or indirectly to the essentials as defined. The type and terms of reorganization should depend upon the calculated supply needed to fulfill Budget requirements. Thus if the coal industry threw up its hands and called for help—as it is perilously close to doing—the beneficiaries should be those more efficient mines capable of producing the 500 million tons or so that the nation annually needs. Displaced miners would have to go on public works, or to some other sector of the economic front. What public works and where? An indication will be furnished in the next chapter.

When we reach the bottom of this matter of capital on the dole, we see how inadequate is the usual diatribe against the profit system ... Fat capitalists are robbing the masses and building large steam yachts with their ill-gotten gains ... As a matter of fact lean capitalists are selling goods or services for less than they cost and beseeching the Treasury to socialize their losses ... The indictment continues: The State must take the factories and plants away from the capitalists and distribute the profits to the people ... As a matter of fact, few factories of the loss battalions are making any profits, and if the State takes them over, the people will, for an unpredictable period, enjoy not a distribution of profits, but a stiff distribution of assessments.

This is the kind of debacle we have fallen into by substituting administrative competition and a rigid price system for the old free market. It makes certain orthodox socialist theories as obsolete as Watt's steam engine. The State is charged with insuring the Budget, yes; but it needs to move with the utmost caution in taking over losing properties. Control them, but do not buy them, unless the bargain be very shrewdly driven. Above all have no traffic with any loss industry which does not produce a manifest Budget essential, except to find jobs for its workers.

CHAPTER ELEVEN

Old Man River: Public Business and Natural Resources

The material resources of the United States cannot be mathematically determined once and for all; and as Zimmerman has precisely stated the case, it is impossible to present a picture of the resources of the United States until we have determined the kind of nation we want to create—made its standard of life budget.*

RESOURCES, or deposits, as Zimmerman more accurately calls them, mean little as such. The Indians possessed more deposits than do we, 400 years later. It is only when they are related to some industrial technology that value appears. Hitherto the relationship has been primarily speculative; to secure the largest possible aggregate return in terms of money before they entered into the industrial process. This has made, as we all know, for waste on a gigantic scale. "During the time," says the National Resources Board, "it would take the ordinary person to read this fifty-page report enough fuel will have been wasted in our gas and oil fields and coal mines to keep at least 10,000 relief families warm during the coming winter."

Beneath the East Texas field, it is estimated is stored $4,000,000,000 worth of oil, eager, under pressure of its accompanying gases, to burst into the light of day. Ethics and ideals of the

* Charles A. Beard: *The Open Door at Home.* Macmillan, 1934.

public weal go haywire under such pressure. Individualism turns rugged, reckless and ugly.*

"Hot oil" is disorganizing an industry already ragged with waste, and forcing the State through Secretary Ickes to attempt a measure of control. The extent of our resources and the rate at which they should be exploited are questions which can be answered only by relating them to the Budget. Conservation as such may prove as barren as saving money in itself. We must know in a specific way what resources the community needs, and how much of them a year. Then we must know which of the deposits, at a given rate of exploitation, are threatened with exhaustion within a measurable period. Clay, stone, gravel deposits are laid down in such quantities that conservation is needless. Iron and coal also exist in great quantities, but for certain grades exhaustion is measurable, and the community interest grows. Forests at the present rate of cutting will be gone in a generation; petroleum may be very costly within a generation. The community accordingly must have the liveliest possible interest in the husbandry of these resources. Clay, stone, iron, coal, lumber, petroleum are all Budget raw materials of the first importance, but the function of public business grows or lessens with the factors of mass and time.**

The Mississippi Valley report

It is no longer necessary to argue that natural resources are on the State's Agenda. Everyone in his

* W. A. Dupuy in the New York *Times*.
** Dr. C. K. Leith of the University of Wisconsin asserts that unless stringent measures are taken the nation's supplies of copper, oil, zinc, and high grade iron ore will be exhausted within a generation.

senses admits it, although there is much research to be done in relating resources to the Budget, and in establishing sequences of control. We have heard the sad story of wastes in coal, oil and natural gas until we are weary of it. We have not heard so much about the waste of soils through erosion, and the manhandling for profit of the hydrologic cycle. The recent dust storms are an indication of the seriousness of the problem. Suppose that we review the report of the Mississippi Valley Committee as something relatively fresh in the conservation approach, and yet typical as showing the urgent necessity of public business in the division of natural resources.

In releasing the reports of the Mississippi Valley Committee and of the National Resources Board in January, 1935, President Roosevelt said: "These documents constitute a remarkable foundation for what we hope will be a permanent policy of orderly development in every part of the United States. I have asked the Congress for four billion dollars. A substantial portion of this sum will be used for objectives suggested in these reports."

The 4 billions are now in his official check book. The reports lie on his desk. The conjunction is unprecedented if not miraculous. For many years I have been reading magnificent reports, done up with maps, colored diagrams, little square men representing 1,000,000 farmers and little square men split in two representing 500,000 farmers, zigzag charts, and lush, lovely tables—telling with great detail and often profound wisdom what ought to be done to make mankind happier on the land it so ardently buys and sells. I have been reading Mr. Lewis Mumford, Mr. J. Russell Smith, Sir Patrick Geddes, Sir Raymond Unwin, the *Survey Graphic,* the Russell Sage Plan for New York, and many others. All were thrilling and exciting, like a detective story. But, in the back of my mind, the question has grown more insistent: Well, why not read a detective story? These are fine plans but nobody is ever going to do anything about them. Brain food for intellectuals, like chicken food for chickens. In the end, they gave me just a touch of nausea. I suppose I overate.

Along comes Morris L. Cooke, an engineer, who has been in the little-man half-man business for years, only he prefers little zigzags each symbolizing 10 million volts or so. He has specialized in giant power surveys. He cares about the relation of nature to man, and has made someone in authority share his concern. The report of the Mississippi Valley Committee, of which he was chairman, is the best report I have ever seen on the intelligent use of land, water and resources for the enjoyment of mankind. I read it from cover to cover, then arose and cheered. And so what? A rousing cheer, and a dark library shelf, world without end . . . buried with all the other hand-illumined reports on planning. By the Eternal, no! Slapped on the table of the most powerful executive on earth, and 4 billion dollars stacked on top of it. Four billion dollars; 10 billion man-hours of work, first and last, more or less. "A substantial portion of this sum will be used for objectives suggested in this report."

What did Mr. Cooke and his engineers find in the Mississippi Valley? What do they ask of Old Man River? This report is live stuff—wheelbarrow, cement mixer, steam dredge, generator, combine, power line stuff; library dust does not gather here. Indeed it may be that dust will be blown from the tops of some of the older planning documents. Mayor La Guardia is now asking for hundreds of millions for New York City, basing his projects on the Russell Sage study inaugurated many years ago. If the heavy industries cannot absorb the unemployed at the old rate, then public works must take the place of the flywheel of capitalism. This means either raking leaves from east to west and back to east again, or it means following carefully developed blue prints for the creation and conservation of social wealth—for real capital, rather than dubious capital like unrentable skyscrapers.

Here is the domain of Old Man River, the midriff, the very bowels, of the nation. It comprises five great drainage basins, the Upper Mississippi, the Ohio, the Missouri, the Southwest, the Lower Mississippi. The Missouri Basin alone exceeds the area of Germany, France and Italy combined. Forty-nine million Americans live in the Great Valley, on 1,235,000 square miles of land—when not under water in floods. Here grow the great staple crops—wheat, corn, cotton, rye; here hogs and beeves are fattened for a continental market; here are huge deposits of coal, iron ore, copper, oil; a forest coverage once vast, now dwindling.

One can grow giddy with the statistical wealth of the Mississippi Basin. But a conversation I had the other day with an old timer from St. Louis is a good specific for giddiness. "No sir, I wouldn't go back there again. I can't stand it; it breaks me all up. Last time was the last. Why, I remember when that valley was a paradise: fat farms, bursting barns, neat painted houses, smiling people, prosperous, happy. It was a pleasure to go up and down from state to state with a horse and wagon. Now what do you find? Misery, unpainted houses, no more smiles, floods, pollution, erosion, dust storms, patched fences, pep meetings by tin horn Chambers of Commerce. Sure, there are more roads, automobiles, radios and movie palaces, but what are they? A lick of paint on a rotten flooring. That valley used to be rich for people to live in, common folks. Now it may be rich for some Easterners, but it's poor to live in. I wouldn't be found dead in it; the heart's gone out of it. Something has made a hell out of what was paradise once. What spoiled it, mister?"

What spoiled it, Mr. Cooke? I pass the old timer's question on. Has the heart gone out of Old Man River? Is he destined to line his banks with peasants like the Hwang Ho; grateful for a cupful of cereal a day? Can people be happy there again?

Erosion

A large portion of the agricultural land in the Basin has lost from three to six inches of top soil, and no less than 25 percent of the tilled lands have actually been stripped to the subsoil. About five percent has reached the gullying stage, and has been permanently ruined for agricultural use. Four hundred million dollars a year is a conservative estimate of the tangible loss to the whole United States. First comes sheet erosion, often imperceptible except for a slight change in the color of the soil and a mysterious loss in fertility. Then "shoe-string" erosion, cracks and wrinkles across the fields. Finally gully erosion, like the last stages of an incurable disease. During this process the standard of living of those dependent on the land is lowered progressively. There is an increase of farm tenantry, tax delinquency, bankruptcies and land abandonment. The income of the whole community is lessened. There is a failure to maintain public institutions and public improvements, a progressive disintegration of the population, lowering of the morale of the people, increase of distress, and dependency on State or Federal relief . . . Once smiling regions become a desolate testimonial to man's folly.

The old timer had eyes in his head; he was not a sentimental dreamer. Over great areas, what was once rich is now poor. The cause lies much deeper than financial depression. It lies in the soil itself.

Erosion on the upper valleys means floods on the great rivers down below. In the Yazoo area in the delta, where levees have been built on both sides of a stream, cases are on record when, in times of dangerous floods, people living on one side of the river have dynamited the levee on the other side in order to release the pent-up water and thus relieve the danger to their own property. "This has led to a state approaching armed warfare, and serves again to emphasize the necessity for coordinated planning." A nice, neighborly repercussion.

Seventy-five percent of all tilled land in the United States is losing fertility by erosion. Soil which has taken a thousand years and more to build is now washing into rivers at the rate of 1,500,000,000 tons a year, there to choke channels, reservoirs, irrigation canals with silt. The loss arises from tilling over-steep slopes; from one crop farming, especially of corn, cotton and tobacco which need cultivation between the rows; from lack of adequate terracing; from forest fire injury; from overgrazing by livestock. Here is a 3.7 percent slope on Shelby loam soil studied for six years by the Missouri Agricultural Experiment Station. On bare land, the rate of movement of soil was 34.8 tons per acre per year—down to the sea. In continuous corn, the rate was 17.7 tons; in continuous wheat, 6.6 tons; in a rotation of corn, wheat and clover the rate drops to 2.8 tons; in sod grass, only .3 tons.

To water erosion when well under way, we must add

wind erosion—a very serious factor today, in the dry and windswept portions of the valley. In a dust storm in May, 1934, soil was carried east 1,500 miles to blot out the sun in some cities on the Atlantic coast. "Unless vigorous public action to check soil erosion is initiated at once, on a scale commensurate with the real situation, it will be too late to save vast areas of our most productive land from permanent depletion." In the dust storms of the spring of 1935, the pneumonia rate increased, and people began to die of lung hemorrhages.

The ideal river, which would have a uniform flow, does not exist in nature. Something has to be done to equalize the flow, or take advantage of variations in flow, if the stream is to resemble even remotely an ideal river. The problem of control involves not only the physical nature of the stream, but the often conflicting claims of various uses and various users. Scientific planning requires a use pattern for each community, district, or region, as well as a geographical pattern which will reflect as fairly as possible the dominant needs of each locality. The same principle must hold when we attempt to prevent a river system from doing damage. There is no one method of flood control which is applicable to the entire Mississippi system. The improvement of natural channels; the building of reservoirs—sometimes well adapted for purposes of irrigation and power; the construction of levees, reforestation, and a change in certain areas from tilled crops to grass crops, may all play a part in slowing down the rush of water to the sea, or in keeping it away from cities, towns and valuable lands. Floods pay no attention to political jurisdictions. Any coordinated system of control will demand the cooperation of neighboring states with each other and with the federal government.

Navigation and power

There are almost 13,000 miles of navigable channels in the Mississippi system—some of them monuments to the congressional pork barrel. Wild fowl squawk in angry astonishment when a scow churns their silent waters. Some of them are of sound use for the passage of people and things, and a grave cause of distress to railway presidents. The stricken officials summon well-paid experts—accountants, economists, professors—precisely as the power trust summoned them under Mr. Insull, and for all I know summons them today. Feverishly they set to work computing the "hidden costs" of these waterways, to the end that they too shall be left to the wild fowl, if any, while the railroads absorb the freight. I have been inspecting these "hidden cost" schedules lately, and from the standpoint of public interest, they are about as straight as a Kreuger gold bond. The report takes no sides in this century-old controversy. It is content to point out where waterways are a public service and where they are not. On the whole it is dubious about further developments.

Of 16 million potential kilowatts of power in the valley, only 2 million have been developed. "If coordination is taken as the key, we see the unfortunate effects of the present set-up in a power map which shows a mass of independent, unrelated units. Congested areas have more installed power than their inhabitants can utilize under present conditions; other areas, especially the rural ones, have little or no electric service, and there is a general underconsumption of power.... The federal government should regulate transmission, regardless of the number of generating plants or transmission lines it may ultimately own." Beyond this lies the great task of rural electrification—the need for which is shown by the fact that only one in ten of the nation's farms, only one in sixteen of those in the valley, buys electricity from power lines.

Forests

About 40 percent of the land of the valley was once forested. Some 20 percent rated as forest land remains, but the rating is optimistic. A large portion consists of cut-over lands or second growth. "Private ownership as a means of maintaining the forests in productive condition has broken down." Some 25 percent of the national forests lie in the valley, to a total of 165 million acres. States and local government units own 11 million acres more. The Forest Service has recently recommended that an additional 225 million acres be acquired. Mere ownership, however, is not enough. There must be protection from fire, insects, diseases; scientific planting programs, erosion control, continuing research. A healthy forest cover not only is the lumber supply of the future, but is indispensable for regulation of stream flow and the prevention of excessive erosion. When an area is denuded, run-off promptly increases.

Water table

The "ground water table" is the level at which water normally lies beneath the surface. A fall in this table is a serious matter for 95 percent of the population of the valley, which lacks access to the water supply of great cities. In the easterly, more humid parts of the valley, there is no evidence that the table has dropped, but in parts of the western watershed, there is an alarming shrinkage. Answered questionnaires were received from 1,482 well drillers in these regions. The returns indicated that during average periods ranging from ten to forty-four years there has been a ground level drop of more than ten feet in Nebraska, Minnesota, and the Dakotas, and of somewhat less than that average in Kansas and Missouri. In western North Dakota, the table has dropped twenty feet, on the Missouri-Mississippi Divide in Iowa, from twenty to thirty feet. In South Dakota, there has been a drop of at least forty feet in twenty years. The shrinkage is progressive, like compound interest.

As the table sinks, wells go dry, springs, ponds, lakes, streams shrink or altogether disappear. A declining water table with no decline in rainfall means that water is running down to the sea too fast because of slaughtered forests, wasteful methods of tillage. Improvements in farm machinery have protected neither the land nor the cash position of the farmer. They have created floods in the delta and overproduction in the market. "The diversified cropping system of the pioneers was easier on the land. . . . We cannot return to pioneer conditions, but we probably should return to diversification, which in turn would mean a better balanced agriculture."

In the fall of 1934, after the drought, I was in central South Dakota. One could take up a handful of black soil, crush it, open his fingers and let the dirt fall out. It left the hand as clean as beach sand; not a molecule of moisture remained. Citizens were quite frank in telling me that their region had reached its economic end. It could not go back to wheat, the only crop. It was not certain that it could go back to buffalo grass, the original cover, because the water table now lay so deep that the roots would wither before they found it. Fine people, on a dead land.

Function of the valley

I have only hinted at the wealth of material, the breadth of approach, the sound sense contained in this report. It falls into two grand divisions—function, and geographical area. The first includes a comprehensive survey of flood control, low water control, navigation, power, erosion, irrigation, forestry, wild life conservation, precipitation and run-off, ground water tables, water supply, sanitation, recreation. The second surveys the valley basin by basin—the Upper Mississippi, Ohio, Missouri, Southwest, Lower Mississippi. The report concludes with an authoritative discussion of planning in general, its application to the valley, and an exciting glimpse of the valley of the future—if and when planned.

The opportunities for Mr. Roosevelt to write checks are set forth in detail. The cost of protection against erosion is but a minute fraction of the cost of erosion. A twenty-year federal program, calling for joint action by states, counties, land districts, and individual owners would cost the national government $20,000,000 a year —about five percent of the measurable annual loss. Plans for flood control are developed basin by basin. To finance them, it is suggested that the federal government pay 30 percent of the cost of labor and materials for projects of chief benefit to local communities, and so on up to 100 percent when the project is primarily of national benefit. The same general principles apply to low water control—where the questions of sewage and pollution become acute. Sometimes a given project may include flood control, low water control, power development, irrigation, navigation and city water supply—a blue-print paradise for any engineer. In the next two decades, half a billion dollars could be well spent on power installations, and another $100,000,000 on independent projects for rural electrification. The report follows the Forest Service in estimating $47,000,000 a year for twenty years for the acquisition and protection of forest cover. Displaced farmers, coal miners, steel workers, lumbermen, have thousands of useful jobs awaiting them in this reconstruction work.

The sun is a great engine, pumping water from the Gulf of Mexico, depositing it as rain and snow over the Mississippi Valley, where gravity takes it in charge. Then down it slides, by gullies, rivulets, brooks, sub-soil waters, little rivers, big rivers, the father of rivers, to the Gulf again—a never-ending hydrologic cycle. In the functioning of that cycle, men live. Failing it, their lands are deserts and they die. Land, water and people go together. Flood control, erosion and low water control, navigation, hydroelectric power, water supply and sanitation are integral parts of the picture, and they tie in to agriculture, irrigation, forestry, recreation, the conservation of wild life.

A drainage basin, big or little, is a region through which water moves. No act of man can permanently halt this flow of power, nor even diminish it to an appreciable degree. The water must come down—we could not stop it if we would. We can, however, figuratively as well as literally, canalize it so that it will do what we want it to do and will not do what we do not want it to do.... Engineering does not exist for its own sake. It is of little use to control rivers if we cannot thereby improve the quality of human living. Therefore, the final and most significant element which the Committee has considered is neither land nor water, but the people who live on the land and who are dependent on the water.

Here is the report in a nutshell, its philosophy, its objective, its method. Observe there is no cringing to a profit motive; no specification that this engineering project or the other will be good for shippers, for property owners, for commercial expansion, for all the dubious claims of a bastard acquisitive culture. This report is for people who live on the land and are dependent on the water, not for those who live on land speculation and use water primarily for balance sheet purposes.

An acquisitive economy has thrust greedy hands into the hydrologic cycle. Forests have been heedlessly butchered, soils denuded of their fertility; the resulting floods have reached unprecedented heights, the low water periods unprecedented lows (like the business cycle), navigation has been neglected here and gorgeously overexpanded there (like the housing of Megalopolis), water powers have run to waste, and when developed, the power map shows "a crazy patchwork of operating areas"; wild life has been decimated, great areas rendered fetid with the untreated sewage of cities. A few more generations of the strenuous pursuit of the main chance, and it is safe to say that Old Man River would roar in lonely majesty, rid of that dirty animal *homo sapiens,* his waters clean at last.*

* Speaking before the American Works Association in May, 1935, Mr. Cooke said: "At the present rate of destruction only 150 million acres of really fertile land will remain in this country in fifty years—an area three times the size of Nebraska. It is my personal opinion that as matters now stand, and with the continuance of the manner in which the soil is now being squandered, this country of ours has left to it less than one hundred years of virile national existence. We have probably less than twenty years in which to develop the techniques, to recruit the fighting personnel, and, most difficult of all, to change the attitudes of millions of people who hold that ownership of land carries with it the right to mistreat and even destroy their land, regardless of the effect on the total national estate."

Fools: do you think a great river system is only a mechanism with which to turn an honest penny? The water will come down; slow and beneficial if you hold the run-offs with adequate forests, terraces, crop rotations; swift and terrible if you neglect them. You have neglected them for a century; many an honest penny has been turned and spent in Chicago, New York, Paris. Now Old Man River presents his bill. You will have to pay it or be thrown into bankruptcy—the bankruptcy of a vast river culture. This report indicates how the bill may be paid; the only way it may be paid: by planning, by subjugating private business to public, by reviving that life which the old timer thought was lost. Fortunately it is not too late. Not quite.

The great compulsions

Man is subject to two great compulsions: nature and his fellow-man. He cannot do what the physical environment forbids, and without courage far above the average, he cannot do what the mores forbid. The first compulsion is less obvious but more fundamental. To outrage the hydrologic cycle, though it take a hundred years, is a more serious matter than to outrage the day by day proprieties.

Among primitive peoples, the two compulsions march close together, for the hand of nature molds the customs of the tribe. In vegetable civilizations there is more latitude, but the compulsions of nature are still visible and direct, and the penalties for defying them obvious and terrible. Men have been killed for polluting a water hole. In mineral civilizations, the base is hidden in a maze of specialized tasks, in the complexities of urban living. But the base is there, and the penalties are terrible if not obvious.

Indeed the penalties may be more severe, for mineral cultures demand coal and oil and metals which once consumed are irreplaceable, while vegetable cultures demand crops, fibres and timber, which are self-renewing. The one lives on its economic capital, the other on its economic income. Sooner or later the capital will be gone. Soils, as we have seen, are not renewing where the tractor and mechanized farming can strip the land cover more ruthlessly than is possible with horse and ox.

Science is very clever, but not yet clever enough to grant any community the right to outrage nature, and to butcher resources, indefinitely. We may find "substitutes" for this and that, and we may not. Hitler, I believe, is having some difficulties at the present moment. He can make gasoline out of coal, but at four times the cost. We can probably grow food for the people of the Mississippi Valley in other sections of the country, but that settles nothing but starvation. There is also the problem of living—on lands to which one has become accustomed, in homes that one loves.

In the attempt to relate man to nature through a farsighted control of natural resources, public business strikes bedrock. Sometimes it seems to me that here lies the profoundest function of the community in its quest for security.

CHAPTER TWELVE

Big Business

THE function of the State in attending to important tasks which are nobody's business, in salvaging profitless enterprises when they render essential services, in conserving natural resources, is demonstrable to all sensible men. All over the world, furthermore, we find governments deeply involved in these divisions, and steadily going deeper. The actual penetration has placed the matter practically beyond argument.

But assuming a 100 percent penetration, the survival Budget is only partially provided for. Even with agriculture, soils, banks, railroads, coal, oil, placed officially upon the Agenda, supply is not assured until many other great industries are prepared to deliver goods and services to community schedule. These industries include meat packing, flour milling, canning, automobiles, iron and steel, aluminum refining, chemicals, agricultural implements, and so on. Only to mention them is to realize that here we come face to face with Big Business, glum, defiant and still very powerful.

Ever since the Civil War, Big Business has dominated the State itself. What it wanted, whether a franchise, a tariff schedule, or a slice of public land, the government has usually given, and only rarely did an income tax law, or a Teapot Dome decision, survive the censorship. We have seen, through the studies of Gardner Means and others, how Big Business has laid free competition away in lavender, and completely transformed the character of our economy. It is now proposed that 80 billions of massed and organized capital, more or less, be asked to serve the public interest by delivering its products on the basis of community need. Considering the history of Big Business, such a demand is little less than colossal effrontery.

Colossal effrontery I feel compelled to offer. Unless Big Business plays ball there will be no Budget, no economic security, no assurance of community survival. Big Business finds it difficult to cooperate, though some of its leaders may desire to. As Dr. Means has pointed out, it generally makes the wrong industrial decisions. There is no method of avoiding battle. Big Business must be faced, and power to make wrong decisions taken away from it, by whatever methods the community can summon, or, and I say this in all solemnity, the community may perish. We shall not nationalize aluminum, meat packing, steel manufacturing, tomorrow, but unless we presently find a way to control them, the outlook is dark indeed.

Big Business, we must remember, is not necessarily bad business. Monopolies, large units, can often drastically reduce the wastes and duplications which attend free competition. For much production—motor cars are an example—they constitute a technological imperative.* The power age demands them. Universally high standards of living would be a hopeless dream without them. Imagine what cars would cost

* Mr. Justice Brandeis in his *Curse of Bigness* dissents from this point of view, but I cannot agree that bigness per se makes for inefficiency.

us if Ford, General Motors and Chrysler were pulverized into a hundred ferociously competing units. Yet if the community surrenders to Big Business, what it stands to gain through technological efficiency may be lost through restriction of output and the maintenance of profitable scarcity. J. A. Hobson puts it thus:

> When business men desire to combine, it is impossible to force them to compete. The alternatives are either to leave the consuming public to the mercies of a monopoly . . . or else impose legal regulations, or finally, to buy out the business, transferring it from a private into a public monopoly.

There we are. Huge industrial units are here; the power age sanctions many of them, but in private hands the objective is normally all the traffic will bear through judicious restriction of output. There is no escape from this dilemma except to control the price controllers.

This brings us back to the NRA and its abrogation of the anti-trust laws. It appears that the United States is entering a period of *cartels,* or permitted monopolies, such as have long been known in Europe. Here also they have been long known, but sub rosa. Under the NRA they came boldly into the open, sanctioned by the State. The Supreme Court has withdrawn official sanction in the Schechter decision, but it is extremely doubtful if the anti-trust laws will be seriously invoked by the government in an attempt to break up the de facto combinations. One of two things may happen. The several cartels, as the most powerful bloc on the horizon, may bolt with the whole economic system, or they may bow to a superior force in the government, which exacts a price for the privilege of monopoly, official or unofficial as the case may be.

That price must be social control, running to such forms as excess profits taxes, complete publicity of accounts, prohibition against shut downs for the maintenance of prices, quality standards for the consumer, fair treatment of workers, veto power on new investment, the prompt distribution of corporate surpluses. If these fail, the price may be outright ownership and operation, as Hobson suggests.

Cracks in the Big Business structure

Many radicals and progressives are convinced that the big boys will bolt with the show. Doubtless they will if they can. But can they? If we put Big Business under the microscope, certain serious cracks and fissures in the structure itself are apparent. Let us examine them carefully. The weaker the structure, the less sanguinary the approaching battle, and the better the hope for the Budget.

In the first place, Big Business is not what it was in 1928. High finance, which provided the glue that bound the whole structure together, has been weakened by frozen assets, Senate investigations, restrictive legislation like the SEC, and bitter public disapproval and suspicion. The whole banking system is moving into the control of the State, which is now furnishing the buying power—some sixteen billions to date—that enables Big Business to balance its books, where books are being balanced. If the RFC, the PWA, the AAA, the FERA, shut up shop, the several cartels would be in grave danger of shutting up shop too. For the moment, Big Business must come to terms with the State, lest the mass income which feeds it be cut off.

A second and more important fissure appears when

we consider the future of capitalism. Big Business *is* modern capitalism. We have examined earlier six good quantitative reasons to doubt the continued operation of the capitalistic formula. If even one of these reasons prove valid, Big Business must either progressively weaken, or shift its technique to a new formula, of which the most probable form is a kind of frozen scarcity, akin to feudalism. Something of the sort may be tried, but it is so alien to the habit patterns of the leaders of Big Business that one doubts if it can be established. Expansion, development, new processes, are in their blood.

The third fissure we have also noted. Many large industries have been shuffled off into the division of loss —especially the railroads and the producers of certain capital goods—to become permanent wards of the State, and so to weaken the brotherhood as a whole.

Other members deal in the exploitation of natural resources—coal, oil, water power, copper, where the drift to public business appears inevitable, splitting the ranks for the fourth time.

Big Business has been developing a fifth lesion by an internal dissension of the utmost seriousness. It has been twisting traditional conceptions of private property upside down. Berle and Means in *The Modern Corporation* show in great detail how the owners of great corporations no longer control them, and how the non-owning "control" often manipulates the property to its own advantage and to the detriment of the stockholders. The law does not yet correspond with the facts of the "control," and the 2,000 or so financiers, dominating the 200 or so corporations which comprise Big Business, are in a precarious legal position. Witness the Van Sweringens. "It is quite conceivable today," says George Soule, "as it was not when capitalism began, that production and distribution could be carried on at least as well if all the legal 'owners' should be buried in an earthquake."

It is hard to overemphasize the importance of this shift in interest which modern corporation methods have brought about. The stockholders and bondholders of Big Business are by definition capitalists, but their interest is now centered in security of return. There is hardly a vestige of the entrepreneur left in them. Their interest has often run counter to the interest of corporate managements; it is on the point, in certain cases, of running parallel to an extension of public business.* Thus the united front of capitalism is broken; important groups of capitalists are against private business here, and for public business there.

Finally, and also significant, is the fact that Big Business is concerned with quantity production dependent on mass markets for its volume and its profit. While the creation of artificial scarcity does often enhance profit or avoid loss, there is a rigorous limit to this technique. If prices are maintained regardless of demand, there may come a time when, like the stock market in the fall of 1929, the whole house comes tumbling down. Many foreign cartels have been through this type of collapse since 1929. They posted their prices and held on. Finally came a day when their gross receipts were so meagre that bankruptcy threatened. The plug was pulled and prices fell into the subcellar literally over night.

"The cartel idea," says David Cushman Coyle, "is an appealing will-o'-the-wisp that haunts the dreams of

* As for instance the holders of the junior securities of the railroads, cited in Chapter X.

harried business executives, and yet the economists know that freezing the price system is one of the best known ways of causing an explosion. Control of production in plain English means firing men and reducing purchasing power. The idea is to make somebody else take the losses on the down turns, and to keep everybody from sharing in the profits on the up turns ... high profits in good times, slow adjustment to slight depressions, followed by a sudden collapse of the market as pegged prices collide with rising unemployment."

Said Mr. Alfred P. Sloan, president of General Motors, in 1932:

> The problem gets down to one of purchasing power. This has been recognized by far sighted industry. The movement for lower wages is not one in which the larger manufacturers of the country have taken the initiative. And the plain reason is that unless wages be high—although the cost of production must be low—there will not be enough purchasing power created to move the finished products.

There is little consciously malevolent about industrial Big Business, and a reasonably good case could be made out for conscious benevolence. It wants its profit, but as contributory thereto, it wants citizens to have plenty of money, plenty of things, and even high wages—preferably if some other manufacturer pays them. It does not take the troglodyte attitude of some British industrialists, that high wages corrupt the worker by making him aspire to goods and services above the station to which God has been pleased to call him. American Big Business has very little class consciousness in this sense; it welcomes rather than resents the sight of workers in motor cars—though it may consider a bricklayer in a Rolls-Royce as carrying matters a trifle far.

Big Business, by the laws of its technological development, can no longer afford to grind the faces of the poor.* This fissure in the structure does not need a microscope to detect. I cannot picture, try as I may, that nightmare where Big Business sits in feudal splendor over serfs and peasants in an economy where business is no longer big.

The real question at issue, it seems to me, is whether the individual leaders of Big Business are prepared to accept a greater measure of state control over their enterprises as the price of continuing those enterprises. Some of them would rather scuttle the ship. Others, and I have talked to one or two, are not disposed to be so arrogant. The fate of Big Business and of the public Budget turns primarily on this question of individual power and prestige, and not on any industrial logic. Probably not more than 2,000 individuals are involved. Should they permanently retire to a golfer's paradise tomorrow, the battle for the principle of state control might be won with hardly a gun fired.

The upshot of all these six fissures in the structure of Big Business, is that the nut is not so tough a one to crack as it first appears. Its market position is precarious and promises to be worse if automatic capitalism cannot be revived. Its legal position is rickety, since control has never been defined. It is surrendering large segments to the State in the loss division and in the natural resource division. Its united front is split by dissension between owners and managers.

From time to time there appear elaborate spiderweb

* Mr. Edward A. Filene, an ex-big business man, goes up and down the land driving this point home.

charts showing a vast tangle of corporate directorships, with Messrs. J. P. Morgan and Company, and Kuhn, Loeb and Company, snugly in the center. Generally the charts are accurate, but the impression they leave on the reader's mind is not accurate. No human being can serve on sixty boards of directors and know much about the underlying companies. Many of the spiders have never even seen each other. J. P. Morgan and Company is no longer the dominant financial power it used to be, as any Wall Street man will tell you. Certain of the companies so tightly bound together on the charts are in reality bitter competitors—lumber versus brick, tobacco versus sugar, rayon versus silk and cotton, newspapers versus radio. There is no "system" in Big Business, in the sense that the nobles of England once had a system under the king. Furthermore, such prestige as Big Business possessed as a system was seriously damaged by the depression, which it did not foresee, and long refused to admit after it had come. Its members made fools of themselves so often that the public took to reading *"Oh Yeah?"* Are they interested in, and are they capable of, the direction of an integrated continental economy?

This is, I believe, sound analysis, but rather general in content. Would you like to examine Big Business at first hand? Here is a classified list of the great corporations which comprise it, taken from *The Modern Corporation and Private Property*. No banks or financial companies are included. I have telescoped certain holding company groups, so that the total number is less than the 200 on the Berle and Means schedule. Nearly every company in 1930 had assets of $100,000,000 or up. Fifteen had assets of more than a billion. The whole group accounted for 81 billions of assets, or more than one half of all corporate wealth. From these corporations some 5 million stockholders, more or less, patiently await their "conventional dividend."

I have grouped them to indicate in a general way the categories discussed above. I have not had the heart to make a separate Loss division, but the reader who knows his financial page can recognize many victims. They appear chiefly in the capital goods group, and in certain sections of the utilities group. The grouping must be somewhat arbitrary. I have placed General Electric on the capital goods list, but as everyone knows, it makes many articles for ultimate consumers—like refrigerators. Berle and Means made their historic study on the basis of assets obtaining in 1930, and so a revised list of the 200 largest non-banking corporations today would show a number of new faces. The lists as they stand, however, give us a good idea of the mass impact of Big Business.

The first group listed is Big Business in the private zone, whose activities are not on the Agenda of the State. These companies do not contribute to the survival Budget as earlier defined—with exceptions to be noted.

Non-Budget Group

Eastman Kodak Co.
General Theatres, Inc. (Fox)
Loew's, Inc. (theatres)
Paramount Publix Corp.
 (theatres)
Warner Brothers Pictures, Inc.

American Tobacco Co.
Liggett and Myers Tobacco Co.
Lorillard Co. (tobacco)
Reynolds Tobacco Co.
Radio Corporation of America

Motion pictures, radio and tobacco are regarded as necessities rather than luxuries by millions of Americans. They are too far from survival requirements, however, to make them public business at this time. Perhaps this is a measure of the danger we are in. The supply of tobacco is for the moment ample and reasonably priced. But labor conditions in many cigarette and tobacco factories are reported to be bad. Wage and hour regulation is certainly needed not only in tobacco factories but throughout the group.

Distribution Group

Drug, Inc.	Marshall Field & Co.
Great Atlantic and Pacific Tea Co.	Montgomery Ward & Co.
Kresge Co.	Sears, Roebuck & Co.
R. H. Macy & Co.	United Stores Corp.
Woolworth & Co.	

Here is Big Business in retail distribution. Are these companies obstructing the flow of goods to the consumer? They are not altogether above suspicion, but on the whole they had better be left alone until the community finds a superior method.

American distribution methods are wasteful in the extreme, and the trade as a whole shows more losses than profits. This is evident in the high death rate of small retail shops. Chain stores and large mail order houses can be more efficient, and render the consumer better goods at lower prices. They constitute another technological imperative. The question remains whether, so long as they are privately operated for profit, the consumer has any certainty of receiving better goods at lower prices. It seems to me that the mail order houses listed have established some claim to that consummation, but that the chain and department stores, by and large, have yet to prove their worth.

Natural Resources Group

Atlantic Refining Co.
Continental Oil Co.
Gulf Oil Corp.
Ohio Oil Co.
Phillips Petroleum Co.
Prairie Oil and Gas Co.
Pure Oil Co.
Richfield Oil of California
Shell Union Oil Corp.
Sinclair Consolidated Oil Corp.
Standard Oil of California
Standard Oil of Indiana
Standard Oil of New Jersey
Standard Oil of New York
Texas Corp.
Tide Water Associated Oil Co.
Union Oil Associates
Vacuum Oil Co.
Consolidation Coal Co.
Glen Alden Coal Co.
Philadelphia & Reading Coal & Iron Corp.
Pittsburgh Coal Co.
Long-Bell Lumber Corp.
Aluminum Company of America
American Smelting & Refining Co.
Anaconda Copper Corp.
National Lead Co.
Phelps Dodge Corp. (mines)

Here we find Big Business in oil, coal, and lumber, in aluminum, copper, lead and other metals. The great oil companies, it is true, tend to limit themselves to refining and distribution, allowing little business to take the speculative gamble on opening new fields and wells. The interest of the State is more in conserving the underground supply than in controlling the process of refining. But the oil industry after all is one great complex, and is tied to the problem of a rapidly diminishing natural resource—where will the refineries be when the wells go dry? It is in the aura if not in the immediate zone of public business. Lumber is urgent public business. Whether the several mining companies should be placed upon the Agenda depends on the needs of the Budget, the extent of the resource, and the resulting length of its life. Coal, copper, zinc, probably belong in the public zone.

Gold and silver have no place in the Budget at all.

Now that we have left the gold standard—if it comes back its reign is likely to be very brief—I see no point whatever in bothering about the supply or the conservation of these metals. Statesmen have always been reverent towards gold and silver. Today they are wasting their time, and the public's time, in drafting legislation, and setting up controls, for a department of public business which belongs to a bygone age.

Capital Goods Group

General Electric Co.
Westinghouse Electric and Manufacturing Co.
Deere & Co. (farm equipment)
International Harvester Co.
United Shoe Machinery Corp.
American Can Co.
American Car & Foundry Co.
American Locomotive Co.
American Radiator Corp.
Baldwin Locomotive Works
Crane Co. (plumbing, valves)
U. S. Realty & Improvement Co.
American Rolling Mill Co.
Bethlehem Steel Corp.
Cliffs Corp. (iron and steel)
Crucible Steel Co. of America
Inland Steel Co.
Jones and Laughlin Steel Corp.
National Steel Corp.
Republic Iron & Steel Co.
United States Steel Corp.
Wheeling Steel Corp.
Youngstown Sheet & Tube Co.
Pullman, Inc.
Koppers Co. (coke and chemicals)

This is heavy industry. Some of these companies, like Baldwin Locomotive, have fallen into the loss division. Some are still solvent but with depleted surplus accounts, like United States Steel. Some are doing nicely, thank you, like General Electric. But all produce capital goods, and the fate of that sector is clouded. Many companies are dependent on the government's public works program for present and future orders. This division cannot afford to be unduly arrogant, for it is bound up with expanding investment under the formula of capitalism.

Public Utilities Group

American Telephone & Telegraph Co.
Associated Telephone Utilities Co.
International Telephone and Telegraph Corp.
Western Union Telegraph Co.
American Commonwealths Power Corp.
American Water Works & Electric Co.
Associated Gas & Electric Co.
Central Public Service Co.
Cities Service Co.
Consolidated Gas Co. of New York
Consolidated Gas, Electric Light & Power Co. of Baltimore
Detroit Edison Co.
Edison Electric Illuminating Co. of Boston

International Mercantile Marine Co.
Middle West Utilities and other Insull companies
Brooklyn Union Gas Co.
Eastern Gas & Fuel Associates
Lone Star Gas Corp.
North American Co. (power)
Pacific Lighting Corp.
Southern California Edison Co., Ltd.
Stone & Webster, Inc. (power)
Tri-Utilities Corp.
United Corporation group of utilities
United Light & Power Co.
United States Electric Power Corp.
Utilities Power & Light Corp.
Duke Power Co.
Electric Bond & Share Co.

Pennsylvania Railroad
Southern Pacific Railroad
Alleghany Corp.
New York Central Railroad
And the other great railroad systems of America

Philadelphia Rapid Transit
Interborough Rapid Transit
Brooklyn & Manhattan Transit Co.
And the other great street railway systems

What memories of the 1929 stock market this list conjures up! Hardly one of these companies but was to make us independent for life—Telephone at 304; New York Central at 256. Ah, happy days.

This entire division has long been regulated by the State in one form or another. Holding companies it is true have escaped, but their subsidiaries have not, and now President Roosevelt moves on the holy of holies. The control of utility holding companies is something he deeply cares about. It is of course ridiculous to regulate the horse without the rider upon him. Only corporation lawyers can see the horse alone. Utilities are public enterprises of the first order, and, writhe as it may, we may expect Big Business in this division ultimately to accept the fact. Drastic control there must be, but whether public ownership is mandatory depends on how far Big Business thwarts that control. We must remember that we live in a power age. These companies deal in our life's blood.

Certain of the holding companies, like Middle West Utilities, have been deflated into the loss section—with perhaps the most appalling losses to be found in American economic history. The cost to Insull investors alone has been placed at close to $1,000,000,000. These pricked balloons cannot present any very stalwart opposition to state control. Their stockholders would be glad to accept any offer above the current price for wallpaper.

The railroads are a legal public service, and also, as a system, in the loss division. Many are already wards of the RFC. The telephone and telegraph companies are now regulated, and public outcries against the quality of their services are not loud. The American Telephone Co. is a public darling as compared with the so-called power trust. For one thing it does not bribe legislators and college professors, so far as the record shows, nor send forged telegrams to Congress.

Budget Group

Borden Co. (milk products)
National Dairy Products Corp.
United Fruit Co.
Armour and Co.
Swift and Co.
Wilson and Co.
American Sugar Refining Co.
Cuban Cane Products Co.
National Biscuit Co.
Procter and Gamble Co. (soap)
Corn Products Refining Corp.
Allied Chemical & Dye Corp.
DuPont de Nemours & Co. (explosives, chemicals)
International Match Corp.
Pittsburgh Plate Glass Co.
International Shoe Co.
Ford Motor Co.
Chrysler Corp.
General Motors Corp.
Studebaker Corp.
Singer Manufacturing Co. (sewing machines)
Crown Zellerbach Corp. (paper)
International Paper & Power Co.
Minnesota & Ontario Paper Co.
B. F. Goodrich Co. (rubber)
Firestone Tire & Rubber Co.
Goodyear Tire & Rubber Co.
United States Rubber Co.
American Woolen Co.
Union Carbide & Carbon Corp.

Here is Big Business furnishing direct supplies for the survival Budget. The list, you will observe, while powerful, is not long. Of course, if we include the great distribution companies, the impact of Big Business grows. Could the directors of these corporations, single handed as it were, prevent the community from guaranteeing the service of supply? The Chicago meat packers have already felt the hand of the State, and their old arrogance has appreciably diminished. I know its quality, because I once tried to regulate packers' profits under the Food Administration. The milk distributors face an increasingly heavy attack. The automobile companies and the rubber companies are not budget items of the first importance, and their control is not immediately imperative. The rubber companies, incidentally, hover on the brink of the loss section. DuPont is a special case. The company makes essential chemicals and textiles, and it makes munitions. Munitions are rapidly coming to be regarded as public business of the highest order. Bills are already before Congress for government ownership of the industry.

On the whole, the above lists go to support the conclusions earlier reached. Big Business does not present a united front. Certain units are beyond the State's purview; certain units furnish capital goods with a highly uncertain future; certain units are legally quasi-public business already, or, dealing in natural resources, are clearly headed for such legal status. The remaining group is not unduly formidable. It may listen to reason. Mr. Gerard Swope of the General Electric Company has seen the handwriting on the wall:

> That industry must evolve and make effective those measures which will first ameliorate and ultimately eliminate these conditions [unemployment, industrial breakdown, etc.] must be the reaction of everyone who gives thought to what is taking place. I say that industry must do this thing, because it will surely be done. . . . Shall we wait for society to act through its legislatures, or shall industry recognize its obligations to its employees and to the public and undertake the task?

Apparently the gentlemen are waiting.

A summary

Let us pause for a moment and take stock.

I want a public business Budget. I believe that more than 90 percent of Americans want it. As I have defined this Budget, it leaves plenty of room for private business and individual enterprise. This room, furthermore, promises to grow with the growth of industrial productivity.

Governments all over the world are consciously, as in Russia, or unconsciously, as in the United States, moving towards a guarantee of social security as the price of survival. Progress is particularly noticeable in the United States in three major divisions:

1. Work which is nobody's business unless it is the State's.
2. The work of unprofitable industries, where private business is withdrawing and seeking to socialize its losses.
3. The control of national resources (which is rendered the more imperative by the threat of war).

These divisions account for a large fraction of the service of supply which constitutes the Budget. But they do not account for all. In the margin stands Big Business. To secure the Budget, Big Business must be controlled. Fantastic! you say, and I cannot blame you. Fantastic the proposal sounds. But under the microscope it appears that Big Business has developed six cracks across its grim face.

There is a battle coming, undoubtedly. But not so one-sided a battle as would have been the case when old J. P. Morgan was generalissimo. I prophesy no pushovers, but I think that the Budget can be secured without excessive fisticuffs. It has the splintering effects of modern technology fighting for it. It has the world trend towards collectivism in its favor. It has a human tropism for social survival on its side.

What may ruin the community, even if it wins the battle, is the selection of unworkable models for public business and the setting of insuperable administrative tasks. This is perhaps a harder fight than that against Big Business. Let us examine the prospects.

CHAPTER THIRTEEN

Models for Regulation and Control

THEORIES and plans for collective controls in the interest of a stabilized economy are legion. I have a filing case full of them, mostly dispatched to me since 1930. They cover every conceivable field from complete world planning to the proper way to run a cooperative corner store. The pages bristle with "ought," "should," and "it is assumed." Some show real thought, many show ingenuity; but in the following discussion, we shall try so far as may be to paint our models from real life. With the world one great laboratory, these paper plans seem rather stiff and remote. Is a community forced to do something about agriculture? Then let us observe how the AAA is working, the Italian wheat plan, the Queensland sugar plan, the British Milk Control, the Finnish cooperatives.

To describe all functioning models since the War would fill a library. They are of all shapes and sizes from a North Dakota flour mill to a complete Soviet Republic. They vary from mild regulation to the most rigorous ownership and operation. But every one of them has interfered with private business, and has had a greater or lesser effect on private profits. All we can do here is to select typical examples, and especially try to appraise the general principles involved.

As we noted in the first chapter, public business takes three main forms, no matter who runs it:

1. Major regulation. (We are not concerned with petty regulation, like factory inspection.)
2. Control-without-ownership, where key industrial decisions pass to the State.
3. Ownership and operation by the State.

These activities in turn may cover an entire national economy, a complex of industries, a specified industry, a given unit within an industry. Again, the control may fasten on production with little regard to distribution, confine itself primarily to distribution, or take up a position between them, like the British Grid. The mind reels at the number of possible combinations. How much simpler it would have been had laissez-faire, whereby nobody need control anything but his own small business, not refused to work in a wayward world.

Financial vs. physical controls

With laissez-faire disappearing as a method of automatic control, planners have been busy with blue prints for putting things to rights on the principle of what the engineers call "least work." What is the next easiest thing to laissez-faire? Many years ago, Henry George evolved one such scheme and called it the Single Tax. By controlling land values alone, the community could go to sleep on all other sectors of the economic front; free competition would care for them. The simplicity of this proposal was appealing; one single fiscal levy and security was won. Personally, I regret that Mr. George's proposal was never put into the national laboratory. In a developing country with population and land values rapidly expanding, it might have worked well. With population growing at a decrement, and land values at a standstill, it is obviously less applicable, but still useful, I believe, as a simple and just method of local taxation.

One does not hear so much of the Single Tax as one did a generation ago, but one hears plenty of other single remedies. Most of them now turn on the control of money and credit; one little law, one little device, and the whole economic problem will be solved. The Social Credit plan of Major Douglas, the British engineer, falls into this category. George would have socialized land; Douglas would socialize credit. Nothing else need be touched, or very little else. I remember talking to one of the Washington Brain Trust not so long ago, who had no patience with Social Credit, but was nevertheless convinced that a wise federal control of money and credit was all that was needed to rescue us from the depression, and to maintain equilibrium thereafter. Probably half the plans in my filing case echo this conviction, though a scrutiny of the several blue prints reveals an alarming diversity in ways and means.

Another favorite lone star champion lies in the judicious application of the income tax. It could certainly be made to reapportion the national income. Legally, the State could take away every cent above $10,000 or $5,000, or any figure it wished to set. What we need, however, is not so much a redistribution of existing income, as *more income,* in terms of available goods and services. The income tax, by changing the ratio between saving and spending, can perhaps act as one powerful lever, but a whole battery of levers is needed

REGULATION AND CONTROL 219

to accelerate physical production and to maintain it at a high level thereafter. Great Britain has had a punishing income tax since the War, but it has not saved her from depression, and a totally inadequate volume of production.

My personal conclusion is that the problem is too complicated to be solved by any one simple model. Perhaps I have read too many plans. When one sits down and dispassionately considers the variables in any given economic situation, one realizes why economics has never become a quantitative science and how sanguine it is to hope for an easy solution. I look on the collective control of money and credit as perhaps the most important variable of all, in a world that has passed from barter to what Bassett Jones calls symbolic money. The gold standard was the last lingering vestige of barter money. Money control is paramount public business, and one of the first jobs to be tackled. But other jobs must go with it. Just what would an adequate credit system do about the progressive deterioration of the Mississippi Valley, for instance? It would insure a sound method of financing any project, but it would not do the planning or the physical work. The hydrologic cycle is not to be controlled by symbolic money, however deftly devised. The community must also come to physical terms with its environment; engineers and industrial administrators as well as financiers are needed. But Henry George, Major Douglas, the income tax distributors, and the money-credit reformers generally, are on the right track in one important sense. Collective business must be done on the principle of least work, or it may not be done at all. The simplest model is always to be preferred. In so far as the Budget can be assured by distributing tickets rather than goods, always use tickets. They are easier to handle and provide greater freedom of choice to the worker and consumer receiving them. Most of us would rather have a five dollar bill than a basket of groceries, however admirable the dietetic balance.

Public business as major regulation

Before assuming the severe administrative task of outright ownership or operation, many States first try regulation. If it does not work, they may go on to control-without-ownership; if this proves inadequate, they may socialize the activity. Soviet Russia regulated wholesale and retail trade under the NEP before taking it over bodily.

At present, regulation is rife in nearly every nation. Laws, codes, licenses, prohibitions, orders, imposts, are piled one on top of another in bewildering confusion, as economic forces fall out of control and demand adjustments and readjustments. Nowhere is regulation more mountainous and burdensome than in foreign trade. Many look on it as the work of official bunglers, eager to plague honest exporters and importers. But this is to miss the point of post-war history. Faced with declining world markets, with serious shortages of raw materials—often the very food supply—the several nations had to regulate their foreign commerce in the interest, not of profits, at this stage, but of economic survival. Look at Germany today, and the desperate measures she is taking to insure adequate food and raw materials.

The newspapers are now full of the failure of regulation in power utilities. Here is a typical story, for instance, from the New York *Times,* March 2, 1935:

REGULATION AND CONTROL 221

UTILITY LISTS LAND 400% ABOVE COST

The Mack Committee investigating public utilities turned its spotlight yesterday on Westchester County and found write-ups and questionable land deals, coupled with high prices. The committee heard evidence showing write-ups ranging from 78 to 400 percent, with 200 percent common ... In one case, the realty agent who handled the sale of a piece of property first for $50,000, blandly valued it at $193,000 in his capacity as appraiser for, and as official of, the company. It was his figures that were accepted by the Public Service Commission ... The Commission's engineers felt that they lacked the scope to go into the values back of the figures.

Perhaps the sublimest exhibit of rate-base padding to date is found in the books of the New York State Electric and Gas Company, a subsidiary of the Associated Gas System.* The company owned an undeveloped water power site, which had cost $2,271,000. The company figured that *if* the water rights were developed, the outlay would come to $3,500,000. *If* the outlay were made, earnings of $800,000 were possible, *if* the current could be sold. The current apparently could not be sold and not a sod was turned. Nevertheless, the company proceeded to capitalize the sum of $800,000 a year at eight percent. Thus the water rights, *if developed,* were estimated to be worth $10,000,000. The $10,000,000 was solemly transferred to the books, but the company was careful to deduct the $3,500,000 which the development would have cost had it been made. The net effect was a shiny new asset of $6,500,000 instead of the old site value of $2,271,000, and the net result to consumers was an additional charge of $250,000 a year, based on the

* Reported in the New York *Times*, February 5, 1935. Testimony before the Mack Committee.

permitted return to the company on the higher valuation. *If* my grandfather had bought the stock which Alexander Graham Bell once tried to sell him, I might now be worth a million dollars. Teller, a hundred grand on account, and make it lively!

In twenty holding company systems, inflation of the capital structure to the amount of $839,395,000 has been officially established.* "The total inflation of fixed capital throughout the country must exceed one billion dollars. Thus with a sweep of the accountant's pen, supported by the diverting arguments of astute lawyers, the customers are forced to pay a 'fair return' on *no* investment for years to come." Well may the wag say that the industry is "afflicted" with a public interest. Professor Danielian notes ten specific methods for stuffing wind into property values:

1. Writing them up to "present worth." (Thus capitalizing a rising price level.)
2. Organizing a new operating company and transferring to it the property of existing companies at inflated values.
3. Writing up unused land and water rights. (The $6,500,000 case cited above.)
4. Loading operating companies with holding company charges for "construction service." This in effect siphons profits out of operating companies to their eager papas, yet the operating companies do not suffer. You and I suffer. The operating company showing these "costs" on its books is allowed to charge rates high enough to cover them. Thus the customer pays the operating company one profit, and the holding company another.
5. Ditto for "organization expenses."
6. Ditto for "going concern value."
7. Ditto for interest on the value of unused land.
8. Ditto for stock and bond discounts.
9. Failure to write down property accounts when items be-

* Professor N. R. Danielian of Harvard in *Harper's Magazine*, June, 1935.

come obsolete. In the traction business, cases are on record of the public paying a fair return on horse car mules which died in the '80's. In the utility business we still pay on paleozoic generators which wheezed their last decades ago.

10. Taking deficits of a predecessor company into the fixed capital of the successor.

Regulating commissions generally, the country over, have "felt that they lacked the scope to go into the values back of the figures." As a result, figures have been rotten with private graft, false appraisals, and metaphysical bookkeeping, while the public has paid rates based on a "reasonable" eight percent, based in turn upon this valuation dung heap. A legislative committee, reviewing twenty-three years of regulation in New York, reported: "On the basis of this intensive investigation, we find that effective public utility regulation in the state of New York has broken down, and that the consumers of the state of New York have been abandoned to the exploitation of the utility companies without any effective restraint by the Public Service Commission."

Since the War, the American merchant marine has been nursed, regulated and subsidized by the government. A Senate committee of investigation reported in June, 1935, that regulation "has resulted in a saturnalia of waste, inefficiency, unearned exorbitant salaries and bonuses, corrupting expense accounts, exploitation of the public by sale and manipulation of stocks, the 'values' of which are largely based on the hope of profit from robbing the taxpayer, and a general transfer of energy and labor from operating ships to 'operating on' the taxpayer."

Regulation, be it observed, divides power and control between public and private business. This is its fatal weakness. The balance wavers from the State to the regulated industry. In times of public wrath, the State may tighten its authority, but usually the industry finds one method or another to pass on its burdens. If the Public Service Commission commands a utility to lower its rates or otherwise serve the public better, the utility promptly rushes to the courts, and the case may drag on for years. The Mack Committee found one piece of legislation which had cost consumers $2,200,000. Mr. Joseph P. Eastman, in presenting his plan for regulating the railroads (January 1935) remarked: "The chief threat to the plan lies in the difficulty which the numerous railroad managements may encounter in acting collectively of their own volition, and in prolonged litigation if the power of the State is exerted to compel such action ... The complex situation created by government regulation of privately owned companies would be much simplified, and there would be far less division of responsibility under government ownership."

Unable to serve two masters, the industry usually serves private business. Each addition to the ranks of regulated business, furthermore, tends to enlarge the gross power opposed to the government. A kind of trade union of animosity develops. "Every increase in the area of regulated enterprise increases the difficulty of control by strengthening the opponents of the State and weakening its advocates. Thus, an industrial system completely regulated on behalf of consumers is almost inconceivable. As soon as the body of the regulated enterprises becomes large enough, the whole regulatory system must be vitiated of power." *

* Atkins and others: *Economic Behavior*. Houghton Mifflin Company.

The NRA was a regulatory model. Under pressure of emergency, it might have worked in a few well chosen industries. When practically the whole private sector was included, opposition became too massive to handle. Chiseling was started from coast to coast. It remains to be seen whether regulation modified to minimum wages, maximum hours, child labor provisions and a few simple trade rules can be restored. There is reason to believe that it can, especially if organized labor helps to enforce the provisions.

The folly of attempting a "partnership" between state and private enterprise is well exemplified in the sad story of the lumber code.* The lumber industry was in a depressed condition even before 1929. The code gave the industry the power to fix minimum prices, based on the cost of production, and to restrict and allocate output between companies. Little was known about costs of production, but a guess was made, and into it went the cost of carrying stumpage, depreciation on excess capacity, interest on excessive values, losses on trade accounts carried over from pre-depression days, a gorgeous pre-depression scale of salaries for officers, and similar cats and dogs. The result was a very handsome cost figure indeed, and an even more handsome price based thereon. In the first ten months of 1934, lumber prices averaged 53 percent higher, relative to general wholesale prices, than in former periods. The boys got away to a flying start, but presently they were stumbling. Stocks piled up; and consumption fell off. "It should also be noted that 5,000 new sawmills were established after the code went into effect, probably con-

* Report of National Resources Board; also article by Constant Southworth in *Plan Age*, May, 1935.

tributing a good deal to excess capacity." Price control, moreover, turned out to be unmanageable in the form employed. It appeared that there were 81,000 items involved which, after discounts and differentials, worked out to hundreds of thousands of separate and distinct prices. "Sweetening" of lumber grades, the illicit extension of wholesale discounts, secret rebates, and other forms of chiseling became general. Rivalries, jealousies, suspicions, developed right and left. The industry could not run itself, and the State had no real power to run it.

"Partnerships" on this scale are possible only with a senior partner whose decision is final. Under the codes nobody was boss. Private business left the initiative to the government, and the government left it to private business. Net effect, zero. Or each side became filled with initiative followed by a dog fight, and again zero. In the background, the courts stood ready to produce more zeros.

The regulatory model on the whole is suspect. It unsettles and disrupts private business by keeping the balance of power in constant oscillation, while benefits to the general public are dubious if not negative. The New Deal as a whole is primarily emergency regulation. Private business is justified in resenting it in many cases, for nothing is definitely settled, and without settled controls, planning for the future is exceedingly difficult. If public business is destined to become permanent, the question of power must be strictly delimited, controls must be defined. One suspects that private business would be happier if it knew with some precision the field in which it was to operate, even if that field were comparatively narrow.

Control-without-ownership

Beyond regulation lies control-without-ownership. Here power is defined and action positive. The State takes over policy and major decisions. Examples are the War Industries Board, the AAA, the British Milk Control. All three are—or were—legally voluntary, but if an individual refuses to come in, he finds his role hard and lonesome.

The result is not far different from the present arrangement in the majority of our great corporations. If for corporate "control" we substitute the State, we have a roughly analogous situation—except that one would wish the State to be less cavalier with other people's property than the corporate control has often been in the past. If 80 millions of corporate property, more or less, can be managed by men who do not own it, who often do not hold even a share of stock, the question is raised whether in the realm of public business outright ownership is essential. Many students believe that in an age of plenty, legal title is no longer so important as it used to be, and that equal or superior results can be obtained by operating strategic controls.

Gardner C. Means is emphatic on this point. Antitrust legislation sought to maintain competition as the maker of industrial policy, and failed because it confused the absence of monopoly with the existence of a free market. The trust busters had apparently never heard of administrative competition. The breakdown of the free market was not a result of monopoly as defined by the courts, but a result of industrial policies made by private individuals in big corporations. The regulation of utilities, furthermore, by freezing the rate structure, tended to aggravate the situation by making administrative prices legal—another serious count against the regulatory model.

Dr. Means believes that decisions as to price and output must pass to the State. But this does not necessarily mean ownership. "Actually the choice does not lie between private ownership and government ownership, because the problem is primarily the distribution of controls, not the locus of ownership." It means a switch from one non-owning group, concerned with its private affairs often at the expense of stockholders, to another non-owning group, concerned with the public welfare, and in a better position to make correct industrial decisions.

In earlier chapters, we have dwelt at some length on the AAA as a control-without-ownership device; industrial decisions as to output pass to the State. In Queensland, Australia, we find a model of a different agricultural control which has been in operation longer, and perhaps is a superior model.

Queensland, like other beet sugar areas, had a boom after the War when the world sugar shortage was acute. Investment poured into the industry, acreage was greatly expanded. Presently, the enterprise collapsed, as it did elsewhere, when the bottom fell out of the world price. The government was implored by farmers and business men to do something. What it did was this: It shut out sugar imports 100 percent. Then it divided the whole sugar area into districts, with one grinding factory in each district. The factory was assigned a quota, not to exceed its previous maximum. Each farmer in the district was given his quota, based on previous production. Next a Sugar Control Board was incorporated, to become the sole sugar merchant of Australia. It sold to Australian consumers all the sugar they could buy at a price as high as they would stand for. Any remaining stock was sold abroad at the world price. The board, with cash from the sales, settled with the factories, which in turn settled with the farmers. Each received his proportionate share. Any farmer, however, can grow all the sugar he wants above his quota, *provided he is willing to sell abroad and take his chance on the world price.* The board will assist him in selling this surplus.

There are important features in this model. While gross income is limited by virtue of the quotas, any enterprising farmer can increase his income by improving his methods and reducing his costs. This puts a premium on scientific agriculture and on individual initiative. No farmer, however, is immediately run out of business by the commercial initiative of his fellows. If he produces his quota, he gets his price with the rest. Only if he is too unenterprising to keep his costs below the cash return will he disappear from the economic scene. Again, low cost enterprising farmers can exceed their quotas if the world price offers them any margin. We have here a most interesting combination of individualism and collectivism. Power is defined—the State to budget and sell, the individual to produce. There is no nonsense about vague "partnerships," and no unproved theory whatever.

Suppose, says Dr. W. O. Willcox in his book *Reshaping Agriculture,* that this device were adopted for cotton farming in the United States. Imports would be shut off and the cotton belt divided into districts, with a gin in each district. Quotas would be allocated to gins on the basis of previous performance. Farmers would be registered and assigned a percentage of the quota. The Cotton Control Board would take the total output and become the only seller of raw cotton in the United States, its directors to include producers, consumers and the government. It would sell to spinners at a fixed price, the balance to be exported and sold by the board at the world price. The farmer would receive his quota payment for both the domestic and export share. He could cultivate more cotton if he chose, but it would have to go into a third pool to be sold abroad. Enterprising cotton farmers would probably tumble over one another to install the new Rust mechanical cotton picker. Newcomers would be shut out. The board would set aside a large product reserve in case of crop failure.

Under the AAA, there is no such security of tenure, no such premium on efficiency and progress; while paying farmers for not producing is a clumsy and morally somewhat abhorrent procedure. Furthermore, an acreage restriction can always be evaded by intensive cultivation which in time will invalidate the whole scheme. It so happens that just at the period when corn acreage was restricted 20 percent, a new corn hybrid was developed by agro-biologists, which gave a 20 percent greater yield.

Australia is not unique in her plan. The Agricultural Marketing Acts of 1931 and 1933 in England offer somewhat similar models. Already a Milk Board, a Sugar Board, a Potato Board and a Pig Board have been set up. In the milk control, every farmer with more than four cows can be registered and licensed. The board fixes wholesale and retail prices and ratifies contracts between farmers and distributors. Quotas are allotted. The farmer sends his bill to the board, which collects from the distributor. Nobody has to come in who does not want to, but a referendum showed 96.46 percent of milk producers, representing 96.51 percent of the British output, in favor of the plan. Rugged individualists voted for collectivism by huge majorities. As in the case of Queensland, a virtual monopoly is set up and newcomers are excluded.

A brother model is found in the Central Electricity Board which operates the so-called British Grid. It is a government corporation, and it owns nothing but transmission lines. It is charged with setting up one efficient supernetwork for England, Scotland and Wales—the kind of network which Mr. Morris Cooke did *not* find in the Mississippi Valley. It is a "controlling middleman," enforcing low cost generation on the one hand, and wholesaling power at cost to local distributors on the other. The average wholesale price in 1932 was seven mills per kilowatt hour. Acting through the Minister of Transport, the Grid has power to revise the rates of distributing companies; and so protect the consumer. The majority of the distributors, however, are not private companies, but municipally owned light and power companies. Many of the generating companies are privately owned, but their scope and their opportunities for metaphysical bookkeeping are severely limited. At the bus bar stands the State.

Competition heretofore has taken two main forms —extending markets and reducing costs. The former is the domain of the salesman, the latter of the engineer. The Queensland plan and the Grid plan eliminate the salesman and encourage the engineer, and thus put competition on its sounder foot. This model should work well in competitive industries like agriculture. It works well for quasi-monopolies like power.

I find no comparable models yet established in manufacturing. The plan is certainly worth a laboratory test in a competitive industry with relatively small units, like textile manufacturing or lumber manufacturing. It is relatively easy for a control board to maintain its authority over production when units are generally small, disorganized and often desperately eager for controlled direction because of a long period of losses.

The lumber industry is rapidly approaching this condition. Thanks to the hard lessons learned under the NRA, and the fact that lumber is in both the loss division and the natural resource division, the industry is ripe for some permanent form of control-without-ownership.* The government now owns many million acres of forest land, and is continually adding to the total. This should be treated as a natural resource reserve in preference to throwing the State into the operation of sawmills. Some day the government may be forced not only to protect the forest cover but to saw it up to meet the national need; but so long as private business has mills, crews and managers available, why not let private business do the work, provided it is willing to surrender the key decisions of quotas and price levels?

Control-without-ownership, in spite of certain dangers which I shall mention later, seems to have wide application for public business in the power age. If it were inaugurated wherever possible, it would save the State the burden of administrative detail, and so apply the principle of least work.

* A plan for such control is blocked out by Constant Southworth in his article quoted above.

CHAPTER FOURTEEN

Models for Public Ownership

IF CONTROL-WITHOUT-OWNERSHIP will not work, the last recourse is public ownership and operation. Models in this department are very numerous. Some of them may have been adopted with little or no study of the former device. Russia of course furnishes the largest model, and it is working well enough to permit unprecedented increases in physical output.

When an economic activity is socialized, a grave source of conflict is automatically removed. The power lobby, or the railroad lobby, or the oil lobby, is liquidated, and with it friction, litigation, counter litigation, Supreme Court decisions, bribery, and a shifting balance of power from industry to the State. This gives the government administration a less storm-tossed area in which to operate, and an opportunity to concentrate on providing service rather than lawsuits. It does not follow, however, that the State inevitably will do the better job. Many other factors must be taken into consideration.

The most significant new form of public business in this department is the use of the corporation. The German Railroad Company was valued in 1932 at 6 billion dollars, making it then the largest corporation in the world. The government owns the capital stock, but the company operates as independently as the American Telephone Company. It is responsible for its own debts. It borrows money on its own credit and risk. It can sue and be sued; hire and fire without red tape restrictions. Corporations of this kind are the despair of politicians. The VIAG is a huge German government holding company with forty industrial subsidiaries, dealing in aluminum, coal, chemicals, electrical equipment, machine manufacturing, potash, metals. Prussia owns three large central power stations, and blocks of stock in the Stinnes Power Company and other plants. Berlin owns all the stock of the Berlin City Electric Company, which furnishes 90 percent of the city's power.

The Hydro-Electric Power Commission of Ontario is a special type of corporation. It is an agency of the Provisional Government of Ontario, to which it accounts, and it is trustee for the associated municipalities of the province, on whose behalf it generates and transmits power. It owns and controls generating plants and transmission lines, and thus goes the British Grid one step further. It can take legal title to property and make contracts. But the province raises the capital. The several municipalities own their local distributing systems, and share in the equity of the commission's property. The investment of the commission is close to $400,000,000; and that of the municipalities in the distributing systems, about $100,000,000. The rates to consumers under this twenty-five-year-old system are among the lowest in the world. Padded valuation accounts are unheard of; litigation is at a minimum. Citizens of Ontario can forget the power problem, as citizens of New York can forget the water problem.

MODELS FOR PUBLIC OWNERSHIP 235

In Chapter IV, we listed a long series of United States government corporations, the RFC with its 4 billions of assets being the largest. The Tennessee Valley Authority is not a simon-pure corporation, but it follows the general pattern. The Inland Waterways Corporation operates steel barges on the Mississippi on behalf of the federal government. Recently I went over its excellent books, and noted the rich details of its accounting controls in the interest of efficiency of service.

Russia has been through the mill in this connection. First she tried factory control by the local workers, which was terrible. Then she tried trade union control which was about as bad. Then she tried government department control—like our Post Office—which was unworkable on the scale required. Finally, in 1923, came the state trusts, a semi-corporate form borrowed from private business. The trusts have now been meeting the pragmatic test for twelve years. They control the major industries, usually by regions. An example is the Ukrainian Sugar Trust, of which I was once the guest. They must stand on their own feet apart from politics. They must meet their debts, assume financial responsibility, keep their costs down, show a profit, except in cases of a few "infant" industries like iron and steel, which have had losses subsidized. Creditors cannot alienate the fixed property of the trust, it is true, but they can alienate its working capital. There is no nonsense about workers' management. A technically trained administrator runs the enterprise, and if he does not produce a profit, or show adequate cause, he is fired. Workers are protected as well as possible from exploitation, but not from laziness, stupidity, indifference or sabotage. Trust profits are divided three ways: to the State, to the workers, to the reserve account for expansion.

A map of collective enterprise today would show the corporate form of ownership spotted far and wide. It has grown enormously in recent years. In the good old debates on capitalism versus socialism, neither side envisaged such a departure. The stock argument about political plums is fairly answered. Mr. Farley himself would have the devil's own time getting appointees into the British Grid, the Russian Steel Trust or the Canadian National Railways. Said Sir Henry Thornton of these railways: "There has never been any politics. . . . Today there is as much chance of politics getting into the Canadian National Railways as there is of an elephant walking a tight rope. Last year the railways, which I am fortunate enough to administer, bought 99 million dollars' worth of supplies. Not one cent was dictated politically." * It might not be a bad idea to incorporate the U. S. Post Office Department, appoint an expert administrator at $50,000 a year, and remove the whole service completely from the political arena.

"It is contended," says A. H. Hansen, "that by operating under a legally incorporated entity under a price system, all the capitalistic devices for achieving efficiency can be carried over into socialism. Such a corporation can not only hire and fire on a business basis without regard to civil-service regulation, it can apply all the calculus of a cost-and-price system to achieve efficiency of operation." It can, and often it does. Cost accounting can be used—and is used—to

* During the depression the Canadian National has run large deficits. One reason is that it took over a bankrupt private system at a high valuation. There seems to be a moral in this somewhere.

measure the relative efficiency of various departments, various plants, precisely as the General Electric Company uses it.

Once a business becomes too big for one brain to handle personally, accounting takes over the job. The principles of cost accounting are uninfluenced by political or moral passions. There they are—for Mr. Sloan's use, or Mr. Stalin's use, or the use of the Danish cooperative societies. All large corporate organizations are now run by remote accounting control. On the records as they come hourly, daily, weekly, monthly, to the central office, the front line administrators stand or fall. Question: What difference does it make to a front line administrator—say the manager of the A and P store in any town—whether the stock in the vast impersonal corporation for which he works is owned by Tom, Dick, Harry, or the State? Answer: The only difference to him is which corporate control gives him the better break. Front line administrators as one talks to them are not inclined to be sentimental about the moral beauties and benefactions of General Motors, the Great Atlantic and Pacific Tea Company, or the Consolidated Gas Company. Neither are they inclined to be sentimental about the joys of serving their fellow men through the Inland Waterways Corporation, or the Home Owners' Loan Corporation. They will serve either, and the mechanical finger of accounting can trace how well they serve. Their preference will be determined, as always, by considerations of hours, wages, tenure of employment, pension plans, chances for advancement, and a little human recognition from the man higher up.

In the great corporation, collectivism and capitalism meet. Administratively it is becoming increasingly difficult to tell one from the other. Old arguments dissolve in this new compound. Capitalism has been socializing its forms through the great corporation, collectivism has been adopting and adapting this most characteristic of capitalist institutions. Administratively there is little to choose; for years there have been no better run corporations in the world than German state utilities.

If the 200 massive corporations which control the bulk of the resources, services and goods supplying the wants of the American people were nationalized tomorrow, through the device of exchanging stockholders' ownership certificates for preferred stock guaranteed by the government, the controlling common stock to vest in the government, the shock would be morally great but physically small. Here would be the same corporations, the same stockholders with different colored pieces of paper, the same administrative staff except the board of directors, the same jobs to be done, the same impartial accounting records. The 2,000 gentlemen now constituting the "control" would undoubtedly be discomfited; the inert mass of stockholders would in many cases be encouraged by a somewhat better prospect for their "conventional return"; the workers and the line administrators would wonder if they were going to get a better break. The public would have the prospect, for the first time in American history, of a steady flow of goods and services.

These great corporate groups are by their very nature closer to collectivism than the scattered hordes of retailers, laundry owners, garment makers, manufacturers of novelties, and other small business men. They are impersonal, cumbersome, bureaucratic, highly organized. Except at the top, the Bell Telephone System does not differ greatly from the Post Office system. Their hordes of employees have the same type of habit patterns and responses. The girls on the switchboard suffer from no more spasms of the profit incentive than do mail carriers. The Bell System certainly has better research laboratories, and perhaps plans better for extension of service. The Post Office system does not have to hop around for stockholders, and does not have to pay nine percent on somewhat diluted stock.

I paint the alarming picture of nationalization not because I believe it will be done tomorrow or the day after tomorrow, or because I am convinced that it is the only thing to do, but simply to show how ripe the great corporation is for collective ownership, so far as physical organization is concerned. The tangible shock when the State acquires common stock control is theoretically no greater than when a Cyrus Eaton beats a Samuel Insull to a string of corporate beauties by fast work on the stock market.

Obviously, the United States government, including the brainiest of the Brain Trust, is now in no position to determine detailed policies for 200 great corporations, and to coordinate the same into one giant service of supply. I doubt if the conception has crossed their minds. What may be emphasized is that, in the world of practical realities, the corporate form is the best form to choose, when and if public business undertakes outright ownership and operation. Year by year, more communities are choosing it.

Louis B. Wehle has laid down the principles which he thinks should govern a public corporation in the United States. Speaking before the American Bar Association in May, 1935, he said:

First, it shall hold its charter directly from Congress.

Second, it should be suable wherever it carries on business in the United States.

Third, it should presumably be free from local state taxation, unless it be in competition with private capital within the state levying the tax.

Fourth, as a monopoly, it should enjoy the sovereign's priority, but if competing with private business, it should be treated as a private creditor, and also taxed on equality with its competitors.

Fifth, even though its funds be given the revolving status, and it be granted its own accounting procedure, it should be periodically held to account to the Controller General.

Sixth, if it have the power to issue bonds or other obligations, they should be clearly guaranteed by the United States, and be issued only at such times and at such rates as the Secretary of the Treasury may approve.

I am not sure that I agree with all these provisions, particularly the last, but they form an excellent basis for discussion. I congratulate the American Bar Association for placing the problem on its agenda. Mr. Wehle in the course of his remarks said that federal corporations were here to stay. Created to fill an emergency need, they have constituted "a brilliant achievement in statecraft which bids fair to lead to a deliverance from much that has limited and inhibited government effectiveness." Incidentally these corporations threaten "to render obsolete some of the executive departmental structure contemplated by the Constitution."

Mr. Joseph B. Eastman, Federal Coordinator of Transportation, has prepared a detailed plan for a government corporation to operate the railroads, to be administered by five trustees. Equally interesting, he has set forth the sources of opposition to such a corporation. (1) Banker's profits would be curtailed, (2) officers of private companies would tremble for their jobs, (3) directors would lose inside information for profitable use on the stock market; and (4) even members of the Interstate Commerce Commission might lose their positions. The advantages, according to Mr. Eastman, are (1) low cost of capital, (2) opportunity to reduce capitalization over a long period, without undue hardship on the public, (3) the end of the "valuation" nightmare which is perpetual under regulation, (4) the increased efficiency of operating railroads as one coordinated system, (5) the constant limelight playing on a great public corporation with open records, which would tend to prevent corruption and inefficiency. Mr. Eastman probably knows more about American railroads and their operation than any man alive.

In many corporate models, the State holds control while private capital holds bonds, preferred stock or a minority of the common stock. The Swedish broadcasting control is a case in point. A limited dividend corporation was organized, with contributions to the stock from private capital. The government held the controlling interest and monopolized the service of broadcasting, as in Great Britain. Revenue comes from a moderate tax on receiving sets. As with the liquor monopoly, profits go first to the private shareholders, limited to a modest return, and the balance accrues to the government. This form of administration of a state monopoly has been so successful in Sweden that it is now being extended to the importing, processing and wholesaling of coffee, and is proposed for the munitions industry.

Summary

I have had time to present only the barest handful of the new models in public business. I have tried to select significant samples, but there are many others of great importance. From this brief survey, we can derive at least certain general principles. If public business on a large scale is to become a permanent feature of our economic life, those installing it may well bear in mind:

1. That the principle of "least work" is the first thing to determine. Use the money-credit mechanism to attain as much social security as possible, before embarking on elaborate methods for the physical control of goods and services.
2. That regulation, except for temporary situations, is useless, and often worse than useless. The regulation of a whole economy is a fantastic conception, for it leaves the question of power hopelessly in the air. Simple functional regulations in respect to minimum wages, maximum hours, child labor, the distribution of national income through taxation, are probably workable within limits.
3. That outright public ownership is an unnecessary administrative burden in cases where control at some strategic point in the industrial stream promises the desired results. Observe the British Grid.
4. That when the State is forced to outright ownership, the independent corporation, administered by accounting control, using all the efficiency devices of contemporary capitalism, is the preferred model.
5. That before locking a delegation of the brain trust in their offices to concoct a model for public business out of their heads, it may be well to dispatch an exploring party around our country and the rest of the world collecting models already in successful operation. Five continents afford extensive exhibits. Any model, of course, must be revised and amended in the light of home conditions.

MODELS FOR PUBLIC OWNERSHIP 243

In the foregoing pages I have hinted how the cotton industry, the power industry, the textile and lumber industries, the railroads, the broadcasting service, might be operated if and when public business is forced to find a more permanent form than the sketchy controls now obtaining in the United States. If space allowed, we might use our general principles, plus a more intensive survey of foreign models, to amplify these pictures and draw others for banks, bituminous coal, petroleum, steel, motor cars, or any other essential industry. We are reasonably sure that consumers' cooperation is probably the best model in the long run for distribution to the consumer, not on any fine theory, but on tangible performance over a century of trial and error.

Space does not allow, and your author would need scores of experts to help him if he made so bold as to attempt the task. All that he is justified in presenting here is the summary of guiding principles, the working models which serve as specimens of others to be found all over the world, and the conclusion that large scale public business is not such a sudden drop into cold, unknown depths as is generally supposed.

CHAPTER FIFTEEN

The Administration of Public Business

NINE Americans out of ten have a fixed idea which nothing can shake—or could not to 1930—that government business is by nature, inherently, from the germ plasm, everywhere, at all times, in any service, grossly inferior to private enterprise. It follows that any wide extension of collectivism threatens the community with penury, corruption, and disaster.

Psychologists know that it is of little avail to argue with an *idee fixe*. I do not propose to do much arguing, but rather to point out one or two administrative considerations in addition to those—like the shift from individual ownership to impersonal corporate ownership—already mentioned. First, however, I should like to quote from Gustav Stolper:

> In order to proceed beyond the beginnings [of civil service, public administration] already made, the American has first to change his attitude towards his State; to overcome his distrust of it. Whether he really wishes this, whether it is even a desirable aim, is not yet a foregone conclusion. But to the European observer, this seems the central problem about which in the coming years all great and fundamental political decisions of America will turn. I, personally, do not believe that in any predictable time the tendency towards ever further extension of governmental interference in economic and social life can be checked. You may hail or deplore that—for the immediate future it is an irresistible process.

A sane man cannot fail to agree with Mr. Stolper as to the unpreparedness of American opinion for large scale public business. But equally he is forced to agree that there is no immediate prospect of withdrawing from the task. If collective administration is in growing demand, a time must come when the supply will meet it. Other nations, exposed longer to collective necessities, like Germany, England, Sweden, Russia, have developed techniques and personnel roughly adequate to the tasks involved. *Necessity* is the dominating consideration, not a spurious psychology which would turn a man's bowels to water the instant he goes on a community payroll. We shall be handicapped, however, for years in this country, because of the curious fixed animosity towards ourselves, collectively considered, which has been inoculated into our very spinal cords for a century.

As a group, the lawyers view recent developments with alarm. They say they are afraid of bureaucracy, but it is fairly easy to see that they fear that the solution of commercial, industrial and agricultural problems will be passed on to men technically trained in these fields, who will act with little regard to the concepts and phrases of jurisprudence. They see too plainly that the legal learning in which they have a vested interest is in very real danger of losing its market value.*

It may be that corporate "control" finds itself in somewhat the same predicament, and shouts bureaucracy and ruin, lest men more responsible sit on the board of directors to make industrial decisions covering output and price. It might even be that bankers are touched with a like apprehension.

The case of Russia is an instructive example of ad-

* E. S. Robinson, in the *Yale Law Journal,* December, 1934.

ministrative skill born from necessity. When the Bolsheviks seized power the situation was akin to a group of grocery clerks boarding the sunken and fire-gutted *Morro Castle* on the Jersey beach and undertaking to put her in good operating condition. The Russian economic system was a ruined hulk, gutted by war, invasion and Czarist incompetence. It is interesting to reread the press dispatches of the years 1918 to 1925, and note the complete finality with which observer after observer foreclosed the idea that Russia could ever stand on her economic feet again. The railroads were a mass of safety pins, such factories as remained from the holocaust of civil war were obsolete and tumble down, applied science was without laboratories and research facilities, credit was non-existent, and above all, the Russians were by temperament poor mechanics, mystical, dreamy, impractical and incompetent; never doing today what could be put off until tomorrow. The indictment was not excessively wide of the mark. But the conclusion was false.

The commentators overlooked the factors of enthusiasm and necessity. Russia, to survive at all, had to be reconditioned from the keel up, and there were a few thousand forceful personalities who asked nothing better than to go to work. Necessity and interest —a dynamic pair. The results, in 1935, lie plain for all to see. Russia has made herself one of the strongest military powers on earth, and one of the leading industrial nations. This has not been done by waving banners or singing the Internationale. It has been done by the stiffest kind of administrative work; work which has killed scores of good men. They have died at their desks and they have died in the field. On their tombstones, it should be engraved that service to the community also commands its competent and devoted administrators.

Germany from the days of Bismarck has never known "politics" in the management of federal and municipal enterprises. "Reasonably high salaries, permanent tenure of office and professional reputation have, it is agreed, placed public operation on a plane as high as that of private enterprise at its best." There is no campaign by private utility interests in Germany or England or Sweden against government ownership as *inefficient*. It would be laughed out of court as preposterous nonsense. It is reported that many of the best engineers in Ontario are turning to the public service as the state hydro-electric system establishes itself as a *fait accompli*, and becomes an important factor in the life of the community. In Sweden, Albin Johansson, the head of the Cooperative Union, is conceded by all factions to be the keenest merchant in the country. Even Wall Street can grow enthusiastic about the honesty, competence and intelligence of the British Civil Service. True, it has been the work of generations through which Eton and Harrow boys went to Oxford and Cambridge pledged from birth, as it were, to serve the State. The Civil Services of Holland, Germany and France are also of high calibre.

Said Sidney Webb, as long ago as 1915: "We have, in a large number of cases, no longer a choice between the individual entrepreneur and the government; what we have open to us is often only a choice between the salaried staff of the State and the salaried officer of the trust." (Again the American Telephone Company versus the Post Office.) The British administrator, according to Webb, has (1) continuity of employment,

(2) an assured standard of living, (3) disinterested management, (4) automatic promotion, (5) a staff recruited with a view solely to the requirements of service, (6) open, competitive examinations, which tend to give the government the pick of the market through a selective device seldom employed by private business.

In the United States, we have to struggle along on what talent we can pick up. Mr. Harry Hopkins, putting 4 million men to work in a few weeks' time on the CWA, is no mean administrator. Mr. Arthur E. Morgan announces that he is building the Norris Dam for the TVA with a labor turnover of less than one percent a month, where private construction jobs of this nature normally run from 25 to 50 percent a month. The dam promises to be one of the cheapest ever built. Here and there good administrators are being molded in the furnace of necessity.

President Conant of Harvard is preparing to meet the demand. "Whatever may be the final answer to such specific questions as the future control and operation of our public utilities, whatever may be the final outcome of a number of the undertakings of the federal government in the last two years, it seems perfectly clear that the training of our future government servants is of the utmost importance." So in January, 1935, he announced new courses at Harvard for training men in public administration. Other colleges, notably the University of Chicago, have conducted such courses for some time. A training school for public service has recently been opened at Washington, sponsored by one of the Foundations.

Late in 1933, a commission of inquiry was appointed by the Social Science Research Council to examine the status and problems of public personnel in the United States.* The commission found 175,000 government units, employing 3,250,000 persons, and spending $4,500,000,000 a year for salaries. (Average salary about $1,400.) On all sides, it found the public service derided, laughed at and spat upon—"tax eaters," "payrollers," "bureaucrats." "Indiscriminate vilification lessens the morale of all public officials, dissuades capable persons from entering the service, and discredits the authority of the government. . . . No one who goes through the country from coast to coast examining the public service, as did this commission, can fail to be impressed by the many evidences of marked ability and loyalty in those who now serve the public. To transfer to these worthy employees the abuse earned by a few bad ones is a most unwholesome piece of demagogy." I confess that I find something not only paradoxical, but morally shocking, in the spectacle of a public servant like President Hoover, charged with administering a collapsing economy, making repeated announcements that the government—that is himself—is lax, inefficient and incapable of large administrative tasks. It is like a general on the eve of battle sending word to the army that it cannot hope to win. If one is plagued with such dogmatic defeatism, he should keep out of public service.

The commission concluded that private business at its best is more efficient than the government average, but that government at its best (say Cincinnati under City Manager Dykstra) is more efficient than the average business. At many of the hearings the testimony ran fifty-fifty—what private business gains through the profit incentive and elasticity is lost through heredi-

* *Better Government Personnel.* McGraw-Hill, 1935.

tary management, labor difficulties, and outside control. It was frequently brought out, furthermore, "that in America, governments have, as a rule, undertaken no services except after private agencies have proved themselves incapable or powerless to conduct them"; in short, until they became nobody's business. "To achieve any measure of success under such conditions is a remarkable accomplishment for public management."

The commission finds precisely the same functions in public service as in private:

1. Administrative work. Managing, planning, budgeting.
2. Professional work. Of engineers, accountants, doctors, lawyers, teachers, research workers.
3. Clerical work.
4. Skilled and trades work. Electricians, printers, machinists, carpenters, masons.
5. Unskilled work. Day laborers.

What government personnel needs above all else, the commission believes, is a "career service," whereby young people from grade school, high school, university or technical school, enter one of the above divisions as a life work, as a career—the same thing that we find in the British Civil Service for the upper two groups. The commission would make American practice applicable to all groups. A strong, sensible procedure and program is outlined to put the recommendation into practical operation.

Particularly important are the recommendations for the administrators—group one. As permanent, protected employees of the government, their function is to tell the duly elected representatives of the people what to do and what not to do. As undersecretaries, they run the secretaries. Secretaries come and go;

Republicans today, Democrats tomorrow, Mugwumps the day after. But public business, if it is to be efficient, cannot come and go. The task of the "career" administrator is to protect it from the political secretaries. "The administrator is the link between the elective and appointive political service, on the one hand, and the professional and the clerical services on the other." Most of our graft and our grief in the past has come from the elective and appointive political gentlemen mixing and blundering into the technical and professional work of government.

Recent Social Trends gives an impressive account, observed in Chapter II, of the rise in the standards of administration since 1900, particularly in respect to local municipal and state service. The executive arm has steadily forged ahead of the legislative, commanding more appointive power, veto power, budget power. The spotlight has been focused on the executive, requiring increasingly competent technical performance. Professionalism has notably advanced. Interchange of information is now carried on by some 400 local government groups organized under the Public Administration Clearing House, established in 1931. The Municipal Sewer Cleaners had a convention in New Orleans recently, replete with technical papers and brothers in dinner coats. Progress is being made, but Dr. Merriam admits that we still have a long way to go before the stigma of "dirty" can be lifted from public business.

Some overall considerations

The overall efficiency of any given undertaking cannot be measured by the competence of the personnel alone. Even more important is the place of the undertaking in the whole economic complex.* Through the depression I have been associated with the very competent manager of a business enterprise. Literally single-handed he brought the business from disorganized prostration in 1914 to a flourishing state of profitableness—a profitableness which in the 1920's appeared solid and permanent. Every department was running smoothly. Yet by 1933, the volume of sales had been cut in half, and the ledger was covered with red ink. Was this the manager's fault? No; he had never worked harder in his life. It was the fault of circumstances over which he had no control. If some central administrative power, however crudely, could have warded off the depression, it would have counted more in the total national efficiency than all the work of all the managerial geniuses in the land.

Under high energy conditions the industrial complex, we should remember, does not need to be driven to its maximum efficiency. There is plenty of room in which to turn around, when one factory, for instance, can make all the automobile frames that the whole nation requires. Operation at 100 percent capacity, day and night, is not mandatory. If we ran motor car factories at peak rate throughout the year, we should swamp the roads. If we ran radio factories at maximum capacity, we should swamp the air. The Budget of essentials can be met at a reasonable tempo, when inanimate energy does most of the work, and particularly when outright stoppages are prevented. A steady 60 percent produces twice as much goods as 100 percent for a month and 20 percent for the rest of the year. American administrators are the envy of the world

* This idea was illustrated by the case of Russia in Chapter V.

chiefly in rush jobs. They can run up a skyscraper in six months, treble their volume for the Christmas trade, show incredible activity in emergencies. Public business is not like that. Its task is to set quotas, standards, budgets, and see that the work moves forward on an even keel, twelve months in the year. Incidentally, any engineer will tell you that the chances of low cost per unit are improved on this basis, though the excitement is less.

Too much efficiency

This brings us to a really menacing aspect of public business. It lies couchant beneath Mr. Eastman's proposals for taking over the railroads, beneath the Australian and British agricultural controls, beneath nearly every extension of public enterprise in a large way, and it gives the lie direct to the charge of inefficiency from the overall standpoint. Why does Mr. Eastman hesitate to recommend immediate government ownership? "The economies which government acquisition and operation would immediately make possible are largely of the labor saving variety." Railroad workers in large numbers would be displaced by consolidating terminals, eliminating duplicate lines, cutting down competitive sales forces. The pit of a depression is no time in which to displace more men. What is going to happen to many sugar farmers in Queensland when the efficient farmers have brought their costs so low that the board, in justice to the consumers, must lower prices, and thus the return to the growers? High cost farmers will have to quit; even as high cost British milk producers, and high cost American cotton growers—if we ever adopt this model.

These threats are real. Doubtless some sturdy individualists will presently use them as added reasons why the government should cease its meddling. What do the threats connote? They mean that equal output can be produced with less manpower, which is the only abiding definition of industrial efficiency. They mean lower operating costs. For its very competence, then, public administration is feared, and justly. The answer, however, is not to proscribe efficiency in the interest of wasteful private employment, but to develop new areas where the displaced manpower may perform useful service. The recent recommendations of the National Resources Board, the desperately needed projects for the Mississippi Valley, are the kind of answers demanded. We could use in worthwhile public works, contributing to the Budget of essentials, millions of workers for many years. But it will not do to shift the argument; efficiency is one question, unemployment another. Only a madman could say that public business is inefficient because it is too efficient.

Private administration, admirable as it often is in detail, never considers the economy as a whole. As a result of the depression to date, 100 billion man-hours of work have been lost through unemployment (an average of 10 million persons for five years at 2,000 hours a year), and goods and services worth from 150 to 200 billions of dollars have not been produced, although the equipment was in place to produce them. It would require, one suspects, quite an effort on the part of a public administration, charged with the performance of the economy as a whole, however green and inexperienced, to better this record of gross inefficiency. In studying the problem of administration, one must keep one's sense of proportion. We are deal-

ADMINISTRATION OF PUBLIC BUSINESS

ing here not with the best method to file correspondence, collect bad accounts, or blow in a blast furnace, but with the best method to keep effective human demand from falling short of the proved and available supply.

In conclusion, let us summarize the assets and liabilities of public administration compared with private:

Assets

1. Public administration in the national branch is forced to consider the economy as a whole, and thus has extraordinary opportunities for the elimination of waste.

2. Public administration can work on a balanced load without the excessive seasonal and cyclical speed-ups and shut downs that so frequently distinguish commercial enterprise. Balanced loads mean low costs.

3. Public administration can give security of tenure, adequate standards of living, selective appointment to its personnel —if British and continental civil service provisions are followed.

4. Public administration can give purpose and interest in work, especially in this period of transition.

5. Public administration can work on a lower obsolescence rate and make provisions for Mr. Coyle's optimum rate. It can help to assimilate new inventions without the customary shocks. We are now, for instance, about to embark on a spirited development of pre-fabricated housing. It is meet and proper that private enterprise should do the inventing, experimenting, early promotion work, and reap a good profit therefrom. But if pre-fabricated houses are going to be dumped on the market by the tens of thousands, our economy will shortly be subjected to certain terrific additional strains. What is going to happen to plumbers, carpenters, masons, painters, electricians and the rest of the building trades? The new house can use only one man in the field for the ten formerly used. What is going to happen to architects and engineers hitherto engaged in construction work? What is going to happen to real estate values as the new houses render old houses obsolete? What is going to happen to a mortgage market already nearly paralyzed? What is

going to happen to community planning? These houses, marketed by private companies, may be desined to choke communities, as motor cars choked the early roads. Unless public administration stands in the background to guide this development we are in for another painful boomerang of progress.

6. Public administration, being constantly in the limelight, must necessarily adopt somewhat higher standards than the run of private enterprise.

Liabilities

1. Private administration can put through a given local job more efficiently, as a rule.
2. Private administration is burdened with less red tape—until we get to the great corporations, where there is not much to choose. It is interesting to remember, in this connection, that the famous staff and line administrative formula of scientific management was lifted bodily from the army.
3. Private administration can develop a new enterprise or a new process with more gusto and dispatch.
4. Private administration gives more freedom of action to that declining minority who represent the simon-pure entrepreneur class.

Most Big Business executives, however, do not have so much freedom of action, for instance, as Mr. Harry Hopkins. When I was with the Federal Trade Commission in emergency situations during the War, I could not raise my own salary or sell the Commission short on the stock market, but I had all the freedom I could provide initiative for. The New Deal executives have tremendous freedom of action, indeed more than many of them can assimilate. They are dazed by the possibilities which lie before them.

And this brings us back to where we began the chapter. Necessity is the mother of administration. In the nineteenth century, the level of public service was low because it was largely functionless. Now the situation is reversed as to function, and in due time we may expect the level of service to reverse itself also. Do not be surprised at an uneven performance in the interim. It will be some time before President Conant's and President Hutchins' battalions come marching down to Washington.

CHAPTER SIXTEEN

On *Changing Human Nature*

WHEN I have written in the past about economic planning and the control of industry, I have occasionally been criticized for underestimating the human difficulties involved. I do not think I have underestimated them so much as I have postponed considering them closely, because of the amount of study they demand, and because they are secondary to the main objects I have been discussing. Until the aim is clarified it is not always of the first importance to scrutinize the means.

Specialists are at work on these means, I am happy to report, and making progress. In the long run their work is perhaps the most significant being done in the world. Human energy in a sense is stronger than the mechanical energy it has unloosed. At present it cannot control the kilowatts except in detail, but it can turn them on and off and misdirect them. The engineering of the future may be expected to concern itself more with emotional voltage than with mechanical.

Students of human engineering, trying to predict political reactions, have two sources of information. One is the past and the other is science. The behavior of Paris mobs in the French Revolution has been studied and restudied for parallels to apply to the future, but the variables are so many that no clear prediction emerges. There were no telephones, radios, machine guns, poison gas, airplanes, high speed printing presses, labor unions, subways, railroads, high finance, transmission lines, in the Paris of 1793. Social scientists have done better by trying to analyze emotional drives, learning processes, and the normal behavior of communities. Until recently, however, these studies have not been developed far enough to permit practical application. From time to time a philosopher arises who tries to combine the two methods, to deduce scientific laws from history. The present vogue for the writings of Vilfredo Pareto shows how much enthusiasm may be aroused by this approach. I do not think it can ever be a good substitute for controlled experiment and careful observation in the present.

In any losing argument against a reform, the last line of defense is automatic: "You can't change human nature." But this line, hardly worth parrying before an intelligent audience, is refuted by both schools. History, no less than psychology and sociology, proves human nature to be one of the most adaptable materials known.

There are, however, two aspects about which even very intelligent people seem to be in doubt. They wonder whether planned and public business will not destroy their freedom—the regimentation question; they wonder whether human beings will work without the intoxication provided by the hope of profits. Answers to both may seem easy and obvious to you, but I assure you that they furnish a great deal of popular confusion even when they are logically met.

The profit motive—and a few others

As for incentives to work without the hope of profit, one need only look at the whole working class. For some millions of them today, idleness is a powerful incentive; they clamor for jobs rather than doles. Cooperative public business in many countries succeeds on a large scale under administrators with modest salaries. Rexford Tugwell finds the profit motive largely obsolete even in this country. He says: "We go on treating motives quite as though our knowledge of men and industry had been derived from a few eighteenth century books rather than from any contemporary knowledge of the world of men. The truth is that if industry could not run without this incentive it would have stopped running long ago."

William Henry Chamberlin lists the non-profit motives that influence workers and managers in Russia as follows:

Power
Perquisites (such as motor cars and opportunities to travel)
Piece work
Preferences in food and housing for loyal workers, opera tickets and similar favors
Decorations—the Order of Lenin, the Order of the Red Banner of Labor
"Socialist competition" among factories and in construction work. Here the profit motive is used, but as an accounting device rather than for private gain. Factories try to show better earnings, or lower costs, than their neighbors in the same industry.

"A main problem of the Soviet Union is to find out how much individualism must be conceded in order to make a collectivist system work, just as a main problem in other countries is to discover how much collective control must be established in order to make an individualist system work." A kind of individualism is being conceded by other means than the direct incentives Mr. Chamberlin mentions. The Russians are trying to live up to their boast that if they do not encourage economic individualism they do more than any other nation for *individuality*. Under the name "psychotechnics" they are conducting intensive research into the physical and psychological variations found in individuals. Workers and students submit to batteries of tests, whose results are applied in their training and activities. A factory boy was recently sent by the government to Milan to study music because a routine test revealed a fine voice and potential musical ability.

Clearly there are other motives for diligence than bags of gold. Money will draw more work from some people, non-economic motives will draw more from others. It depends on the person. Even among economic motives I do not believe that profit is supreme. In a sense it is close to gambling, as I have suggested earlier, and thus irrational and very potent with some people. But a secure livelihood is also a powerful motive, not unfamiliar to recruiting sergeants.

Regimentation

Regimentation is an abstraction of a lofty order, higher even than capitalism. So is the word liberty. The word paternalism is only a few levels down. They mean one thing to me, another to you, one thing today, another tomorrow; their associations and emotional color are constantly changing, and their power proceeds entirely from these emotional connotations. Dr. Tugwell argues with much force that the New

Deal is fighting regimentation; his enemies contend that the New Deal is promoting it. In this year's melodrama regimentation is the villain with the long black beard. Part of the beard may indeed be real; at least half of it is false.

Complete regimentation is biologically impossible, but so is its opposite, complete differentiation. We should be as shocked to see faces without noses as to see faces, like the Bokanovsky multiple twins in Aldous Huxley's *Brave New World,* identically repeated. In nature the two tendencies are constantly interacting to reach a balance. They might be expected to interact in human society, as in fact they do. "No one," said Havelock Ellis, "needs individualism in his water supply, and no one needs socialism in his religion."

It has been pointed out that the capitalist system itself, the stronghold of so-called economic individualism, is not innocent of regimentation. I have collected statements to this effect from authorities of the most varied political complexion. Here are a few samples:

Of the 49 million people in the United States who today carry on the work of the country, at least 35 million are regimented in detail for at least eight hours of each working day.
—Lewis L. Lorwin in *Plan Age,* February, 1935.

In America many of the magnificent material things have had to be achieved at the sacrifice of individual liberty, the sacrifice of things which in the old world are regarded as the greatest victories of civilization.
—Andre Siegfried (paraphrased by Everett Dean Martin).

Agencies of mass impression subject the individual to stimuli of sight and sound that may serve to make him think and act, in some measure, like millions of his fellows. With the concentration of these agencies the control over his behavior is increased.
—*Recent Social Trends,* chapter on Communication.

Change is so much faster than it was formerly that what is known as opinion management or pressure politics or the technique of public relations or group leadership can assert itself much more effectively. That is why it might be said with justice that we are living in a regime of government in every phase of our activity (I don't mean government in the political sense) by propaganda.
—Edward L. Bernays. Interview in New York *World-Telegram*, April 9, 1935.

Super-capitalism would have all men born of the same length, so that all cradles could be standardized; it would have babies divert themselves with the same playthings, men clothed according to the same pattern, all reading the same book and having the same taste for the movies ... because only in this way can capitalism do what it wishes.
—Benito Mussolini. Speech reported in New York *Times*, December 3, 1933.

When we tremble at the thought of regimentation by a strong central government, we really envisage two dangers. The first is the danger of having our choices and thoughts controlled from outside. The second is the danger of having that control monopolized.

The first, repulsive as it may be, need not frighten us unduly because it is already a fact. Our thoughts and actions are swayed this way and that by a hundred interests and pressure groups. The air is thick with successful propaganda.

The second danger is also a fact in any dictatorship; I hope it can be avoided in this country. But to the extent that it replaced commercial persuasion with persuasion in the interest of the whole community it would be welcomed. Would you rather be propagandized about public health, safety, literacy, and the virtues of the proletariat, as in Russia, or about canned foods, cancer cures and the nobility of utility companies, as in the United States? The Federal Radio Commission recently had to warn twenty-one broadcasting stations that their licenses would be forfeited if they continued to advertise a certain fat reducer condemned by the pure food and drug authorities. Government ownership of the British Broadcasting Company, incidentally, has not monopolized the control of opinion. Minorities are conscientiously represented—even musical minorities; and Britons point with horror at the comparative lack of freedom on American ether waves.

Propaganda might be defined as the deliberate use of high order abstractions to arouse emotion, and to control action. The technique is unpleasant for four reasons: (1) the hypocrisy with which it is frequently used; (2) the sense of helplessness it gives the victim, since we all like to believe in our personal free will; (3) the anti-social ends it so often achieves; and (4) the belief that emotion is less trustworthy than reason.

Eliminate objections (1) and (3) by assuming the propaganda to be honestly used for admirable ends, as it quite frequently is even today, and we have left a sense of helplessness, and a distrust of emotion—two subjective reasons which are not unassailable on psychological grounds.

So long as we have competing armies of propaganda we feel safe. Is not truth sure to win if all sides are stated? We tend to believe in a beautiful theory of the laissez-faire of ideas. But laissez-faire works hardly better in ideas than in industry. It is not always the truth that wins either the vote or the customer's money. The principle of free speech was bitterly invoked against the Tugwell pure food and drug bill by advertisers who had lied about products which literally poisoned their users.

If we resigned ourselves to the supposed evils of government propaganda, we might find it less terrible than the abstract conception. The City of Detroit has made sound films to show taxpayers how their money is spent, for schools and parks and policemen. A sound film reaches more citizens than a printed report, and may reach their feelings as well as their minds. I see no reason for calling it unethical propaganda.

Against any method yet invented for influencing opinion there is sure to be a reaction by one minority or by several. The group in power may thus have to devise reverse methods for reconciling those whom they have prejudiced in the first place—an allowance for spoilage in the mass produced article. Not only is the technique of propaganda likely to be crude, so that traitors are led to make disconcerting remarks about the cost of the king's jubilee, but it arouses in many people a perfectly predictable negative reaction. You could perhaps find the exact percentage on the law of probability. I think that all the European dictatorships underestimate the power of this anti-suggestibility.

Public business, say the capitalists, will regiment the public. It has certainly regimented their water supply, and now moves into various other departments; which departments these are I have tried to show earlier. It will regiment behavior in respect to traffic lights and communicable diseases, and has already done so to a degree. If the public health service does its job it may regiment bodies and minds to the extent of eliminating many ailments and defects. No one can confidently say that collectivism (or capitalism for that matter) will not go further than this, or that it will not go too far. Again I have collected opinions on the lengths to which regimentation will go.

Walter Lippmann thinks that the citizen will be a conscript in any directed social order ... "The people ... must be overwhelmed. They must be drilled. They must be stuffed with the official view of all things ... of the constitution of the universe and the providence of God." David Cushman Coyle thinks that planning of the engineering type would require the death penalty; he therefore prefers planning of the policy type. George Bernard Shaw says that the business of government "can be done only by devising and enforcing rules of social conduct codifying the greatest common measure of agreement as to the necessary sacrifice of individual liberty to the good of the community"—a very sensible formula which should be committed to heart by all statesmen. Aldous Huxley of course has provided the reductio ad absurdum of nightmares about regimentation in the unforgettable picture of his Bokanovsky twins, and their treatment in the Social Predestination Room of the Hatchery and Conditioning Center.

All this alarm is quite natural. Certain temperaments always exaggerate perils in the future. When the X-ray was invented, there was a panic among people who expected to lose their freedom and privacy because their neighbors would look through windowshades and walls and even their clothing with X-ray machines. An English merchant advertised "X-ray proof clothes for modest ladies." Similar fears are now being repeated about television. The Postmaster General of London has found it necessary to broadcast an assurance that television does not involve "the possibility of looking into other people's houses." I wish he would also announce that a program of public business does not mean that people will have to wear the same clothes and think the same thoughts and like the same dish of strawberries and cream.

Even Mr. Coyle takes perhaps too limited a view of engineering control. Consider for instance engineering techniques for controlling behavior in situations where it is impossible to detect a trace of repression. Many safety devices fall in this class. Where is obnoxious regimentation in an elevator that refuses to fall forty stories even if the operator faints away? Where is tyranny in one way streets? Where is the blow to freedom when one goes in where its says ENTRANCE, and comes out where the sign reads EXIT? Such engineering controls should be widely extended. We have all too few of them. Ship designers, for instance, could reduce the number of shipwrecks, and the opportunities for panic, cowardice and heroism, if they were allowed to design ships for safety instead of for a display of interior decoration. Private business in shipping has promoted tragic risks in order to multiply bookings. I give you the *Morro Castle.*

Technical controls to carry out democratic decisions would save citizens a great deal of bewilderment on election day, and save legislators much hard work for which even the more intelligent of them are not equipped. The alternatives to such scientific decisions are three: a genuine democratic choice, which political methods rarely allow; a supposedly democratic choice manipulated by propaganda and time-honored political expedients, and a choice imposed by governmental power alone. The technical method seems to me incomparably the best, except in broad matters of policy, where the voice of the people should be heard as clearly as new scientific methods can arrange to transmit it.

Dr. Merriam pictures the government as a kind of broker between technical experts and the masses. "The better acquainted men become with the engineer and the physician," remarks E. S. Robinson, "the more skeptical they feel about the ideas of statesmen, jurists, and politicians."

As set forth in Chapter IX, I cannot honestly see why the minimum control necessary for the Budget of essentials should be unduly irksome even to practicing individualists like myself. I have declared my deep antipathy for the moral regulation of personal behavior by the State. I hope that whoever manages our coming collectivism will share this antipathy. And I most earnestly and solemnly hope that he will not undertake to dabble in eugenic controls at the present stage of ignorance of this science. Sterilization is perilous enough; selective breeding makes one blanch. The best safeguard against such abuses would be the cooperation of intelligent and tolerant people. Too many of that small and important class are doing nothing more to assist the transition than shutting their eyes and shaking violently with Mr. Huxley.

Sometimes, through accident or disease, an individual becomes paralyzed and unable to perform automatic acts like walking or taking food. Later, I am told, he may learn to perform those acts by conscious control. The cerebrum takes over the task and replaces the automatic work of the cerebellum. This seems to me a good parallel for the conscious planning of economic activities when laissez-faire ceases to perform its automatic function. Whether or not it is a misfortune to have lost the free market, its balance is now gone, as we have seen in much detail, and it is time for higher brain centers to take over the function. They must take it over, for the only alternative is the nihilism of Oswald Spengler.

Demand for regimentation

Not only is the popular meaning of individualism a fiction to scientists, but there exists a definite anti-individual impulse, a desire among large numbers of people to have their behavior controlled and their lives planned. Dr. W. O. Willcox says, discussing the British milk control described in Chapter XIII: "They little understand the common man who underestimate his yearning for economic security. The British dairyman with his dozen cows is less interested in having held open for him the opportunity of speedily acquiring fifty cows than he is in the guarantee that he will have a fair return on his actual twelve." Why do people rush to the army, the church, the horoscope monger, the psychoanalyst? Why are there perennial students, who spend their lives taking course after course in bridge-playing, art appreciation, child rearing, even in social problems? Because they want advice and authority to lean on. This need probably shows weakness and almost certainly immaturity, but there it is. To refuse to admit such people to the army or the church or the parlor of a psychoanalyst, might be condemned as harsh interference with their liberty. The decline of religion increases their need for authority. The desire can be exploited, or it can be satisfied in a way that will gradually increase their independence. Any good psychoanalyst knows the difference.

This helplessness of individuals increases with the complication of their surroundings. In the village of Chan Kom, the environment is negotiable. Mental diseases are rare, though physical ailments should be better cared for. People in mechanical cultures need medical assistance—clearer diagnoses, clinics, birth control information; they may need vocational assistance even when they are earning a good living. More people than ever are out of gear emotionally. Insane asylums are filling at an alarming rate. The public has to be helped even to play, and so kept from developing mental breakdowns with the wrong job, or no job, or with the sheer pressure of living in great cities. The breakdown may take the form of turning the sufferer into a chronic criminal. *Recent Social Trends* emphasizes repeatedly the growing helplessness of the individual faced with the personal hazards of a complex and unmanageable industrial age, helplessness which causes "an unremitting pressure upon government to intervene to protect the common man." Paternalism? Certainly. But how else can we keep the modern community healthy?

The French sociologist, Emile Durkheim, studying causes of suicides more than thirty years ago, found one for which he had to invent a name. He called it *anomie,* by which he meant the planlessness of society as compared with a small controlled group (like Chan Kom) in which every individual has a function and a useful role. *Anomie* had killed some promising young men and women. It probably kills more today.

Not long ago my mail contained a letter from a young engineer who had diligently worked his way through college and technical school, to come out into a world which had no use for him. After two years of fruitless job hunting and frustration, his mental equilibrium had broken down. He wrote damning me for an optimistic fool—which perhaps I am. He enclosed a beautifully detailed working drawing of an infernal machine which he had designed to go into a box. The box was to be insured for $20,000, and exactly three days, fourteen hours, twelve minutes and twenty-one seconds after it left the pier, the steamship which carried the box would be blown to pieces. The scheme was obviously too wild to merit taking up with the authorities, but the picture of that young man, working, skimping, saving, for eight long years to make himself a trained and useful member of society, turning on society with bitter vengeance, and all the technical skill at his command, has haunted me ever since. A little paternalism would have saved this engineer; it may save him yet.

Greed and egotism

Are there cases on record in which a large group of people have acted collectively in opposition to personal interests? There are plenty of them. Every war is such a case. The supposed national interest impels soldiers to neglect not merely property and material advancement, but even their strongest motive, self-preservation. They neglect it not merely in a burst of anger, as a fighting animal may do, but over long periods, through depression and discouragement and physical wretchedness.

Armies could be logically criticized as against human nature, a point which so far as I know the pacifists have never developed. So could monasteries. George Santayana admits he finds it logical and appealing to live in a cell, or in a communist State, thus solving the economic problem, and gaining leisure philosophically to contemplate the higher values. True, monks like philosophers are a selected group. True, monasteries offer them economic security. True also, and perhaps most important, they have the satisfaction of a powerful group emotion.

The Russian people, under a long continuing group emotion, have quite generally submerged their egos and their acquisitiveness. It is no longer respectable for a young Russian to contemplate a private business career. This has been accomplished in part by compulsion, but I do not think compulsion is ruled out of theoretical means for changing human nature. Greed and egotism count, but other stimuli also count. We cannot generalize from only part of the field.

Changing human nature

If the State is to pursue its course in controlling economic activity, side by side with progress in technical administration, it will have to use thoroughly modern psychological methods. It will have to develop techniques for arousing popular interest, for dealing with recalcitrant minorities, and for helping citizens in their personal adjustments. Julian Huxley, in his book *Science and Social Needs,* calls for a psychological arm of the government. He says: "Government cannot be successful unless it either has great power and is very autocratic, or unless it gets the understanding and interest of the population it is governing."

How do pressure politics of our day differ from those of the past? Dr. Merriam finds certain new political elements which are common to almost all countries and power groups. For instance: Changes are now faster than in any previous historical period and adaptations must keep pace with them. Science and invention, which cause many of the changes, will bring more regulations in their train. There will be medical crimes and industrial crimes. Take for instance the case of a child in Westchester County whose parents refused to have her operated on for an eye tumor. A judge ordered the operation and it was performed successfully. Incidentally, this judge was no regimenting tyrant. He not only pleaded for the operation with tears in his eyes, but he offered his car to the family for visits to the hospital. When the publicity became unbearable, he arranged to have them hidden from reporters in the house of his secretary. An example of the new phenomenon of the industrial crime is the armed refusal of many owners of small oil wells in the Texas Panhandle to have them capped, following the output quota.

Critics of collectivism have two contradictory complaints: they say first that government ignores individuals; second, that it interferes with them too much, "institutionalizes" them. But institutional methods are not so stupid and cruel today as they used to be. Compare penology now and a century ago. In the constant see-saw between individual and collective methods, techniques of individual study have advanced so far that the institution often knows more about the real problems of an inmate than he knows himself. It is complained with some justice that handicapped children in public institutions secure the best individualized training anywhere to be found. Millionaires cannot buy the equivalent of what paupers secure gratis.

The best techniques for assisting individuals to solve

their own problems cannot be applied in a society economically disorganized. Psychiatric social workers, eager to help their "clients" to express themselves, develop their individualities, become independent, have had to go back to passing bowls of soup during the depression. The resulting change in the political opinions of the social workers has driven them to the left in a large red wave. Many of them are demanding a basic collectivism, in which to exercise their talents for re-creating individuals.

These methods, when we have enough economic security to try them, bid fair to substitute a realistic brand of individualism for the romantic kind. Dr. Frankwood Williams says that the new individualism will be inductive—studying the individual; rather than deductive like the old—declaring his freedom since he *is* an individual.

Human nature can adapt itself to any program of public business if the program is confined to a limited area and not pushed to the point of universal conscription, and if the directors of the program have enough common sense to take fair advantage of the techniques discussed above. *Public business does not have to be done by dictatorship or a fascist State.* Because I profoundly question the common sense of most fascists, I doubt if their particular variety of public business is consistent with human nature in the long run. It may collapse as suddenly as it arose. Certainly if economic disorganization is as threatening as it seems to be under the old dispensation, there is reason to believe that the great mass demand for security and stability can be canalized into forms of public business which, after a certain period of experimentation, will meet the pragmatic test both administratively and biologically.

CHAPTER SEVENTEEN

An Order of Business

THE invisible hand of Adam Smith has failed us. Communities must now control their economic life according to some deliberate plan, or sink into decay. In the early chapters of this book, I have drawn up inventories showing the enormous penetration of collectivism, both here and abroad, in an attempt to find workable controls. This penetration did not burst suddenly from a single industrial depression, but has been cumulative for many years. The camels of public business are in the tent, and the problem is no longer how to keep them out, but how to handle the living beasts. If they stink, our course is not to follow the Liberty League and hold our noses until we suffocate, but to wash them.

Having surveyed the facts of collectivist penetration, I attempted to give them meaning and direction by setting up a Budget for community survival, as a suggestion for the Agenda of the State. This Budget was not designed to make citizens happier—though hopefully it would do so—but to keep the community, specifically the United States, from progressive degeneration. The details of such a Budget were then examined: the classes of goods and services which must be controlled; the extent of control already obtaining;

the non-Budget area remaining for private enterprise; the probable objections on the part of Big Business, and the specific corporations which might be expected to object. The six lesions in the Big Business organism were set forth; models for operating public business were displayed; the problem of administration was discussed; the sanctions of human nature in a collectivist society explored. The upshot of the analysis was that without the conception of the Budget as a definite economic and political aim, the modern trend was meaningless, and that there was perhaps better than a fighting chance to achieve that aim within the measurable future. Many grave obstacles were found and duly scheduled, but no insuperable obstacle. Without some such definition and estimate of needs, I do not see how a guaranteed standard of living can ever be achieved.

There is little objection to the ideal of a guaranteed standard of living—until some vested interest is disturbed in the process of securing it. There is, however, much wagging of heads over possible demoralizing influences. Many people are so constituted that a doubt about the farthest effects of the most remote achievement can inhibit them from acting on even a modest and reasonable immediate program. There are two considerations to offset the influences they fear. First, the absence of security is now creating demoralization, crime, disease, hopelessness, worry and social misery on a scale which only relief workers can adequately realize. Second, psychologists assure us that while human wants are not unlimited, they tend to follow a fairly definite law of relativity. If a foundation of health and decency were cemented home under every American family, the conflict for power, prestige, display, would simply move out of the basement into the next story. Instead of a struggle for bread, we should have a struggle for cake. People would work for comforts, luxuries, goods and services above and beyond the Budget. The whole middle class has been doing so for fifty years. In the struggle would be many heartaches, worries, envies and perhaps a suicide or two. But it would be *above the line.* Below it, hunger and cold and nakedness, the bulk of crime and disease, and all the dreadful monsters which creep from stark, material poverty, would have been exterminated.

The power age can afford to give citizens all manner of goods and services which vegetable cultures could never give them. Already it has given them public schools, cement highways, urban water supply, health clinics, and many other things. Is it seriously contended that these "gifts" have pauperized Americans and caused them to lose their initiative? Professor Hansen has pushed the conception one step further in his inquiry whether the community for its own protection should not provide decent houses for citizens to live in, and so reduce the breeding places of gangsters, the focal points of epidemics, and other degenerative effects of slum living. Many foreign States have answered this question in the affirmative.

In the Budget, we push the conception forward again, perhaps to its logical conclusion. For its own protection against dissolution, the community, aided by power age techniques, might guarantee not only education, water and playgrounds, but food, clothing and other essentials as well. Indeed this is not so much a new morality, as an extension of a morality already sanctioned for many years. If water, why not milk; if roads, why not an automobile to run upon them?

The instant objection, of course, is that there is a limit to the gifts a community can bestow upon its citizens. Certainly there is. The limiting factor is manpower. Wealth cannot be produced without labor. If citizens are to have a Budget, they must work for it. But work in the power age is different in kind, and briefer in duration, than mankind has ever known before. What if no work is available? We cannot escape the conclusion that the Budget must be distributed regardless. No other answer is permissible unless we want to starve, torture and finally kill our fellow-citizens. One of the collateral items in our Budget, however, was to find work for everyone capable of performing it. The obvious place to find it was in some department of the public works authority. The worker on erosion control does not produce bread for the bread he receives from the community today, but he makes possible the supply of bread for tomorrow. There is a time lag, but he is paying his way.

By default or by fight?

Nobody fought for the New Deal. There was no philosophy, strategy, propaganda, before its inauguration; no devoted adherents on soap boxes giving their lives to the cause. There was no battle, struggle, determination to win; none of the accredited phenomena involved in the deliberate attempt to change social institutions. It came by default. And it has changed more institutions in two years than all the reformers have been able to do in a generation.

We can expect more collectivism to come by default, but hardly a whole collective program. From the actual history of the last six years, we can confidently predict that capitalists will not fight very hard for property which shows a net loss. For existing profits or a reasonable hope of profit, we may expect them to fight.

The question of default or fight turns primarily on the outlook for losses and profits. When the economic mechanism sags, collectivism is likely to come precisely as it is coming in the New Deal. I look for more losses than profits in the next decade, and so a greater advance by default than by battle.

Too much democracy

Another deep rooted objection to the idea of a national minimum is that it is too democratic. Of course, the objection is not cast in these terms but such is what it amounts to. There is something morally shocking to some of our best people at the thought of negro share-croppers in trim, decent houses; pick and shovel men in new Chevrolets; while the possible change in attitude of domestic servants is matter for genuine, if secret, alarm. Note the word secret. America really has a kind of democratic tradition almost unknown elsewhere—unless it be in Canada or Australia. Our so-called upper classes know better than openly to flout those whom they consider their inferiors. One does not address a garage mechanic as "my good man." American democracy is political and only partly social, but it is an institution not to be extensively trifled with. Guaranteed security, when all is said and done, is nothing but an extension of democracy to the economic field. True, it has never entered this field before—except in the loose form of permitting a poor boy here and there to become, by methods which do not always bear scrutiny, a financial magnate. Most poor boys have remained poor.

Universal distribution of the Budget would give substance to democracy of which we have heretofore had largely the shadow. It would give Americans an equal base, a true equality of opportunity, from which to start. They would not be condemned from the cradle, as millions are today, by hopeless poverty, slum dwelling, rural decay, through which only the hardiest can emerge into the sunlight of a decent and civilized existence. Every child would have a chance to show what was in him. Compared with this conception of democracy, the political brand is watery indeed. Yet the Budget is opposed, and will be increasingly opposed, on the grounds that it makes a tyrant out of government, and stifles the pure vapors of freedom, democracy and the rights for which our forefathers laid down their lives. A tiny class, but noisy, raises the hue and cry. The great mass of Americans know what food, a house, a job, mean right enough, but their notions about freedom and the principles of the forefathers are hazy, and remind them uneasily of school lessons. A democracy is not made up of a handful of intellectuals.

When I hold economic security in my right hand, and balance it against the ballot in my left, I would exchange all the political democracy ever heard of, and all the constitutions, and all the founding fathers, for the real democracy of the universal right to be born clean, to grow strong, and not to be crawling on one's belly to a petty tyrant for a job. I would suffer an economic dictatorship to secure this happy state. If Sweden, however, provides a workable model for us, she indicates that economic democracy, given time enough, can be achieved by parliamentary methods. I confess

I admire parliamentary methods profoundly; but my admiration for them does not extend to a mandate for perpetual misery and poverty. Given time enough, we could follow Sweden. But at this particular juncture of history one sometimes wonders if we have the time.

Any such statement bears the onus of favoring fascism, or communism, or some other ism. I favor the use of collective forms now so abundantly in evidence, to secure economic democracy through a guaranteed subsistence Budget to the last family in the United States by all or any reasonable means. If this be a dangerous ism, make the most of it. I want delivered on the doorstep, as it were, a six-room pre-fabricated house or its equivalent, with modern conveniences, electric current, fuel, an order for such food as is found in an A and P store, Sears Roebuck clothing and equipment, a Ford, gas and oil, public and high school education, skilled medical attention, adequate insurance against old age, accident, sickness, and loss of work.

Order of business

The essential strategy of the next decade, it seems to me, is to accept the aim of an adequate standard of living, and to stand ready to promote that aim with every available law, constitutional revision, administrative technique, tested model for public business. The New Deal did its part, but the preparation was inadequate. We should profit by the experience. From it and from our earlier analysis we can project certain obvious steps.

The *first* is to keep the economic ship afloat. This at least the New Deal so far has done. An interlocked productive mechanism cannot be allowed to halt, no matter how admirable the new design. We have to keep the trains running while we rebuild the station. Russia could halt the trains, because of her large area of agricultural self-sufficiency, but this is impossible for us.

The *second* step is to permit Congress to legislate for economic controls without such constitutional handicaps as the interstate commerce clause, which operates to check national controls unless the industries involved can be shown to send their products from one state to another. Extreme centralization we must try to avoid, but the unhampered right to lay down wage, working hour, child labor provisions, and to control natural resources, agriculture, coal, and such other industries as are primarily national in character, is a necessary legal tool of the modern community. If regional differences affect some of these controls, they could be varied, and administered through six or seven wide districts. Forty-eight districts are too many. Complete states' rights are, as President Roosevelt has said, a vestige of horse and buggy days. The power age has built a national economy *de facto;* and it is manifestly contradictory and infantile to consider it *de jure* as a series of local, unrelated geographical units. Public business can perhaps be carried on without such constitutional changes, but it will entail much legal hypocrisy and back door logic, with always the possibility of the Supreme Court's slamming the door as in the NRA decision. This is no way for a great nation to do business. Mr. Justice Holmes, we remember, said that the Supreme Court in the long run will do what the public demands. Let the public make its demands explicit through a clean, open constitutional amendment of the interstate commerce clause, and if this is not enough, through a redrafting of the whole instrument.

With the amendment on the books, Congress may be expected to proceed to the enactment of minimum wage and maximum hour legislation, covering the whole country, but with careful differentials as between industries and geographical districts. Such provisions would give the Budget a most necessary foundation. No job, anywhere, could be offered at a wage below subsistence, or at hours which destroyed health and freedom. Evidence is accumulating of thousands of cases of reduced wages, lengthened hours, child labor, since the NRA codes were abolished.

With constitutional sanction, the AAA would be subject to continuous improvement. There is no dodging the responsibility of the community for its food supply, or the breakdown of that supply under pure private initiative. The problem is to find and apply the best collective model. On the production end, the Australian sugar control, as we have seen, is working well and conserves much individual initiative at the same time. It is well worth an experiment here for a crop like cotton, following a popular referendum.

The *third* step would be to bring the control of money and credit into the division of public business. No real progress towards community survival and the Budget can probably be made without this step. It is needed for financing public works, for guarding against inflation and sickening changes in the price level, for reorganizing such members of the loss battalions as come down upon the State—like the railroads; it is needed for financing the whole program of social insurance and security. We have noted how profound the penetration already is under the RFC, the Treasury, the farm credit and home owners' credit institutions. Private banking, furthermore, is by way of joining the loss battalion itself, as the interest rate drops towards an ultimate zero.

The specific mechanism may be control-without-ownership, or outright ownership of the banking structure. My guess would be that from control of the Federal Reserve System, the government will go on to ownership of the system, and so to ownership of the member banks. The ownership of all private banks may or may not be necessary. Precedents show, however, that only trouble can come from a division of power between public and private banking. If we are to accept symbolic money as an energizer of economic activity, it becomes supremely important. If we will not or can not accept symbolic money, then we may have to go on to a straight rationing of all necessities, a cumbersome and regimented process. Certain commodities like water may be best handled by rationing or its equivalent, but one stands bewildered before a whole economy rationed.

A *fourth* step is a method for financing public works on principles which will not increase the public debt until it ends in runaway inflation. Two approaches are open. The first, and the more logical, is the use of the income tax to produce more revenue, especially from the higher brackets. This not only helps the government to pay as it goes, but has the important secondary effect of reducing the amount of capital seeking new investment. It cuts down the accumulation of idle funds, and redresses the lopsided balance between spending and saving. Now that private investment, due to the decline in capitalist expansion, is at a standstill, public investment has to take its place, as a mechanism for distributing wages and salaries.

The other method for financing public works is the creation by the government of a credit fund *without interest,* or at a very low rate of interest. Income tax levies, even if very severe, cannot provide adequate revenue for all the State must spend.* A revolving fund of 10 to 20 billions, loaned to local governments for local improvements, without interest, would go far towards making up the deficiency. The loans should of course be amortized over a period of years, payments going into the revolving fund for further loans to states, municipalities, school districts and the like. Mayor La Guardia of New York is a proponent of this general plan. It could hardly be put into effect until the banks were nationalized, for private banking could not stand the competition of state credit at one eighth of one percent, or zero percent, with their own creation of credit at five or six percent. Simple kindness would suggest that the banks be spared this strain on their feelings and their assets.

A *fifth* principle would be to hold models in readiness for the strategic moment to apply them. The State will follow the "least work" theory by taking over no more industries, regulating no more activities, than the pressure of circumstances warrants. When the railroads throw up their hands, then is the time to act, to a model already carefully prepared, such as that of Mr. Eastman. When the coal mines go down for the third time, act, again according to a carefully prepared plan. When the textile industry is one long groan, act. It is so much easier to deal with an indus-

* If all individual income above $5000 were taken in taxes, the yield in 1933 would have been only $2,451,000,000.

try haggard with losses than one proud with profits. This program will not be relished by reformers who want collectivism to march by predetermined schedule. It is admittedly a Fabian strategy. Recent calculations indicate that an industry which has ceased to expand can never make an economic profit. It automatically falls out of the profit system and becomes ripe for public business.

Fabian methods, however, would be inapplicable for those industries which monopolize a Budget essential and obstinately restrict production in the interest of high prices. Here it is useless to avoid the battles which we have already anticipated. Electric power, aluminum, meat packing, come to mind. For this reason, it seems to me that the utility holding company bill now before Congress is a good fight in a good cause, and that the President should receive our belligerent support. The bill, of course, is only a beginning. Perhaps control-without-ownership on the British Grid model is the next step. We may have to go on to outright ownership, like the Ontario Hydro.

Again, conservation of natural resources calls for action in advance of the majestic course of capitalism's decline. Here are more battles, although many petroleum operators, for instance, are swinging into line with the idea of state control of output. Erosion work, afforestation, the control of the hydrologic cycle, are urgent public business and whatever vested interests stand in the way must be fought unremittingly. Incidentally, the power gentlemen will be found on the opposite side of this battle, too.

All of the above steps hinge on the functioning of a national planning authority. Secretary Wallace has proposed an Economic Council of four members "who would be as revered and trusted as the Supreme Court." They would be appointed by the President and have power to determine by direct referendum the will of the people on key questions of national policy, including amendment of the Constitution. Such a council might be broadened to act as a planning authority as well. Again, the National Resources Board is already functioning, and could be turned into the kind of authority we have in mind. The duties of such a board are primarily to calculate Budget requirements, measure them against both actual production and capacity production, and keep the government constantly informed where shortages occur and why. Private industries which were doing their job could be let alone, but where serious restrictions of output occurred, or where inadequate supplies were being produced—as in the case of milk today—the Council could not only point out the fact but recommend carefully prepared models for legislative action. Especially important, to my mind, would be its function in preserving local, regional and decentralized economic activity to the limit of its applicability. Its experts should spend a great deal of time on the dividing line between industries preeminently national in scope, and industries preeminently regional, or local. Railroads, power, telephones, mails, coal, meat packing, petroleum, are obviously national, and demand centralized control. Laundries, tailoring establishments, water supply, retailing, barber shops, restaurants, are primarily local. A whole book could be written on this distinction, and if it were well done, it would be a very important book for future reference.

First, keep afloat; then clear the road to straightforward control through revision of the Constitution;

then wage and hour regulation for all industry, but differentials for local conditions; then improvements in agricultural controls; then a long term policy for money, credit and the banks; then income taxes and revolving funds of public credit to finance public works and jobs for everyone not otherwise employed; then the control of power, natural resources, monopolies in essentials; then public business for railroads or textiles or what other industries can no longer pay their way. The order is of course subject to change. Perhaps income tax legislation should precede control of the banks; perhaps certain steps should proceed simultaneously. These however are the steps indicated by our earlier data; these the kind of problems with which Democrats, Republicans, Progressives or Socialists will have to reckon in the years before us.

Into our minds, battered with six years of trying to understand a world depression, comes a daily tornado of facts, half-facts, quarter-facts, plain lies, rumors, opinions, pronouncements, prophecies, dogmas, loose generalizations, and frequent blasts of the lofty patois of international diplomacy. We know that nine tenths of what we read, and an even higher percentage of what we hear, means nothing, leads nowhere ... Trivia, dramatized by coatless, weary men in copy rooms, to a stale dramatic formula. Yet under the whirling confusion of headline, rumor and gossip, we feel a sense of impending danger which grows rather than recedes. What is going to happen to us in a year or ten? If we ride out this depression, what of the next? What is going to happen to our children?

Peace, a chance to work, a chance to live, a modicum of security—that is all most men want. A few want power, meaning material possessions. Until recently, such assets were severely limited, and those who seized power did so at the material cost of those who wanted only peace, work and security.

Now the equation has changed. Modern technology offers material possessions adequate for comfort and security to the last man. Facilities are available in the United States to provide every family with mass production goods and services to a value of between four and five thousand dollars, which is about all that any family can use. Above that line lie luxuries and goods carrying scarcity values. These too can be produced in large quantities for those who desire them. Energy, materials, manpower are available. It is a situation without precedent in human affairs.

Peace, a chance to work and live with some ease of mind. From every continent rise millions of outstretched hands. Decent people, kindly people, willing to live and let live, reach out and grasp nothing. We read the headlines, and the fingers of our minds grasp . . . nothing. Yet we know that what is need not be. Somewhere must lie a pattern, a shape, a trend, which men can take hold of, build policy around, and so check the insane slide into the abyss. Learning, specialized knowledge, the mastery of a block of facts, help us little. Specialists abound, busy now on new methods for lethal warfare. Wisdom does not lie here. It lies rather in an understanding of relationships between disparate groups of facts. For mathematical variables, the Massachusetts Institute of Technology has designed a differential calculator which can grind out the answer without possibility of error. Better bridges, skyscrapers, streamlined motors, can be designed from the laws laid down. Unfortunately no such machine is available for human and social variables.

It may be that the variables in the life of a human community are so numerous, and so complex, that they defy the capacity of any mind, however wise, to define their relationships and plot a curve of possible development towards peace and reasonable security. Perhaps no dependable theory of relativity is possible in sociology as it is in physics. But no one can now say that it is impossible to establish trends, rough relationships, well grooved movements, leading to a general pattern and to specific policies built thereon. Never were there such mountains of data to assist in plotting relationships. Never was there so great a margin of safety between population and food supply. Never was there such tangible, accredited evidence for the liquidation of economic misery. While the final pattern remains undrawn, there is no turning back for men of good will.

This book is an attempt to trace the pattern of community business and survival. Here, possibly, is something to tie to, something which persists after the proof readers have gone home to bed. It contains no plea for any dogma to save the world. I have only tried to plot what is, and to follow the curve a little way into the future.

Index

Ackerman, Frederick L., on credit, 110
Adams, A. H., on buying power, 98
Administration, in public business, 244ff.; assets and liabilities of, 255, 256
Africa, South, 91
Agenda, 4, 5, 13, 275; Keynes on, 42; principles of, 118ff.; problems of consumption basis of, 129; defined by President, 131; the State and the Agenda, 148; personal view of, 155ff.
Agricultural Adjustment Administration, 39, 41, 46, 52, 55, 142, 227, 230, 283
Agricultural Marketing Acts, British, 230
Agriculture, 52, 178; failure of, 39
Akron, Ohio, 166
Alabama, 64
Alcohol, 53
Argentina, central bank in, 88
Arts and sciences, 162ff.
Australia, 71; agricultural control in, 228; Sugar Control Board in, 228, 229
Austria, 71

Baldwin locomotive works, sales and income of, 175
Bankhead bill, 42, 53
Banking and credit, 53
Banks, for cooperatives, 59; as holders of government securities, 60; Federal Reserve, 146
Barton, Bruce, 160
Bavaria, 81
Beard, Chas. A., 19

Bennett, Rt. Hon. Richard B., Canadian Prime Minister, 87
Bentham, Jeremy, 4
Berle, A. A., Jr., 100, 111
Berlin City Electric Co., 234
Bernays, E. L., 263
Biddle, George, 163
"Big Business," 114, 115, 199ff.; classified list of, 207-213
Blackstone, V. A., 64
Bonn, Prof. M. J., 117
Borah, Senator, 115
Boulder Dam, 57, 165
Brandeis, Justice, 126
Brazil, 70
British Milk Control, 227
Buchanan, President, 33
Budget, 131ff., 155, 275ff.; Executive, 61; "survival," 148, 149ff., 199; financial and physical mechanism of, 169
Buying power, 98ff.

Canada, 71; New Deal in, 87, 88
Canadian National Railways, 236
Canal Zone, 25
Capital goods, 105; list of, 137, 145, 146
Capitalism, decay of, 93ff.; definitions of, 94ff.; passing of, 117; a profit-and-loss system, 174; Collectivism along with, 237, 238
Cartels, 82; approved by NRA, 200, 203
Central Statistical Board, 52
Chamberlin, W. H., 260
Chan Kom, Yucatan, 9ff., 15, 128, 270
Chapin, A. L., 19
Cincinnati, 249

City managers, 31
Civil Works Administration, 151
Civilian Conservation Corps, 55, 68, 151ff.; camps, 144
Cleveland, Grover, 33
Clothing, 135, 142
Coal, 1, 54; Guffey bill on, 54
Collectivism, 3, 4, 5, 6, 17ff., 78, 159; New Deal, 33ff.; world trend to, 215; in great corporations, 237
Colombia, 71
Committee on Economic Security, 56
Committee on Recent Social Trends, 24
Commodity Credit Corporation, 52, 58
Communication, 55
Compensation, Workmen's, 174
Conant, President, of Harvard, 248
Connecticut Valley Authority, 64
Conscious planning, 18
Constitution, 30
Construction, 55
Consumers' Goods, list of, 134
Control-without-ownership, 227, 232
Cooke, Morris L., 57, 185
Coolidge, President, 29
Cooperatives, units of, 64, 65; lists of, 89, 90; five great patterns of, 91
Cotton textiles, losses in, 176
Courts, their relation to Agenda, 121
Coyle, David C., 203, 266; on capital goods, 105ff.
Czechoslovakia, 88, 89

Danielian, Prof. N. R., on property values, 222
Debt and credit, 108ff.
Deficits, list of industries showing, 176
Democracy, 279
Denmark, Cooperatives in, 90, 91
Dennis, Lawrence, 117
Detroit, 265
Division of Subsistence Homesteads, 55

Douglas, Major, 218, 219. *See also* Social Credit plan
Drainage basins, five great, 186
Duffus, R. L., 41
DuPont de Nemours Co., 214
Durkheim, Emile, 270
Dutch East Indies, 71, 91
Dykstra, City Manager, of Cincinnati, 249

Eastman, Jos. B., 57, 224; railroad plan of, 240
Eastman, Max, 162
Economic Council, proposed, 286
Economic Security, Committee on, 56
Education, 135, 142, 143
Efficiency, dangers of too much, 253
Electric Home and Farm Authority, 56
Ellis, Havelock, 262
Emergency Crop and Feed Loans, 53
Emergency Housing Corporation, 58
Erosion, 187ff.; fertility lost by, 188; control of, 194. *See also* Soil Erosion
Essentials, summary of, 147
Executive Budget, 61
Expansion, of State functions, 171ff.; survey of, 172, 173
Expenditure, increase in government, 27
Export-Import Bank of Washington, 55, 58

Fabian Society, 70
Farm Credit Administration, 52, 53
Fascism, 2, 78ff.
Federal Alcohol Control Administration (dissolved), 53
  Aviation Commission, 53
  Communications Commission, 55
  Coordinator of Transportation, 57
  Emergency Relief Administration, 40, 45, 46, 142
  Farm Mortgage Corp., 52, 56, 58
  Housing Administration, 55

INDEX

Institutions, 1912 to date, 29
Land Banks, 40
Ownership, area of, 28
Power Commission, 56
Federal Prison Industries, 59
Reserve Banks, 146
Reserve Board, 39, 53
Savings and Loan Insurance Corp., 53, 56, 58
Savings and Loan System, 53, 55
Subsistence Homestead Corp., 55, 58
Surplus Relief Corp., 45, 53, 58
Finland, 78
Flood control, 193, 194
Florida, relief in, 48
Flynn, John T., 66
Food, 134, 139, 140
Food and Drug legislation, 159
Foreign countries, public business in, 70ff.
Foreign Trade Zones Board, 55
Forests, 55, 191
France, social insurance in, 88

Gay, Chas. R., 93
Geddes, Sir Patrick, 184
Geological Survey, 145, 153
George, Henry, 217, 219
German citizens, status of, 83
German Railroad Co., 233, 234
Germany, 247; control of by government, 81ff.
Glasgow, 72
Gold and silver, 209, 210
Gosplan, Lenin's, 74
Grace, Eugene G., 66
Grand Coulee Dam, 57
Grant, Ulysses S., 33
Great Britain, Collectivism in, 84; her shift to protection, 85; social security, 85; Milk Control, 227, 269; Agricultural Marketing Acts, 230; the "Grid," 231, 286; Civil Service, 247
Guffey coal bill, 1, 54

Hale, Robert L., 124
Hall, Dr. Ansel F., on CCC and CWA experience, 151
Hanfei, Chinese philosopher, 160

Hansen, Prof. A. H., 236, 277; on housing, 141
Harcourt, Lewis, 72
Harding, President, 4, 29
Harvard University, 128, 248
Health, 135
Hoagland, Dr. H. E., 54
Hobson, J. A., 67, 200
Holland, 71
Holmes, Justice, 126, 282
Home Owners' Loan Corporation, 54, 56, 58
Hoover, Former President, 24, 33, 34, 249
Hopkins, Harry, 45, 68, 248, 256
"Hot oil," 1, 182
Housing, 55
Hungary, 71
Huxley, Aldous, 262, 266
Huxley, Julian, 272
Hydroelectric power, 194; in Ontario, 234, 286

Illinois, relief in, 48
Income taxes, 161
Industries, of "public interest" (list), 122, 123
Industry, control of, 43ff.
Inheritance taxes, 161
Initiative, individual, 154ff.
Inland Waterways Corporation, 5, 235
Insull, Samuel, 212
Insurance, RFC loans to companies, 56
Insurance, social (table), 173
Interdepartmental Committee on Trade Agreements, 55
Interstate Commerce Commission, 25, 57
Invention, science and, 163, 164
Italy, 71, 78ff.

Japan, government operation in, 71, 89
Johannson, Albin, 247
Johnson, Gen. Hugh, 43
Jones, Bassett, 25, 219; on growth of production, 108ff.; on compounding interest, 169

INDEX

Jones, Jesse H., 37

Keynes, John Maynard, 4, 19, 118
Korzybski, Alfred, 94
Kreuger, Ivar, 78
Kuhn, Loeb & Co., 206

La Guardia, Mayor, 186, 285; his public works proposal, 64
Laissez-faire, 4, 119, 129, 264; individualism under, 113
Lamar, Justice, 125
Land Bank Commission, 53
Land program (PWA), 53
Land value taxes, 161
Lehman, Governor, 63
Lenin, V. I., his "Gosplan," 74
Lippmann, Walter, 24, 266
Liquidity, 100ff.
Lloyd George, David, forces old age pension act, 85
Lorwin, L. L., 262
Loss, in industry, 16
"Loss Battalions," 174ff., 180
Lumber industry, 55, 225, 226, 232

Mack Committee, 221, 224
McReynolds, Justice, 2
McVickar, Rev. John, 18
Martin, Everett Dean, 262
Massachusetts Institute of Technology, 287
Mattresses, protest against government production of, 46
Means, Dr. Gardner C., 111, 199, 227, 228
Merriam, Dr. Chas. E., 5, 7, 29, 268
Merrimac Valley Authority, 64
Mexico, six-year plan in, 88
Mississippi Valley, 254
Mississippi Valley Committee, report of, 185
Missouri Agricultural Experiment Station, 188
Models, for regulation and control, 216ff.
Monroe, President, 33
Morgan, Dr. A. E., 20, 242
Morgan, J. P., & Co., 206
Morgenthau, Henry, Jr., Secretary of the Treasury, 146

Mumford, Lewis, 184
Mussolini, Benito, 117, 263; on capitalism, 79

National Association of Manufacturers, 48
  Emergency Council, 52
  Employment Service, 52
  Industrial Conference Board, 93; tabulations by, 59
  Labor Relations Board, dissolved, 52
  Power Policy Committee, 57
  Recovery Administration, 34; its three principles, 43; a regulatory model, 225; its approval of "cartels," 200
  Resources Board, 50, 52, 144, 182, 254, 287
  Survey of Potential Product Capacity, 148ff.
Natural resources, 136, 137, 144, 145, 182ff.
Nature, changing human, 258ff.
Navigation, 189, 190
Nazi party, 81
Nebbia v. New York Case, 126
New Deal, 2, 15, 16; summary of, 65ff.
New Economic Policy (Russia), 74
New State Ice case, Justice Brandeis dissents in, 126
New York City, relief in, 63
New York Power Authority, 63
New York State Electric & Gas Co., 221
New York State, relief in, 48
New Yorker, cartoon in *The,* 128
New Zealand, control of agriculture in, 89, 91
Non-Agenda, 4, 5
Norris Dam, 248
North Carolina, textiles in, 44
Norway, 71

Ohio, relief in, 48
Oil, 56, 182ff.; industry, 1
Ontario, Hydro-Electric Power Commission of, 234, 286
Overhead, 103ff.

INDEX 295

Pareto, Vilfredo, 259
Passamaquoddy project, 57
Paternalism, 177
Pederson, Miss V. J., 100
Pennsylvania, relief in, 48
Petroleum Administration, 56
Planning, conscious, 18
Post Office Department, 3
Potential Product Capacity, Natl. Survey of, 148ff.
Power, 56, 190, 191
Power, buying, 98ff.
Prices, 111ff.; percent drop in, 111
Priestley, J. B., on English conditions, 86
Production, percent drop in, 111; individual area of, 158
Production Credit Corporations, 53, 59
Profit, 14
Profit motive, 260
Progress, major divisions of, 215
Prohibition, 31, 160
Propaganda, definition of, 264
Property values, ten methods of inflating, 222
Prussia, 71
Public Administration Clearing House, 251
Public ownership, 233ff.
Public Service Commission, 223, 224
Public works, 55
Public Works Administration, 55, 68; land program of, 40; railroad loans by, 58
Puritanism, survival of, 160

Queensland, agricultural control in, 228

Railroads, 175, 178; in loss division, 212
Rautenstrauch, Prof. Walker, 167; on overhead, 103ff.
Rayburn, Congressman, 179
Reconstruction Finance Corporation, 32ff., 35–39, 42, 52; balance sheet, 36; railroad loans by, 58; RFC Mortgage Co., 58
Recreation, 135

Redfield, Robert, 9
Regional Agricultural Credit Corporations, 58
Regional markets, proposed for N. Y. State, 63
Regulation, of business, 13, 14; wide spread of, 220
Relief, figures on, 45; grand total estimated, 46; proportion of, 47ff.; in various states, 48; work relief, 50; in N. Y. City, 63
Resettlement Administration, 55
Roberts, Justice, 126
Robinson, Dr. E. S., 132, 245, 268
Roosevelt, President, 1, 15, 30, 34, 44, 45; on aviation, 53; defines Agenda, 131
Roosevelt, Theodore, 144
Rural Electrification Administration, 57
Rural Rehabilitation Corporations, 40, 53, 59
Russia, 71, 74ff., 245, 246; consumers' societies in, 89, 90; experience in public ownership, 235; non-profit motive in, 260, 261

Santayana, George, 271
Schacht, Dr. Hjalmar, 83
Science Advisory Board, 52
Science and invention, 163, 164
Securities Act, 57
Securities Exchange Commission, 57
Serbia, 71
Services, list of, 137
Shaw, George Bernard, 2, 266
Shelter, 135, 140, 141
Shipping, 57
Siegfried, André, 262
Sloan, Alfred P., on purchasing power, 204
Smith, Adam, 119, 172, 275
Smith, J. Russell, 184
Social Credit plan, 218. *See also* Douglas, Major
Social insurance (table), 173
Social Science Research Council, 248ff.
Social security, 215

Soil erosion service, 53
Soule, George, 203
South Africa, 91
South Dakota, relief in, 48
Southworth, Constant, on lumber code, 225
Spain, 70
Spengler, Oswald, 269
Standard of living, steps towards maintaining, 281ff.
Stock Exchanges, 57
Stolper, Gustav, 84, 244
Subsistence Homesteads, Division of, 55
Sugar Control Board, in Australia, 228, 229
Sullivan, Mark, 144
Supply, flow of, 133
Supreme Court, 1, 44, 51, 282; in NRA decision, 30, 43; decision in hatters' case, 121; in Schechter case, 200
Survival necessities (lists), 134–137
Sweden, 71, 76ff., 247
Switzerland, 71
Swope, Gerard, 214

Taft, Chief Justice, 125
Tasmania, 91
Taxes, Federal, State, and local (tables), 26; government expenditure from, 26, 27; limits of, 161, 162; income, inheritance, and land value, 161
Tennessee Valley Associated Co-operatives, Inc., 58
Tennessee Valley Authority, 34, 56, 144, 235
Terra, Gabriel, Uruguay president, 88
Thornton, Sir Henry, 236
Trade Agreements, Interdepartmental Committee on, 55

Transportation, 57
Treasury Department, 39; as an investment trust, 59; drain upon, 179
Tugwell, Rexford, 6, 141; on regimentation, 260, 261
Tyson case, 125, 126

United States Chamber of Commerce, 43, 119
United States Information Service, 52
United States Shipping Board, 57
Unwin, Sir Raymond, 184
Uruguay, "Third Republic" in, 88
Utilities Securities Corp., 37

Van Buren, President, 33
Veblen, Thorstein, 6

Wages, inadequacy of relief, 50
Wallace, Secretary, 41, 111, 286
War Industries Board, 227
Water table, "ground," 191; ground level drop in western states, 192
Webb, Sidney, 91, 247; on public business, 70, 72
Wehle, L. B., 239, 240
Willcox, Dr. W. O., 166, 269; on cotton farming, 229
Williams, Aubrey, 48
Williams, Dr. Frankland, 274
Wisconsin, unemployment insurance in, 174
Wisconsin Finance Authority, 64
Wolff Packing Co. case, 125
Workmen's Compensation, 174
Works Progress Administration, 55
World War, 3, 24, 73

Yale, 132
Yazoo delta, dynamiting levees in, 188